TRAINING

FOR CHANGE

Activities to Promote

Positive Attitudes to Change

**SUE BISHOP &
DAVID TAYLOR**

**KOGAN
PAGE**

First published in 1994

Apart from any fair dealing for the purposes of research or private
study, or criticism or review, as permitted under the Copyright, Designs
and Patents Act, 1988, this publication may only be reproduced, stored
or transmitted, in any form or by any means, with the proper
permission in writing of the publishers, or in the case of reprographic
reproduction in accordance with the terms of licences issued by the
Copyright Licensing Agency. Enquiries concerning reproduction outside
those terms should be sent to the publishers at the undermentioned
address:

Kogan Page Limited
120 Pentonville Road
London N1 9JN

© Sue Bishop and David Taylor, 1994

British Library Cataloguing in Publication Data
A CIP record for this book is available from the British Library.

ISBN 0 7494 1226 7

Typeset by EXCEPT*detail* Ltd, Southport
Printed and bound in Great Britain by
Biddles Ltd, Guildford and King's Lynn

T

TRAINING
FOR CHANGE

Kogan Page Training Activities Series

Contents

Acknowledgements

Our thanks must go to a large number of people whom we have not personally met, plus a few we have, and on whose writings and research we have drawn in putting together the activities. We have, for example, included activities whose genesis lies in the books of Tom Peters. There are many others, less well known, perhaps, but expert in the field of change management.

Our thanks, in particular, to Mags, Val and Niel for their forbearance and support.

We hope the users of these activities will gain as much satisfaction – and, occasionally, enjoyment – out of using them as we did in writing them. We would welcome any comments.

Sue Bishop
David Taylor

Introduction

When introducing change the journey is at least as important as the destination.

Change is a messy, iterative process. Just when you think you've arrived you find you've hardly begun.

(Tony Turrill: Change and Innovation – A Challenge for the NHS)

ABOUT US

We were especially pleased to write this volume on Training for Change, a process we have been immersed in, as trainers, over many years.

We both became trainers when 'chalk and talk' was still popular. Training was something that was done 'to' you. It was essentially a passive process; the trainer knew best! Consequently the result was often something to be endured, and the best that could be said for it was that it was a break from work.

We suffered this approach as 'victims' and as people who were expected to train in this style. We enjoyed neither experience, and met plenty of others who were also dissatisfied with this method of training. We felt instinctively that there had to be a better way; a way that encouraged 'active' learning. The arrival of participative learning methods signalled this for us and we have been committed to developing activities in this mould ever since.

ABOUT COURSE PARTICIPANTS

In our experience – and there is a good body of theory to support it – adult learners must be motivated in order to learn. They need to be engaged actively in learning and be self-directed; less dependent on the trainer. They should be able to relate the learning to their own experience, needs and situation. Several of the activities in this volume build directly on this theory and attempt to bring out the relevance of it to change-managers.

Participants are likely to be managers or supervisors responsible for initiating and implementing change or who are having change imposed upon them in the form of new responsibilities, new job, company reorganization and so on. Some activities are written with junior managers or supervisors in mind. Others target middle or upper management while a small number are designed for senior policymakers.

It is important to recognize what experience (of life and of work) people bring with them on courses. This should be valued by the trainer – and, indeed, by the change manager – and all of the activities in this volume reflect a fundamental principle: that the group itself is a vital training resource.

ABOUT YOU

You may be an experienced trainer or manager or a trainer still new to participative training methods. However, you will almost certainly have too little time to spend in mapping out training activities and deciding how they should be processed. This volume is intended for you! Use the material as it stands – which is how we have used it – or adapt it to meet your own or your group's needs. Use our processing notes if they are helpful to you but if you prefer to develop your own, feel free to do so.

ABOUT THIS VOLUME

We believe that participant dissatisfaction with some training events stems from having to endure or survive management 'games' which are either inappropriate or have been insufficiently processed.

In our view, any activity should include five main elements:

- setting the context
- running the exercise itself
- unpacking the participant experience of the exercise
- processing the activity and drawing out the learning points
- considering how to apply the learning in real life.

The last three elements are too often neglected, or even omitted, which leaves participants wondering 'What was all that about, then?' We have tried to avoid this common failing and the step-by-step methodology and processing notes contained in the text are the result.

This volume contains a wide variety of activities. They range from the simple and light-hearted to the complex and risky. Many different training methods are used. You will find questionnaires, physical activities, games, role-plays and simulations. A well-constructed course should contain a mix of methods and this volume reflects that philosophy.

Managing change involves dealing with the unexpected. When other people are involved we can never be entirely sure of their reactions. These activities suggest ways of reducing the risks associated with this, but managing change means reviewing the process and intended outcomes as you go along. The same goes for these activities. The conclusions drawn by one group will often differ greatly from those of another, and yet the activity itself may be the same. You should not be surprised by this. Unpredictability can, in itself, be very rewarding for all concerned. We do hope, however, that the detailed processing notes and suggestions will allow trainers to feel more confident in handling this very unpredictability.

Tom Peters in his book *Thriving on Chaos* (1989) goes so far as to suggest that organizations cannot hope to survive if they are not able to respond to change – indeed, to love it – so neither do we expect these activities to be set in tablets of stone. Do not be afraid to put your own personal stamp on them. This is precisely what we have done in writing this volume.

ABOUT THE ACTIVITIES

Section 1 – Openers, in-betweens and closers – contains a range of activities which are designed to promote good group cohesion and motivation during courses on managing change.

Sections 2, 3 and 4 cover respectively:

- Managing the *process* of change (activities which address strategic/ 'political'/organizational change and/or introduce specific change management techniques).
- Helping *others* to manage change (activities which are designed to equip people to bring about change, for example by offering ideas on how to overcome resistance to change).
- Helping *oneself* to manage change (activities which present a range of ideas designed to support individuals at a personal level as they confront change).

Both functional and attitudinal change are covered and the activities include, for example, stress, redundancy, retirement, creative thought, information technology, leadership and teamwork.

Each activity is presented in a uniform way:

- *Activity number and title* The order of appearance in each section is alphabetical, by title.
- *Description* A short outline of the activity.
- *Objectives* What the activity is designed to achieve.
- *Participants* Guidance on size and type of group.
- *Time required* This is an estimate only and timing will depend on the group and the depth in which you may wish to pursue learning points.
- *Resources needed* For the sake of brevity, we have omitted the most

important resource for each activity which is, as stated above, the group itself.

- *Method* The various steps present an at-a-glance guide to running the activity. These are immediately followed by guidance on timing, processing issues, background information and suggested discussion points. In order to initiate the discussions we have in many cases, provided, some questions the trainer might use.
- *Documents* These are in a form which can be readily photocopied. They will be either exercises for use within the activity or handouts which will generally not be prescriptive, but provide a summary of some of the more important learning points from the activity.
- *Observer Sheets* These are in a form which can be readily photocopied. They normally supplement exercises.
- *Trainer's Notes* These notes provide either further background information or precise details of materials required for the activity. They are not intended for distribution.

Some last words on terminology. We refer throughout to 'the trainer'. The approach advocated is more properly that of facilitator, but we use the word 'trainer' as this is more familiar. The word 'exercise' is used consistently and purposely to refer to an activity within an activity. 'Participant' is used rather than course member or delegate, and this reflects our beliefs about the importance of participative (ie active) learning.

Activity summaries

SECTION 1: OPENERS, IN-BETWEENS AND CLOSERS

As the section heading suggests, these activities include the getting-to-know-you type exercises to be run at the beginning of a course of training; ice-breaker activities to engage the attention and interest of the participants, to introduce the subject of the training and to clarify concepts and assumptions about the content; activities which can be run as 'light relief' to the more cerebral exercises and discussions; and course closure and post-course activities.

1 Changes (p. 21)   A course-closure activity to help participants recognize the learning which has taken place and to apply it back at the workplace.

2 Chase me (p. 24)   A course-closure activity which, through post-course follow-up, helps ensure that commitments made during training are put into practice back at the workplace.

3 Cogs, fats and dish (p. 31)   An activity which encourages creativity. It could be used as an ice-breaker or a light-hearted course closure.

4 Get knotted! (p. 35)   A 'fun' activity which involves participants becoming involved in change in a literally physical sense. It is intended to help the group relax or 'lighten-up' during a training course.

5 Group laugh (p. 37)   It is widely recognized that laughter is one of the best means of relieving stress. Tension can easily arise just from talking about, or undergoing training on, change. This is a simple way of getting the group to relax.

6 Impressions (p. 39)   An activity which is about the effects of colour and how it affects our thinking, moods, attitudes and impressions. Peripheral to the more serious aspects of change, it could be run between more cerebral sessions, or is ideal for that after-lunch period where a light-hearted exercise is called for.

7 Metamorphosis (p. 47)   An icebreaker with team-building elements.

8 PUNchlines   (p. 51)   A competitive icebreaker concerned with language, and the barriers experienced when communicating with people whose first language is not English.

9 Quick fire (p. 55)   An icebreaker with the two-fold purpose of quickly learning the names of fellow participants, and sharpening and concentrating the mind in preparation for the training to follow.

10 Sit in a circle (p. 58)   An 'active' physical activity to reduce group tension and/or enhance group cohesion.

11 Treats (p. 60)   A light-hearted activity to be run during a course, 'Treats' suggests one way of relieving stress.

SECTION 2:   MANAGING THE PROCESS OF CHANGE

This section deals with managing the organizational, political and strategic aspects of change. While, inevitably, there is a 'people' dimension to this group of activities, they look more at process than human-resource issues.

12 Barriers to equality (p. 67)   This is a non-threatening activity designed to provoke thought, and raise awareness of discriminatory practices within organizations.

13 But we've always done it this way (p. 72)   This activity looks at ways in which organizational culture might suppress change, and suggests how managers might motivate and encourage initiative in their staff.

14 Coblocks (p. 75)   The core of this activity is a questionnaire designed to help highlight company blockages in organizations where change may be needed.

15 Crossing the line (p. 84)   This activity uses a simple visual technique to help managers assess areas of support for, and resistance to, change. It suggests a strategy for turning resistance to support.

16 Cynic's guide to change (p. 89)   A high-speed, light-hearted activity with a serious message: that encouraging 'noises' to good ideas from bosses, peers and subordinates does not necessarily mean that action will be taken! It looks at the deviousness of both those introducing, and those resisting change.

17 Handling redundancy (p. 95)   This activity is intended for managers who may have to conduct termination interviews with their staff. It suggests methods which reduce to a minimum the negative organizational and personal impact of redundancy.

18 How am I doing? (p. 115)   A self-evaluation post-course activity which gives individuals a means of monitoring progress in chosen areas of personal development.

19 Learn to love it (p. 118)   An activity which considers alternative strategies for organizations so that they can embrace, and thrive on, change.

20 Push-me-pull-you (p. 127)   Intended for groups of senior managers, this activity analyses factors impacting on change situations, and explores means of implementing suitable strategies.

21 So far, so . . . good? (p. 135)   This activity should be run during a course of training to assess whether the sessions are meeting the needs of the participants. It demands from the trainer a degree of flexibility and willingness to adapt the programme within the remits of individual and organizational needs, and the objectives of the course.

22 Who manages IT? (p. 137)   An activity intended for senior managers with responsibility for the introduction of Information Techno-logy at a corporate level. It examines some prerequisites for the successful introduction of organizational-wide change based on IT.

23 Worldly wise (p. 154)   A light-hearted activity with a serious mess-age, this exercise tests managers' ability to work effectively under pressure. It has the additional optional spin-off of opening discussion on the importance of international awareness.

SECTION 3:   HELPING OTHERS TO MANAGE CHANGE

This group of activities has the central theme of how managers and others can support colleagues facing change, either imposed or chosen.

24 Acronym (p. 165)   This activity should be run early in a course on change. It is not demanding, but is intended to focus participants' minds on general issues and attitudes regarding change.

25 Back to the real world (p. 168)   An end-of-course activity to help participants reflect on what skills they can use, as agents of change, to help others acquire, develop, or modify knowledge, competence or atti-tudes.

26 Flavour of the month (p. 174)   This is a competitive game which is intended to make participants aware of those techniques of change management which should be avoided.

27 Games (p. 178) Creativity is often a vital element in managing change effectively. This activity considers how to maximize creativity under pressure.

28 Jargoner's question time (p. 181) A light-hearted activity to break down the barriers of 'technophobia' – a condition resulting in part from the use of computer-jargon – which prevents many managers from making the most of technology at work.

29 Mobiles (p. 190) A hands-on activity which requires the use of set materials, this exercise compares the strengths and weaknesses of written and oral communication in planning and conveying new ideas to others.

30 Perspectives (p. 195) An activity which looks at how problem solving might differ depending on the viewpoint of the protagonists. It examines the effects of altered group membership on group dynamics.

31 Tell me about it (p. 200) This activity explores counselling styles and suggests appropriate techniques for helping others who are experiencing problems with transition and change.

32 Towers of strength (p. 210) A competitive, hands-on activity, to explore the effectiveness of planning and implementation, working in tandem, when introducing a new concept or managing change.

33 Where do you stand? (p. 219) A powerful activity which addresses the strength of people's attitudes and prejudices when faced with a controversial issue.

34 Why me? (p. 224) By using ready-made scenarios as a starting point, this activity explores some of the reasons for resistance to change.

35 X, Y or Z? (p. 236) Based on a self-report questionnaire, this activity is designed to help participants identify their present preferred managerial style, and compare this with alternative styles perhaps more appropriate to managing organizational change.

SECTION 4: HELPING ONESELF TO MANAGE CHANGE

This section contains activities which look at personal change, and are more inwardly focused. The central theme is how managers and others can develop personal strategies for coping with change, either imposed or chosen. Some activities on relaxation and stress management are given, for example.

36 Camouflage (p. 255)   This is a wordsquare – a short, 'fun' activity to focus participants' minds on managing personal change.

37 Career move (1) (p. 260)   This activity is targeted at managers who are to face some major change at work, because of a career move, new or additional responsibilities, or because of impending redundancy. It helps participants recognize and communicate their strengths, transferable skills, and achievements.

38 Career move (2) (p. 269)   This activity follows naturally from 'Career move (1)', but would be most suitable for participants who are about to be made redundant in that it addresses the issue of the job market, and how to manage the process of getting the next job offer.

39 How will I cope? (p. 277)   For use with managers who have some identifiable change ahead of them, this activity allows participants to examine their own reactions to change, and to develop a strategy for coping at a personal level.

40 I am, therefore I can (p. 285)   This activity would be usefully run early in a course concerned with re-training, job-search or interview technique. It is a morale-boosting exercise to instil confidence, help recognize self-worth and generate motivation.

41 Jeopardy (p. 292)   Based on the game-show of that name, this is a light-hearted activity. Two teams compete to suggest the *question* to a statement encapsulating an *answer* read out by the trainer. The questions and answers are on five topics relevant to progress and change.

42 Lifeline (p. 304)   An activity to be run early in a course on managing change – perhaps after an ice-breaker. It is designed to help participants' identify personal major changes and significant life events and coping strategies, and to consider relative stress levels.

43 Relax (p. 309)   Change invariably involves pressure, and pressure can lead to stress. This activity offers several ways in which individuals can relieve stress through relaxation techniques.

44 Retirement (1) (p. 316)   An activity to unblock negativity about retirement. It explores the pros and cons so that people may plan effectively for retirement in a balanced and rational way.

45 Retirement (2) (p. 320)   Like 'Retirement (1)', this activity stands alone perfectly well, but can also be used as a follow-up to it. It provides a structure for looking at the financial implications of retirement.

46 Skill stories (p. 327)   This activity complements, or can be run as an alternative to, 'I am, therefore I can'. It is intended for those who are to undergo a career change, and is designed to raise awareness of capability and skill strength.

47 That's the limit! (p. 333)   This activity explores the causes of pressure and tension at work, acknowledges the stress factors involved in managing change, and suggests some ways of dealing with them.

48 Transferable skills (p. 337)   Designed, in part, as a morale-boosting exercise, to help participants develop a more positive self-image, this activity illustrates to individuals that they have innumerable skills, some of which will be untapped in their present positions.

49 Transitions (p. 340)   This activity is intended for those who are confronting, or are about to undergo, a major change in their working lives. It identifies recognized 'landmarks' in the transition process, and helps individuals see where they are in terms of a current transition.

50 Work will be the death of me (p. 344)   Confronting change can upset an otherwise regular pattern of work habits. This activity invites participants to explore their normal systems of work; to become more aware of how change is likely to impact on their work patterns, and to consider alternatives.

SECTION 1

OPENERS, IN-BETWEENS AND CLOSERS

Activity 1

Changes

`

Description

A course-closure activity to end training on managing change.

Objectives

By the end of this activity participants will:

- have considered all the differences and changes which have occurred during the course of the training programme
- recognize the learning which has taken place, and have considered ways to put the learning to practical use back at the workplace.

Participants

Number: Any
Type: Any

Time

30–60 minutes

Resources

- Paper and pencil/pen for each participant
- Flipchart stand, paper and marker pens

Method

Step 1: Introduce the activity, explaining procedures and timings

Participants will be asked to jot down any change or difference which has occurred, or they have perceived, during the hours/days of the training course, either to themselves or to the group as a whole.

These changes may be as flippant as desired, physical, emotional, cerebral or involving a change of attitude. Participants should also address the effectiveness of the course content and the impact of the training as media for change.

Although participants can produce individual lists, they can work with a neighbour or small group in order that individuals can bounce ideas off each other.

Participants will have 15-20 minutes to complete their lists, the contents of which will then be shared in plenary session, so that a collective list of changes can be compiled, and issues discussed.

Step 2: Issue sheets of paper and pencils/pens to participants
Pairings or small-group membership should be decided by the participants themselves. If necessary, and if appropriate, groups could move to 'quiet' areas to discuss their lists.

Step 3: After the allocated time ask participants to re-group for a plenary discussion
Ask each participant/pair/group in turn to call out a difference or change which they have perceived. Flipchart these, and continue to rotate around groups until all lists have been exhausted. Of course, the lists will be different with every group and with every course depending on the content, but the sort of responses you are likely to get are as follows:

- *I am three days older than I was at the beginning of the course*
- *Janice changed her hair colour on Tuesday*
- *I have worn two different shirts and four different ties*
- *I am more relaxed than I was two days ago.*

And more seriously:

- *I have a completely different picture of Dave now that I know him socially*
- *I am more aware of the difficulties experienced by payroll, and will be more tolerant and less aggressive towards them in the future*
- *I now realize that I am not the only one with problems*
- *I didn't realize how aggressive and defensive I become when my views are challenged.*

And concerning the training itself:

- *The training has made me more aware of the need to motivate my team*
- *I have a different attitude towards delegation and teamwork*
- *I realize now how complacent I was - we all have to adapt and grow if we're to survive and beat our competitors.*

Step 4: Using the lists as a basis, draw out the learning points from the course
Participants should be encouraged not just to recognize the learning that has taken place, but also to formulate plans to put the learning into

practice back at the workplace. Ways of achieving this can be discussed by the group.

Questions you might use:

- *Why had you not contemplated making this change before?*
- *What possible obstructions are you likely to meet at the workplace if you implement this change?*
- *Who is involved/needs to be consulted?*
- *How could you forestall opposition to the change?*
- *How should you go about introducing the change so that you carry your team with you?*

Step 5: Close the activity referring back to the objectives

Activity 2

Chase me

Description

A course-closure activity designed to ensure that commitments made during training are put into practice back at the workplace. This activity can be used on any course, but is specifically designed for training programmes concerned with the management of change. It requires a commitment from course members that they will undertake some follow-up work during the weeks after the event, but provides useful networking so that participants have contact, should they need help and support, subsequent to the training course.

This activity is based on the assumption that the preceding training will have highlighted, for individuals, learning points which need to be put into practice back at the workplace, and that this will involve change of some sort, both for the individual and for other colleagues and subordinates - maybe even bosses.

The activity relies on participants' willingness to share their work telephone number with at least two other participants, and also their commitment to contact these two people at a mutually agreed time subsequent to the course to ascertain progress in the implementation of change.

This should be established early in the activity. Anyone who is reluctant to participate fully can still join in the discussions, steps 1-5, and should not be pressured into revealing phone numbers if they do not wish to be included in the networking process following the training course.

Objectives

By the end of this activity participants will:

- have considered changes which should take place in their place of work or within their teams
- have prioritized changes and broken them into manageable chunks for implementation
- have considered any obstacles to success, and methods of overcoming any opposition
- have shared plans of implementation with at least two others who

will support and give advice if required
- have agreed to 'chase' at least two others regarding implementation of changes they need to make, offering support and guidance as required.

Participants

Number: Any
Type: Any

Time

60–90 minutes

Resources

- One copy of Document 1 for each participant
- One copy of Document 2 for each participant
- One copy of Document 3 for each participant

Method

Step 1: Introduce the activity, referring to the objectives, and explaining procedures

During the last few hours/days of the training course, it is to be hoped that each participant has learnt something new which she or he would like to put into practice back at work, or has recognized that some changes need to be made for more efficient and effective working. This could involve just the individual, although very few things happen in a vacuum; most actions have spin-offs for others. The changes might well involve teams – even whole sections – and could therefore affect other departments within the organization. The changes could be small and relatively minor; in some cases major upheavals are called for.

Whatever the change, it has to be carefully planned; people need to be consulted and considered; too much cannot be done all at once, so priorities have to be set; even small changes need to be achieved in small, easily assimilated stages, involving everyone, with as much harmony as can be achieved.

This is a closing activity which will ask participants to consider which changes need to be made, in what priority, and how these changes can be successfully implemented. It requires commitment from each individual that they will not only take steps to put the learning on the course into practice, but that they will continue to keep in telephone contact with, and give support to, at least one other course member over the course of the next few weeks. In return they too will receive this support from at least one other course member, in their own pursuance of the implementation of effective change.

Initially participants will work alone to establish which learning points they intend to put into practice, or which change should take priority when returning to the workplace. Participants will then be put into small groups of 3 or 4 to work out a plan of campaign for each individual. When this has been achieved, each individual who has agreed to the networking stage of the activity will complete copies of a pre-printed form, stating their commitment to implement the change agreed with the group. One copy will stay with the 'owner' and the other copies be given to each of the other group members for their retention. Members will agree to contact each other at a given time in the future to ensure that some action has been taken towards change, and to offer advice and support as needed.

Step 2: Issue Document 1 and ensure that everyone has a pen/pencil

Participants have 15 minutes to complete this part of the exercise. Most participants should find no difficulty in establishing which learning point needs application and/or which changes need to be considered back at work. If anyone appears to be having difficulties, however, a brief recap of the preceding training sessions should help them establish areas which need to be looked at back at work.

Step 3: After the allocated time, split participants into groups of 3 or 4, issue Document 2 and set them to work

For this part of the exercise 30–45 minutes should be allowed. After working together for several hours over the preceding sessions, participants may wish to choose their own groupings. If this is not practical, use any arbitrary method to decide syndicate groups.

After 30 minutes, check how the groups are working and how much more time, if any, they need to complete this part of the exercise.

Step 4: Re-negotiate timings if necessary

Step 5: At the end of the allocated time, re-group participants for a short plenary explanation of the importance of following up plans made on training courses

Acknowledge the difficulties every individual faces when returning to work from a training programme. Often, from a supportive, enthusing environment, people return to find the 'brick wall' treatment. Management and subordinates alike will often resist any changes proposed unless the situation is handled with great skill. It is also often the case that what seemed a good idea in a training environment becomes too much like hard graft 'back at the ranch'. 'Why rock the boat?' 'Why should I bother?' 'Why alter the status quo?' become the internal arguments which block commitment to change.

To use the analogy of an overweight person trying to diet, it is easy to promise to stick to a healthy eating routine when with other like-minded people, but resolutions are easily broken when at home, trying to win the battle alone. This is why slimming clubs are so effective. Members have to meet regularly and account for their actions; by so doing most keep to their eating plans and lose weight rather than lose face.

This is why participants have been asked to give their work phone number to at least two other people who are asked to 'chase' them after an agreed period of time, to ensure that their commitment doesn't falter. Like the slimmer, they are more likely to keep to the task if they have to keep face with their training colleagues.

The other aspect of this method is that often, like the slimmer, they may feel very alone – the only one with problems – again when they return to work. They have the assurance that at least two other people are there to offer support and advice at the end of the phone should they require it.

Step 6: Issue sufficient copies of Document 3 to each participant so that each member of the syndicate group has a copy
Instruct each participant to duplicate the information required on Document 3 so that each of her/his colleagues has a copy for their retention. The original stays with the owner.

Step 7: Ask participants to consult diaries to decide on a mutually convenient time to contact each other
This can be approximate, and should be at least two weeks after the final day of the course, but no later than one month after.

Step 8: Confirm that there are no difficulties, thank participants for their co-operation, wish them luck, close the activity

Chase me – Document 1

List below all learning points which you would like to put into practice, or changes which you would like to implement, after the course, back at your place of work. Make your statements specific, eg 'I will not buy cakes from the trolley, and only have chips at the canteen once a week until I reach my desired weight of 10st 4lb' rather than, 'I will lose weight' or 'I will speak to Martin about his timekeeping on Monday afternoon' rather than 'I must do something about Martin's attitude'.

A ....

....

B ....

....

C ....

....

D ....

....

E ....

....

F ....

....

G ....

....

Now, taking the same statements, list them in order of importance as you see them in relation to your job, the most important being number 1.

1. ....   5 ....

2. ....   6 ....

3 ....   7 ....

4 ....   8 ....

Chase me - Document 2

Discuss your statements with your group. You have about 30 minutes to do this, so concentrate on each group member's highest priorities.

Things you should discuss:

- Are the statements specific enough?
- Do they encompass too much?
- Is the statement listed as most important too difficult to begin with – in other words, would it be more sensible to tackle something smaller first?
- If the priority statement involves a major change, but is really important, how can the implementation be broken down into manageable parts?
- What obstacles might there be to successful implementation?
- What can be done to prepare the way, thus minimising resistance?
- Who needs to be consulted?
- Who needs to be informed?

Chase me – Document 3

Complete the form as indicated:

NAME.......................... PHONE NO...........

LEARNING/CHANGE I INTEND TO PUT INTO PRACTICE.......

....

OBSTACLES I FORESEE.............................

INITIAL IMPLEMENTATION PLAN..................

DATE FOR PHONE CONTACT.......................

NAME.......................... PHONE NO...........

LEARNING/CHANGE I INTEND TO PUT INTO PRACTICE.......

....

OBSTACLES I FORESEE.............................

INITIAL IMPLEMENTATION PLAN..................

DATE FOR PHONE CONTACT.......................

NAME.......................... PHONE NO...........

LEARNING/CHANGE I INTEND TO PUT INTO PRACTICE.......

....

OBSTACLES I FORESEE.............................

INITIAL IMPLEMENTATION PLAN..................

DATE FOR PHONE CONTACT.......................

NAME.......................... PHONE NO...........

LEARNING/CHANGE I INTEND TO PUT INTO PRACTICE.......

....

OBSTACLES I FORESEE.............................

INITIAL IMPLEMENTATION PLAN..................

DATE FOR PHONE CONTACT.......................

Keep one copy yourself and give one to each of your syndicate group colleagues.

Note in your diary who is going to phone you and when. Also the agreed time you will 'chase' your colleagues to check on their progress

Activity 3

Cogs, fats and dish

Description

An activity which encourages creativity. It could be used as an ice-breaker, or as a light-hearted course closure.

Objectives

By the end of this activity participants will:

- have worked closely with one other course member and presented shared work to the group
- have looked at the advantages of change in a 'fun' non-threatening context
- have identified and analysed problems, considered solutions and devised methods of implementation.

Participants

Number: Any
Type: Any

Time

60–90 minutes

Resources

- Floor/table space for pairs to work on flipchart sheets
- Flipchart paper and coloured markers for each pair
- Means of attaching flipchart sheets to wall (plastic adhesive, drawing pins, etc)

Method

Step 1: Introduce the activity
Explain that this is a 'fun' activity to push inventiveness, ingenuity and

creativity to the limits. Participants will work in pairs, and will be asked to invent, draw and name a fantasy animal and to then describe their creation to the group. It should be stressed that the ability to draw well is not a prerequisite for the activity.

Step 2: Explain the activity, giving timings and procedures

As the twentieth century progresses, more and more animals, fish and birds are in danger of becoming extinct. There are also increasing threats to the animal kingdom in the form of rabies, AIDS-type viruses and diseases for which there is, as yet, no cure.

Participants are asked to imagine a fantasy time in the future when domestic animals, as we know them today, have ceased to exist. Thanks to vast improvements in genetic engineering, in this futuristic time, animals, birds and fish will be created to individual's specifications, to meet practical as well as aesthetic needs.

Working in pairs, participants will create, on a sheet of flipchart paper, a mythical creature. They should invent a suitable name to describe its uniqueness. They will have 15 minutes to do this. The drawings will be pinned to the wall, and pairs will describe their animal to the rest of the group, explaining why it was given its particular name. Each presentation should last no longer than 5 minutes.

Step 3: Divide group into pairs

If used as an ice-breaker exercise, pair people who didn't know each other before the course. If used later in the programme, participants may get more enjoyment if they work with someone with whom they have shown they are compatible.

Step 4: Issue each pair with flipchart paper and coloured marker(s)

Remind pairs that they have 15 minutes to invent a creature, to draw it on flipchart paper, and to name it.

Step 5: Set pairs to work

Observe pairs, giving advice or instructions if necessary. Creations can be as fanciful as desired; animal, bird, fish (or combination!); names should show ingenuity and demonstrate the animal's unique qualities.

Step 6: Close exercise after 15 minutes, or when each pair has drawn and named their animal

Ask each pair to pin their flipchart sheet to the wall.

Step 7: Ask pairs, in turn, to describe their work

They should explain its special features and the reasons for them, and why they chose its name. Other group members can, of course, ask questions, offer suggestions for improvements on the design and so on.

Step 8: Lead a general discussion on the learning points of the activity

It is, of course, a light-hearted activity, with no profound implications! However, the following observations could usefully be put to the group:

Unless individuals have small children of their own, it is unlikely that they will have had such a free hand at being creative since their own childhood. Children are uninhibited in their inventiveness; they do not recognize the constraints of science, finance, or those imposed by 'society'. Their fantasy world knows no bounds.

In this activity, participants have been given the opportunity to be unrestrainedly creative; their task – to bridge a gap created by uncontrollable change, in this case brought about by a hypothetical situation.

However, being adaptable, having to find alternative solutions, using lateral thinking in order to overcome problems created by change are issues which are affecting, and will affect, all of us in the course of our social and working lives.

Questions you might use:

- *What sorts of issues governed your thinking when creating your mythical animal?*
- *Did you work from 'the known' eg your knowledge/experience of domestic cats, pigs, budgerigars etc?*
- *Did you consider external appearances first? or functions? or attributes?*
- *Alternatively, did you envisage a need, and base your creation on aspects which would meet this human need?*
- *If you approached the task from this perspective, did you pursue vertical or lateral thinking methods to suggest solutions?*
- *Did having to give your new species a descriptive name clarify your thinking about its function? Did this process involve modifying your design?*
- *Did you appreciate just how creative you and your colleagues could be?*
- *Can you see practical applications of the very basic principles involved here, in today's working environment?*
- *If now, having the benefit of several other ideas on the same theme, you were asked to work together as a whole group on this project, could you design one or two prototype creatures much more efficient and effective than individual efforts? In other words, could the whole be greater than the parts, or would the opposite apply?*
- *Can you think of analogies within your own place of work?*

Step 9: Close the activity

Trainer's notes

You may wish to participate with the group in this activity, or it may help for you to give an example. If you begin from 'the known' concept, you could, for example, invent a creature which not only fertilizes arable land, but does it in a systematic way ensuring even distribution across a given area. The domestic cat is very particular in its toilet behaviour, digging holes and covering in, never using the same place twice. However, it will only dig into soft material, so if, say, a piece of grassed land needs digging over, the domestic cat could perhaps be crossed with a 'digger' such as a badger or rabbit. If this new creation could acquire the pacing behaviour of caged wild cats, the digging and fertilizing could be controlled by moving this mythical animal's enclosure systematically across the field as it paces, digs and fertilizes, thus effectively ploughing and fertilizing all in one go. The animal would have to be a herbivore . . . etc, etc.

If, however, you look at the problem as one of meeting new needs, you would perhaps start by considering what it is that animals have provided in the past which (if animals as we know them suddenly ceased to exist) we would have to replace. They provide food, but soya protein is a more cost- and space-effective substitute. They provide clothes, but synthetic materials are available. They provide companionship. How can this need be met in the future? Mechanically by robots?

You have here two ways of addressing the same problem – two ways that can easily be translated into solving work issues. The manager who favours the former approach may, for example, look to redeployment, job redesign and so on if faced with retrenchment, whereas the manager who favours the other approach may be less inclined to adapt the old, but may look to technology and more efficient systems in solving retrenchment issues.

Both approaches are equally valid. There are, of course, others. The important learning point is that managers should be aware of the options. 'There is more than one way to skin a cat', as the saying goes.

Activity 4

Get knotted!

Description

Activity 43 – 'Relax' – offers some ways of helping *individuals* relax. This activity offers a quick, simple way for getting the *group* to relax. Discussion about, or training on, change can in itself be stressful and this activity can be used to release tension and help the group relax. However, we don't wish to suggest that 'Get knotted!' can only be used under conditions of stress – it's possibly even more effective when the group is already having fun!

Join in, as trainer, and enjoy it!

'Get knotted!' can be used in almost any kind of training but we have found it especially valuable in the change arena, since it involves change, but in a very physical sense. It scarcely needs any processing – indeed, we strongly recommend that you do *not* attempt to process it, since to do so would drastically reduce its impact.

Objectives

By the end of this activity participants will have participated in a group activity designed to reduce group tension and/or to enhance group cohesion.

Participants

Number: Any
Type: Any

Time

About 10 minutes

Resources

None

Method

Step 1: Introduce the activity
Simply state that you are going to do something different.

Step 2: Getting knotted
Get the group to stand in a wide circle, facing in towards the centre. Each person should be about half a metre away from their neighbour. Ask everyone to close their eyes and to keep them closed as they stretch out their hands in front of them and walk - very slowly! - towards the centre of the circle. The aim is to find first one hand (belonging to another participant) and then another (preferably belonging to a different participant). When, and only when, each participant has linked up both hands, eyes can be opened.

Step 3: The task is for the group to metamorphose, or 'untangle', into the simplest possible structure, but without letting go
The group should cooperate with each other to get out the 'knots'. The final outcome can vary, from a complete circle (with or without a 'knot' in it) to two or more circles, either separate or linked. Laughter always results – and should be encouraged.

Step 4: Close the activity

Activity 5

Group laugh

Description

Activity 43 – 'Relax' – offers some ways of helping *individuals* relax. This activity offers a quick, simple way for getting the *group* to relax. Discussion about, or training on, change can in itself be stressful and this activity can be used to release tension and help the group relax.

However, we don't wish to suggest that 'Group laugh' can only be used under conditions of stress – it's possibly even more effective when the group is already having fun!

Join in, as trainer, and enjoy it!

Objectives

By the end of this activity participants will have participated in a group activity designed to reduce group tension and/or to enhance group cohesion.

Participants

Number: Any
Type: Any

Time

About 10 minutes

Resources

None

Method

Step 1: Introduce the activity
Simply state that you are going to do something different.

Step 2: Run the activity

Ask participants to stand in a circle, facing inwards, holding hands. There needs to be plenty of clear floor space. The task for the group is to maintain the circle, but with every person facing out, with their backs to the centre, without letting go hands.

Whether or not this is ever achieved is immaterial. The laughter that the contortions generate is enough. It is important that hands remain linked, because laughter is infectious; even those normally quite reticent, get 'charged' by this completed circuit, and the laugh becomes a collective one.

Trainer's notes

'Laughter is the best medicine.' In the business of releasing tension, this old adage is quite true. In the USA, and more recently in the UK, laughter therapy sessions are being used to treat patients suffering from stress. It has been proved that laughter can reverse some of the unhealthy side effects of stress, such as raised blood pressure. It is even thought that while laughing, our bodies undergo a chemical reaction which gives off a sort of scent, in itself 'infectious'.

Activity 6

Impressions

Description

A light-hearted activity, peripheral, but relevant to change. It is intended as a break between more serious sessions, run, perhaps, immediately after lunch – always a difficult time to motivate participants; or as the final session of a day during a course on managing change. It looks at colour, and how it affects our thinking, moods, and impressions.

Objectives

By the end of this activity participants will:

- have a greater awareness of the importance of first impressions
- have looked at how different colour combinations affect our moods, energy levels and so on
- recognize that colour choice, whether in interior decoration, clothes, packaging, design or promotions, can result in success or failure, harmony or discord
- realize that changes which encompass colour – wardrobe, workplace re-decoration, salesroom layout and so on – need careful planning to achieve the desired effect.

Participants

Number: Any
Type: Any

Time

30–60 minutes

Resources

- One copy of Document 1 for each participant plus one extra copy per syndicate group
- One copy of Document 1 for trainer use

Method

Step 1: Explain the purpose of the activity

Not to be taken too seriously, this activity alerts individuals to the value of careful consideration of the use of colour, whether in dress, decoration, product promotion or design.

With dress, we can only make one first impression, so it has to be a good one, whether we are attending an interview, a meeting, addressing an audience, or meeting an important client for the first time. Different cultures have firm ideas about formal dress, so when dealing with overseas visitors, or travelling to their country, it is as well to know the form.

How workplaces are decorated makes a difference to energy levels; the colours chosen to paint washrooms, or restaurants, or staffrooms can be chosen to create required ambience – the wrong choice can produce feelings of unease, even if these feelings are only registered at a subconscious level.

Participants will work in small groups of 3 to 5 to consider some of these issues by answering a simple multi-choice questionnaire. The aim of the activity is merely to raise awareness, not to suggest that there is a right or wrong colour formula to apply to every situation.

Step 2: Divide group into syndicate groups of 3 to 5 people

Use any arbitrary means to decide groupings.

Step 3: Issue one copy of Document 1 to each participant, plus one extra copy per syndicate group. Explain procedures and timings

Instruct participants that they should look at each question, as a group, and make a collective decision regarding the most appropriate answer. Mark up just the group copy. *Syndicate groups have 15 minutes to do this. When each syndicate group has completed the exercise, the trainer will give the 'correct' answers, with further explanations, to the whole group; individuals can tick the appropriate box on their own copy, and retain this, should they wish, for future reference.*

Step 4: Allow syndicate groups 15 minutes to complete the exercise

After 15 minutes, re-assemble the group.

Step 5: Remind participants that they should now mark up their own questionnaires with the correct answers. Go through each question, giving explanations where necessary, using the trainer's notes on pp. 42–44 as a guide. (these could be duplicated and issued as a handout if preferred)

Individuals may well want to take issue with some of the 'answers'. These are merely suggestions, backed by research; but with a subject so vast (colour hues and tones being so various) this activity can only deal in generalizations. The activity is intended to make participants pause for thought – to make them more aware of the subtleties of colour choice, especially in areas where there could be change, eg interior decoration of offices, choice of outfit for an interview and so on.

Step 6: Close the activity referring back to the objectives

Trainer's notes

According to research, the correct answers to the questionnaire are as follows:

1 (a) Bill will be dressed formally, smartly, and wisely in that grey suits allow others to concentrate on what you're saying, not what you're wearing. Dark blue is the colour of respectability and reliability.

In this choice of tie colour, Bill is displaying his integrity. Dark blue ties represent the need to be trusted, and to be seen as trustworthy – in all, the ideal combination for interview dress. Black shoes should always be preferred to brown in the business context.

If groups thought (b) was appropriate dress, it should be pointed out that this combination represents the 'power dresser', and whilst appropriate in some business contexts, it could convey arrogance, or intimidate in an interview situation.

If groups chose (c), they should be made aware that whilst brown is a good teamwork colour in that it suggests equal status with colleagues, it is not a colour of authority. When combined with yellow, as in this case, it reflects diminished status. This impression could convey itself to the wearer's subconscious as well as to those interviewing, so this is a poor colour combination choice for an interview.

2 (a) Experiments have shown that people perceive darker colours as heavier than light. This mental perception can become 'reality' when, for example, staff have to lift packages such as these. Management need to consider the lorry drivers, the shop and supermarket staff, and all those involved in lifting the boxes if they are to avoid complaints. An experiment proved this in a factory where workers complained that dark blue boxes were too heavy to carry. A change of design and box colour solved the problem without reducing the weight of the contents.

3 (c) It is important that customers get off the carpeted area, on to the display patch if sales are going to be made. Light spaces are easier to walk along; people prefer to get off dark floors as quickly as possible if there is an alternative.

4 (b) Apart from the fact that red and yellow are now synonymous with fast food, so this choice would be appropriate, it has been proved that people eat more quickly when surrounded by these colours. This is obviously important for the fast-food market, but equally so when there needs to be a rapid turnover of diners, as

in this case. Red and yellow are also warm, friendly colours appropriate for staff recreation periods.

Answer (a) is not a good choice for a fast-food bar as these colours, though cool, are soothing. People will tend to linger. Answer (c) is a cold, austere choice. People may not want to stay long, true, but the scheme, with a hint of colour, is more appropriate to sophisticated wine bars than sandwich and burger bars which should be quick, but fun.

5   (a)   Red is a power colour for women. It not only represents success and authority, but is a choice when wanting to impress colleagues. Wearers of red usually find it improves their confidence.

Green is not a successful business colour for men or women, and should be used as a colour for recreational or casual clothes. Black is a smart colour, and one of respectability, but also tends to obscure individuality. In Mary's situation, it could convey a desire to be one of the crowd, rather than the person 'out front', hoping to inspire with her presentation.

6   (c)   Research has shown that people are not comfortable with this colour combination in indoor decoration, and want to leave the area as quickly as possible. Tingwell's do not want their staff spending long breaks in the washroom, so this would be an ideal choice!

The combination of pale grey and burgundy suggests elegance and luxury, and would be appropriate for a cloakroom in an upmarket hotel, perhaps, where guests are encouraged to pamper themselves, but not in a factory where time is money. Similarly, golden yellow and white is bright, sunny and inviting – just the place to linger perhaps.

7   (c)   Japanese see it as a sign of disrespect to attend a meeting in shirt-sleeves. They would not consider a businessman serious in intent if not dressed in the darkest of suits, and sombre tie. They consider bright colours to be ostentatious and inappropriate to the world of business.

In Japan, during a spell of very hot summer weather, Japanese businessmen were allowed to report for work dressed in light-weight safari suits, but it was unanimously agreed that serious business suffered as a result of this, and staff were made to revert to customary dress – dark suit, white shirt, and dark, subtly and soberly patterned tie.

8   (a) or (b)   Either method of decoration would make the room appear

wider and less corridor-like. In addition, a bright, white ceiling would increase the feeling of spaciousness.

9   (b) Tests have shown that most people think that (exactly the same strength) coffee tastes richer in red cups, stronger in brown, and weaker in yellow. So, to save money, and to cut down on caffeine intake, serve weaker coffee in brown mugs!

10 (b) In the high street, different colours give out different messages. Red and yellow spell out speed, whether fast food or delivery services. Green is probably the colour of the future, telling people's subconscious minds that such products or services are environmentally friendly. Purple is the colour of self-indulgence and luxury. Many chocolate and tobacco products are packaged in distinctive purple. Blue, however, is the colour of many banks and financial houses, implying security and safety. It is the 'respectable' colour; the colour of trust and integrity.

Impressions - Document 1

Although there is no *definitive* answer to the following questions, research has shown that some colour schemes create moods, reactions and emotions different from others; therefore some colour choices are preferable to others. Discuss these questions in your group and try to identify the most appropriate response.

1   Bill is going for an interview as a practice manager at a large health centre. He has decided to wear a business suit. What colour combination would be most suitable?

   (a)   Grey suit, white shirt, dark blue tie, black shoes.
   (b)   Dark grey/black suit, white shirt, red tie, black shoes.
   (c)   Brown suit, cream shirt, yellow tie, brown shoes.

2   Bloggs and Co produce tinned pet food. To brighten their image, they intend to pack the tins in coloured cardboard boxes, each box containing 24 extra large tins and weighing 20kg (approx 44lb). Management have two choices for the predominant colour. Which should they choose, and why?

   (a)   Pale golden yellow.
   (b)   Royal blue.

3   Williams and Son are renovating their electrical goods showroom. They intend to display televisions, videos, and hi-fi equipment along one wall, and kitchen appliances along the other. They will paint the walls in pastel shades, have light wood flooring on the areas in front of the displays, and a carpeted walkway down the centre of the showroom. The carpet would obviously be hard-wearing, easy to clean, and chosen not to show dirt and wear and tear, but what colour would be a good choice, and why?

   (a)   A mid-tone mixture, picking up the pastel hues of the walls.
   (b)   A neutral tone.
   (c)   A dark, contrasting colour.

4   With the new amalgamation there is a 25 per cent increase in the number of staff at Winninghams. Management has decided to offer an alternative to the existing restaurant facilities and provide a snack bar where staff can order sandwiches or burgers. There would still need to be a rapid turnover of diners to accommodate all the staff during the lunch period. What would be a suitable colour-scheme for this bar?

   (a)   Pale blue, pale green and white.
   (b)   Red and yellow.
   (c)   Black and white, with lots of glass and stainless steel.

5 Mary is lacking in confidence, but has to give a talk to a group of her peers. She needs to appear energetic, enthusiastic, authoritative and above all, convincing. She is fortunate in that she can wear most colours successfully, and has outfits in most hues. What colour should form the basis of her clothes for the day of the presentation?

 (a) Red.
 (b) Green.
 (c) Black.

6 The washrooms at Tingwell's factory are due to be repainted. What colour should management choose, and why?

 (a) Mainly pale grey, with burgundy paintwork.
 (b) Golden yellow with white paintwork.
 (c) Mid-green, with darker green paintwork.

7 It is summer, and a group of Japanese businessmen are visiting Andrew's company with a view to opening negotiations on a large deal. How should Andrew dress to give a good impression?

 (a) Light-grey trousers, short-sleeved white shirt and dark blue tie.
 (b) Beige, summer-weight suit, white shirt and bright tie.
 (c) Dark grey/black suit, white shirt and dark patterned tie.

8 The general office of Brown & Co is a long, narrow room with a high ceiling. Staff say it's like working in a corridor! How could it be decorated to give the impression of more width and space?

 (a) Paint the ceilings a dark colour, the walls light, and use carpeting of the same hue as the ceiling.
 (b) Paint the two long walls a light colour, and the two end walls dark, preferably in a warm hue.

9 Research has shown that people can be made to believe almost anything through the use of colour. If identical coffee was served to people in either brown, red, or yellow mugs, which would give the sensory impression of being the richest, and most full bodied coffee?

 (a) Brown mug.
 (b) Red mug.
 (c) Yellow mug.

10 When looking at shopfronts, logos, business insignias and so on, what colour most often represents respectability and reliability?

 (a) Purple.
 (b) Blue.
 (c) Green.

Activity 7

Metamorphosis

Description

A form of ice-breaker, suitable for starting a Managing Change type of course, or one where team-building is an important element.

Objectives

By the end of this activity participants will:

- have physically 'moved' about the training room to find a partner or small-group colleagues
- have 'broken the ice' by speaking to several course participants
- have spoken in front of the whole group
- know some personal information about all participants (and the trainer if you decide to join in)
- have given some thought, albeit in a superficial way, to the positive aspects of change and teamwork.

Participants

Number: Any, (depending on the number of appropriate word clusters you use)
Type: Any

Time

45–60 minutes

Resources

Pre-printed word cards (see trainer's notes on p. 50)

Method

Step 1: Introduce the activity explaining its purpose and objectives
This is a light-hearted way to do three things:

- to split up groups of participants, usually colleagues, who will otherwise form inseparable cliques
- to give participants the opportunity to meet at least two group members and find out more about them
- to ensure that everyone is known to the whole group.

Step 2: Explain procedures and timings

(Prior to the activity, you will have established the number of participants, and selected and shuffled the word cards to ensure that everyone will physically have to move from their neighbour in order to find their group. It may well be advisable for you to join in so that any latecomer to the course can take your place in one of the groups).

*The object of the first part of this exercise is to find the two or three people with whom you are going to form a small syndicate group. Explain that you will give out one card to each participant. Written on the card will be a word or words which connect with word cards held by other people. By questioning others, find out whether you 'connect' with them – ie whether your combined words link in some way; eg one person may have 'hands', another 'face' and a third 'strap'. These connect as they are parts which make up a wristwatch. The three people holding these cards are a syndicate group. Obviously, if the person holding 'face' is looking for colleagues with cards depicting parts of the body, she or he may find 'hands' but will have to re-think the syndicate group theme when no other body-part card-holder is located. **There must always be three or four members to each syndicate group**.*

Step 3: Issue cards

See note above regarding pre-course preparation.

Step 4: Begin the exercise

Encourage participants to move around rather than shout across the room 'does anyone link with "grass"?'

Step 5: When everyone has located their syndicate group, ask them to re-arrange seating so that they can sit with their group

While they are doing this, and to keep the activity 'light' you could ask if the 'egg' immediately found 'cygnet' and 'swan' or tried to team up with 'tadpole', or whether there were other confusions which had to be sorted out.

Step 6: Explain the procedure and timings for the second part of the activity – introductions

Individuals should now introduce themselves to other members of their group, including information such as name, place of work, what their work involves and so on, plus as much personal information as they wish to *share. **It should be emphasized that individuals should only share what they want to share. This is not a self-disclosure activity**.*

Ten minutes will be allowed for this part of the exercise.

Step 7: Give a time reminder at 8 minutes to ensure that everyone has the chance to introduce her/himself to the syndicate group

Step 8: After 10 minutes, instruct individuals to introduce a colleague from her/his syndicate group to the main group, giving as much information as can be remembered

To ensure that everyone speaks to the main group, and to share the syndicate group 'link' (from the word-associated topic cards) it may be useful to ask 'spawn' to please introduce 'tadpole' to the group; then 'tadpole' to introduce 'frog' and finally for 'frog' to say a few words about 'spawn' and so on around the syndicate groups. This maintains a light-hearted approach to what some participants may find stressful, ie talking in front of the whole group during the early stages of a course.

Step 9: After all introductions have been made, lead a short discussion of the process the group has just experienced

First, thank the group for participating and sharing. Explain that this is part of the supportive process which will continue throughout the course.

As this is an ice-breaker to begin a course which will look at change, it may be useful to draw some learning points from the first part of the activity – the groupings.

To follow up the example given earlier; if two people, 'hands' and 'face' found each other, and continued to look for another part of the body to form the third member of the syndicate group, (a) they wouldn't find their third colleague from this group and (b) 'strap' would be left alone without a logical group to join. The necessary change of approach is fundamental to problem solving, ie a change from vertical, logical thinking, to creative or lateral thinking. This is a very simple example of a process important to the concept of change. If there is a problem, or a situation which is getting nowhere, don't continue to bang your head against a brick wall; try looking at things from a different angle; explore all options.

Nobody likes change. The first reaction to the prospect of anything new is for people to resist, refuse or block the change. It's human nature. Most of us, if given adequate reasons to justify change, will soon adapt – even welcome the challenge of the new.

The first part of the activity could be seen as a very simple argument in favour of change. Each element in the groupings has a validity of its own, but through adaptation, combination, amalgamation and change an equally valid, arguably better, end product is achieved.

Change, in itself, is not something to be resented or feared. It is something which is happening to every one of us, all the time, in some way. It is important that this is recognized and that, through sharing, teamwork, and a positive supportive attitude, change in the workplace can be challenging, motivating and rewarding.

Step 10: Close the activity referring back to the objectives

Trainer's notes

The following word-associated groupings will give you six syndicate groups: four syndicate groups of 3, and two of 4, allowing up to 20 participants. If there are to be more than 20 on your course, think up other groupings of words whose elements 'evolve' (eg from spawn to frog) or which are major constituent parts of a whole (eg wings, tail, fuselage and engine).

Caterpillar - Pupa - Butterfly

Yeast - Flour - Dough - Bread

Tail - Wing - Fuselage - Engine

Egg - Cygnet - Swan

Spawn - Tadpole - Frog

Mung bean - Beansprout - Chop suey

Activity 8

PUNchlines

Description

A competitive ice-breaker which demonstrates the difficulties experienced by people whose first language isn't English when trying to understand some of our business language; an important concept when organizations have increasingly international links.

Objectives

By the end of this activity participants will:

- have become cohesive as a group, and be more relaxed in preparation for more serious course sessions
- be more aware of the need to choose written and spoken language carefully when communicating with those who have only a basic English vocabulary.

Participants

Number: 6 to 14
Type: Any

Time

30–45 minutes

Resources

- Flipchart stand, paper and marker pens
- Set of subject cards (photocopied from Document 1)
- Access to photocopier and scissors (for preparation of subject cards)
- Egg-timer or watch with second hands

Method

Step 1: Explain the activity

The group will be divided into two teams and each team will be given a set of subject cards which should be kept hidden from 'the opposition'. On each card is a word commonly used in business circles, but which, if split into its component parts, could suggest to someone who has little English a very different concept from the true meaning. For example, we all know what moonlighting is, but what would that term convey to someone who has only a rudimentary command of the English language? English business language is full of jargon, but what would that word convey – Jar-gone: a glass container missing?

Each of the words on cards lends itself to punning definitions. Some are visually ambiguous eg moon/lighting, each part meaning something entirely different if taken separately (consider the word 'therapist' in this context!) Other words are ambiguous by virtue of their sound, like jargon. Teams will take it in turns to issue a card to a member of the opposing team who will then go to the flipchart and either draw the word by illustrating each of its component parts, or write a pun (not a dictionary) definition, similar to the 'jargon' example above, again from the component parts of that word.

As with similar games, there will be a time limit of 1 minute for the team to guess their colleague's word. Award 10 points for a correct guess; 5 points to the opposing team if the person at the flipchart talks, writes any part of the word on the card, or gives other than a pun definition. The trainer will act as referee.

Step 2: Explain procedures

Each team takes it in turn to nominate one of its members to go to the flipchart. The game continues until everyone has had at least one attempt to convey a word by pun or drawing. There are sufficient cards for 14 people to have two attempts; however, the game can be halted at any time by the trainer, as and when it appears that the players have relaxed and are ready to move on.

Note that the purpose of the game is (a) to break the ice, and (b) to illustrate the point that English is a language which can and does cause confusion when communicating with someone whose command of it is rudimentary. This second point is soon grasped. How long the game is pursued therefore depends on the group and has to be at the discretion of the trainer.

Step 3: Divide the group into two teams; issue half the cards to each team

Instruct teams that they should decide which order their members are to go to the flipchart to convey a word via a pun or by drawing.

Step 4: Teams take it in turn to receive a card, illustrate or define the word printed on it so that their team can guess what the word is

Individuals should be given a few seconds' thinking time. When they are ready, the trainer should turn the egg-timer or start the watch. After a minute, if the team has not guessed the word, they can be told. If they do guess the word within the minute, the trainer awards 10 points to that team.

Step 5: When both teams have had an equal number of turns, and at a time decided by you, end the game announcing the winning team

Explain that the game itself, the quality of the drawings, the winning or losing is not really important. After this activity, individuals should feel alert, part of the group, and ready to progress to the course proper. There are some learning points to be drawn, however.

Increasingly organizations are doing business, and therefore communicating, with foreign nationals. We live in a time of rapid growth and change; the world has become much smaller; national and international boundaries have less importance as more and more companies merge, achieve multinational status and so on.

Whilst, ideally, people whose native language is English should learn the basics of other cultures and languages, it is recognized that much business is done in English. Other business people, whether European or Asian, are expected to use English. It is only fair, therefore, that we make an effort to use words which are as unambiguous as possible. The small sample of words used in this activity gives some indication of the confusion which could arise in quite basic business communication, so care must be taken in the choice of vocabulary used.

Step 6: Close the activity

PUNchlines – Document 1 (for reproduction by trainer)

INDUSTRY	LEGISLATE
ASSENT	ILLEGAL
ACCOUNTABLE	BRAINSTORM
BACKLOG	CAPACITY
DAMAGES	EXCISE
FUNDING	FORFEIT
GLOBAL	HYGIENE
INCOME	INVESTMENT
LABOUR	MARGIN
NEGOTIATE	OFFER
OVERDRAFT	RECYCLE
WASTAGE	SOURCING
TURNOVER	VARIANCE
UNDERWRITE	WINDFALL

Activity 9

Quick fire

Description

An ice-breaker which could be used at the beginning of any course, but especially appropriate to training concerned with managing change.

Objectives

By the end of this activity participants will:

- be more mentally agile and alert in preparation for the learning process of the training sessions to follow
- have learnt the first names of other group members.

Participants

Number: Any
Type: Any

Time

15–30 minutes

Resources

- Seating arranged in horseshoe formation for participants
- A name plate for each participant (this can be a piece of card measuring approximately 5in × 12in folded lengthways)
- Bold markers for writing on name cards

Method

Step 1: Give each participant a card and circulate marker pens. Instruct participants to print their first names (or how they would like to be addressed throughout the course) on the card leaving an approximately 5in space at the right-hand end
In all training situations, it is important for individuals to feel comfortable

and at ease with their environment and with their colleagues. Establishing how each person would like to be addressed from the outset is a way of helping people feel accepted and acknowledged as individuals. For example, there have been many 'Margarets' on courses who (it is subsequently learnt) are usually called Maggie, or Peggy, and would have felt far more at home if those names had been used. Others are referred to at work by nicknames (eg Hugh Richardson known as Richie) who would feel more relaxed if their usual term of address were used.

Step 2: Counting round the room from left to right, or in a clockwise direction, instruct participants to write their appropriate number, and corresponding letter of the alphabet in the space on the right of the card

For example, John who is sitting in the first chair on the left of the horseshoe would write 1 A next to his name; someone sitting further round the horseshoe might be 'Julie 8 H'.

Step 3: Instruct participants to place their card on the floor in front of them with the information facing into the middle so that other participants can read them

Although it is not essential that everyone can see each name – in fact it would be virtually impossible to arrange this – chairs may need to be rearranged slightly so that most of the names can be seen by the majority of people.

Step 4: Explain the first stage of the activity

The trainer will begin by identifying one course member, at random, by name. This person will then repeat her/his own name, and call out the name of any other participant; eg

TRAINER: 'Karen'
KAREN: 'Karen, Mike'
MIKE: 'Mike, Sarah'

and so on until every participant has given their name to the group. (In fact, the group will have heard the name at least twice by this method of repeating own name first before nominating another.) Participants should be encouraged to respond as quickly as possible, and to nominate in random fashion, ie not necessarily to name the person sitting next to them, or directly opposite. It helps if you include yourself in this activity.

Step 5: Begin the activity

Continue this quick fire naming and nominating until everyone has spoken at least once.

Step 6: At a suitable point, halt the proceedings and explain how the activity is to progress

Depending on the group, several stages could be introduced, eg 'Next, follow the same procedure of naming and nominating, but this time use just identifying numbers as printed on the name cards' or 'Next follow the same procedure, but use the letters printed on the name cards.

Alternatively, the group could progress at once to a quick-fire interchange of name/number/letter combinations; eg
  'Karen, John'
  'John, H'
  'H, Bradley'
  'Bradley, 10'
  '10, K'

In each instance the person named or whose number or letter has been called should respond by repeating their name, number or letter, and then nominating someone else either by name, number or letter, at all times keeping the responses moving as quickly as possible.

Step 7: At a suitable point, close the activity referring to the objectives

By now everyone should be fully alert, their brains attuned to speed of reaction, quickly changing and adapting. Explain that this is the ideal situation for opening a course concerned with managing change, where adaptability, alertness and quick thinking are qualities which should be developed.

Ask if anyone felt stressed by the exercise, acknowledging that unfortunately stress is a by-product of our rapidly changing work environment. If appropriate, look at ways of dealing with this stress, or explain that stress will be looked at later in the course if this is to be the case. Or follow this activity with one of the exercises in Activity 43 ('Relax') before launching into the course proper.

Stress the importance of the activity as a means not only of breaking the ice and stimulating the brain in preparation for the training to follow, but also as a means of learning, and using individuals' preferred names.

Activity 10

Sit in a circle

Description

Activity 43 – 'Relax' – offers some ways of helping *individuals* relax. This activity offers a quick, simple way for getting the *group* to relax. Discussion about, or training on, change can in itself be stressful and this activity can be used to release tension and help the group relax. However, we don't wish to suggest that 'Sit in a circle' can only be used under conditions of stress – it's possibly even more effective when the group is already having fun!

'Sit in a circle' can be used in almost any kind of training but we have found it especially valuable in the change arena, since it involves change, but in a very physical sense.

It scarcely needs any processing – indeed, we strongly recommend that you do *not* attempt to process it, since to do so would drastically reduce its impact. Join in, as trainer, and enjoy it!

Objectives

By the end of this activity participants will have participated in a 'group change' activity designed to reduce group tension and/or to enhance group cohesion.

Participants

Number: Minimum of 10; no maximum
Type: Any

Time

5 minutes

Resources

A carpeted floor

Method

Step 1: Introduce the activity

Simply state that you are going to do something different.

Step 2: The group stands in a circle, one behind the other, hands on the shoulders of the person in front

The following criteria need to be met if this activity is to succeed:

- the circle should be as small and exact as possible
- all the feet on the inside of the circle must be touching, heel-to-toe, and forming a perfect circle.

  Check both of these before proceeding to step 3.

Step 3: Everyone should now sit in the lap of the person behind them

Stress that this must be both a simultaneous and a very slow movement. It may need two or three practice runs before it succeeds.

Step 4: The circle should now attempt to change its position, through a rotation of 90 degrees (quarter circle). (This means that a participant sitting at 12 o'clock will finish up at 3 o'clock if the group is facing clockwise.) Explain that this requires a coordinated effort

This change of position sounds difficult but it can be made successfully – help the group out if it fails on its own. (Moving simply requires that all left feet are simultaneously moved forward, followed by the right feet, and so on until the final new position is achieved.)

Step 5: Continue until such time as you decide that the group (or gravity) has triumphed!

Activity 11

Treats

Description

A very short activity for the end of a hard day's training in the middle of a course. It's not really suitable as a course-closing activity but it can be used, with care, elsewhere.

Objectives

By the end of this activity participants will:

- acknowledge the value of small pleasures as a way of helping reduce stress at times of change or particular challenge
- have identified a number of ideas for future 'treats'.

Participants

Number: Any
Type: Anyone involved in managing change of any kind, personal or organizational

Time

15 minutes

Resources

- Flipchart stand, paper and marker pen
- One copy of Document 1 for each participant
- Paper (one sheet) and pencils for each participant
- Cardboard box or some other receptacle; an old shoe box is ideal

Method

Step 1: Introduce the activity

Pedler, Burgoyne and Boydell in their book A Manager's Guide to Self Development *(1986) argue that the secret of managing stress is the ability to undertake pleasurable activity from time to time* without guilt. *The emphasis is significant; even in the 1990s, we still seem to be conditioned by the Victorian ethic that work and non-work should be kept strictly apart and that work somehow requires stern rectitude and selflessness. Yet do we not meet people we envy enormously whose work is their life and their love? 'Enjoying what you do and getting paid for it' is something we would probably all aspire to. Pedler, Burgoyne and Boydell argue strongly that enjoyment and productivity are perfectly compatible, so why not bring an element of enjoyment into our work lives, even – and perhaps especially – if our work currently represents a stressful situation through change or some other major challenge?*

This activity is deliberately short and the timings and processing suggestions brief. Since treats should be pleasurable there is no point in investing too much analysis in them, or they lose their appeal!

Step 2: Give out copies of Document 1 to each participant and ask them to spend a couple of minutes completing the first part of it (it is self explanatory)

Step 3: Briefly process the exercise
Don't take more than a couple of minutes to do this.

Questions you might use:

- *How easy did people find it to think of five treats? If difficult, why?*
- *Did men find the form more difficult to complete than women? If so, does this suggest any possible link with the fact that men tend to die earlier than women?*
- *Do we feel guilty about treating ourselves when work pressures are mounting and need to be dealt with?*
- *Are productivity and enjoyment incompatible in the world of work?*

Step 4: Now ask people to complete the right-hand section of each entry – writing down how long it is since the person last treated themselves in this way
Allow two minutes altogether. It is best not to dwell on this too much, but it is common for people to realize with a jolt just how long it has been since they last treated themselves. A general question, simply asking for any observations on this part of the activity, is all that is needed. Above all, don't allow the discussion to descend to a bitter analysis of all the obstacles that prevent people from treating themselves (these can be endless – job, family and so on).

Step 5: Explain that you would like to increase people's range of ideas about how to treat themselves. Ask each participant to write down their favourite treat (from their list) anonymously on a piece of paper. The paper should be folded

and placed in the box. The trainer then draws out each in turn and writes them up on the flipchart. People can add to their own list ideas they are attracted by
This will only take two or three minutes. People can own up to their own treat if they want to, or if any need explanation but no one should feel pressured to do so.

Step 6: Wind up the activity by suggesting that little treats, especially by way of a reward when things have gone well or a difficult goal has been achieved, but perhaps even more so when the going is tough, are not 'the answer' to handling stressful situations (that would be escapism); but they can help us keep feeling good about ourselves which helps to keep things in proportion
We just want to stress here that this activity should not last more than 15 minutes or it loses its appeal. Essentially it needs to be quick, intuitive and fun. Participants should finish it feeling motivated to go away and try an old favourite or try someone else's great-sounding idea!

Step 7: Close the activity by referring briefly to the objectives

Treats - Document 1

Please list below five ways you 'treat' yourself. If possible, list things that are quick, simple and inexpensive but which give you particular pleasure or help to recharge your batteries. They can be things you do regularly or things you only do occasionally. Above all they should be *achievable* and not some flight of fantasy!

Examples could be:

- Having a long, hot bubble bath
- Walking along the river bank in the early morning
- Listening to a play on the radio

. . . and so on

Column 1

Column 2
(Leave these lines blank until instructed)

1 ....
2 ....
3 ....
4 ....
5 ....

Stop when you have done this. If you haven't managed to list five, don't worry.

Do not complete the section below until instructed.

New ideas I will try:

1 ....
2 ....
3 ....

SECTION 2

MANAGING THE PROCESS OF CHANGE

Activity 12

Barriers to equality

Description

This activity is designed for use in organizations which may be moving towards the implementation of a policy of equality of opportunity in their recruitment practices. Its aim is to help personnel officers and managers involved in recruiting staff to recognize discriminatory selection procedures. This activity is modest within the whole area of equality at work – but people need to start somewhere and this is a simple, non-threatening exercise designed to provoke thought and raise awareness.

Objectives

By the end of this activity participants will:

- recognize common barriers to fairness within the area of recruitment
- be able to detect unfair procedures and remedy them.

Participants

Number: Any
Type: Personnel officers or other managers involved in the recruitment of staff by an organization committed to equality of opportunity in selection

Time

1 hour

Resources

- Flipchart stand, paper and marker pens
- One copy of Document 1 for each participant
- Optionally, an overhead projector and transparency could be used during step 2

Method

Step 1: Introduce the activity
In their infancy, equality of opportunity programmes in organizations are

often seen by staff as 'nothing to do with them' but rather the province of 'the equal ops officer' or 'personnel'. In fact, for such a policy to work, it needs commitment at all levels.

The recruitment process is notorious for discriminatory practice, the law notwithstanding, and all those involved, whether 'personnel' or line management, need to recognize their own responsibility for implementation. This is often quite simple, as this activity aims to show!

Step 2: Suggest to the group that there are 4 main types of barriers to equality of opportunity in recruitment. These are:

Personal prejudice and stereotyping
Attitudes towards groups such as women, black people, those with a disability which stem from prejudice and traditional 'images' of how such people normally act and behave.

Subjective, arbitrary and/or traditional selection criteria
Selection criteria which effectively discriminate against particular groups. The criteria may just not have been reviewed for a long time, or they may actually be framed in order to attract certain types of applicant. The exercise which follows will reveal examples.

Pressure from others to discriminate unfairly
This can be pressure from superiors, from peers/team members or from subordinates who have their own subjective ideas about the sort of person they want to see on the team: 'Is he one of us?'

Unsatisfactory procedures
The recruitment process itself may be at fault; for example, it may by-pass certain groups or may allow unfair questions at interview.

You may like to flipchart these as you go along. Allow 10 minutes.

Step 3: Issue Document 1. Divide the main group into smaller groups of 4 to 6 members. Ask each group to carry out the exercise specified in the Document
Allow 15 minutes.

Step 4: Re-form the main group. Run through the 10 questions and get overall agreement to which barriers are identified
Allow 20 minutes.

The answers are:

1   Unsatisfactory procedures and stereotyping
    Word of mouth recruitment is an unsatisfactory procedure as it tends to exclude potential applicants. There is also a stereotype here that local authority manual work = male work.

2   Subjective or arbitrary selection criteria

Why should a candidate for bus inspector be required to pass a test in written English?

3 Stereotyping and traditional criteria
   Wheelchair users are not necessarily always confined to their wheel-chairs. Even if she was, how essential is it to the post in question that she reaches all the shelves?

4 Personal prejudice and stereotyping
   Research has shown that people with certain accents, eg Yorkshire, Cockney, are often discriminated against. The stereotype is that people with accents (ie 'not like us') are somehow less intelligent.

5 Prejudice and stereotyping
   Maybe she has fully recovered? The stereotype is of the 'poor woman' who couldn't take the pressure.

6 Traditional, subjective and arbitrary criteria
   'Smart' is here being defined in terms of the white British view of what constitutes smartness.

7 Unsatisfactory procedures, subjective criteria, stereotyping
   If there were fair selection procedures, designed to flush out the best candidate in terms of experience and skills then they were flouted here. 'Fitting in' is a very subjective notion and is usually code for 'one of us', in itself stereotypical.

8 Pressure from others, personal prejudice, stereotyping
   'People would feel uneasy' is a familiar cry in recruitment circles and is often used to disguise personal prejudice and stereotyping on the part of the speaker. It may, of course, be felt to be true, in which case it is pressure from others.

9 Traditional criteria, unsatisfactory procedures
   Traditional criteria such as these will always discriminate against women who are usually the ones who are involved in child-rearing – though not always!

10 Personal prejudice, stereotyping, subjective and arbitrary criteria
    This is about a perception of how all Asians tend to behave in their dealings with others – prejudice and stereotyping. The information given would also appear to suggest that there are subjective or arbitrary selection criteria in use. They may – or may not – be fair for the post in question. We don't know.

Step 5: Take three of the examples – we suggest you use those closest to the participants' own working lives – and ask the group to say what they would feel they needed to do if they came across the situation while involved in a recruitment exercise
Allow 10 minutes.

Suggestions for each of the cases follow:

1   Remove the word-of-mouth system and advertise more widely. Target
    men and women.

2   Consider whether the duties attaching to the post actually need the
    standard of written English required by the test. If not, scrap it. Even if
    they do, would someone's track record not provide sufficient evidence of
    facility at the appropriate level?

3   Check with the candidate the precise nature of the disability. If she
    seems the best qualified candidate, and she is confined permanently to
    the wheelchair, can the job not be restructured in some way so that she
    is not required to reach the top shelves? Has anyone asked her how she
    might reach the top shelves?

4   Ask if the candidate is the best qualified to do the job. If so, appoint her.
    Someone's accent is no guide to their abilities. Remember that, to them,
    you *are the one with the accent!*

5   Leaving aside the comment that few people walk away unscathed from
    such an experience she may now be perfectly recovered and there is no
    reason to suppose there will be a relapse. The root problem here is the
    stereotypical view of women as in some way feeble and emotional.
    There are plenty of men who cannot take pressure.

6   Muslim women can be just as smart – or not – as the next person. This is
    really about a perception which is culturally based and increasingly
    anachronistic and which dictates that men should wear suits and
    women skirts.

7   The procedures should not allow this to go unchallenged in an equal
    opportunity environment. The best person for the job in terms of how
    they meet the criteria should be appointed regardless of subjective
    feelings about who will fit in best.

8   It's not clear whether the selector or the team is at fault here. Either way
    there is no reason to suppose that a lesbian's sexuality will interfere
    with her work any more than a heterosexual's would.

9   Why is the five years' continuous experience rule in force? What can the
    justification be? If it's about being up-to-date could not a period of
    induction training be provided?

10 First the procedures should be clear about the level of communication
    skills required to do the job. Second, it is no more true to imply that all
    Asians find it difficult to get to the point than it is to say that all white
    English people are splendidly articulate

Step 6: Close the activity by referring briefly to the objectives

Barriers to equality - Document 1

You have just looked at four main types of barriers to equality of opportunity in selection. They were:

- personal prejudice and stereotyping
- subjective, arbitrary and/or traditional selection criteria
- pressure from others to discriminate unfairly
- unsatisfactory procedures.

Use these four categories to determine which are operating in the following brief case studies. There may well be more than one.

1   A firm employs a large number of male manual workers who are recruited locally by word-of-mouth.

2   Candidates for the post of bus inspector are required to pass a written English test before being considered for promotion.

3   A candidate for a clerical post in a library is turned down because she uses a wheelchair and it is felt she would not be able to reach all the bookshelves.

4   A candidate for a receptionist post is turned down at interview because she has a broad accent which is not local.

5   A woman who had six months' sick leave as a result of depression following the death of her child is refused promotion because the post she has applied for involves heavy pressure of work and it is felt she would not be able to cope.

6   A Muslim woman who always wears trousers is not offered a sales job because she 'doesn't dress smartly enough'.

7   After seeing Kim, Hilary, Pat and Chris, panel members appoint Pat. Although Kim and Chris were better qualified in terms of experience and educational background, Pat seemed pleasant and would fit into the current office set up.

8   A lesbian fails to be appointed as a Head of Section because it is felt that some team members would feel uneasy.

9   A woman who wishes to return to work after a two-year break for child-rearing is not shortlisted for the post of engineer because it requires five years' continuous work experience (she has all the relevant qualifications).

10 An Asian man is unsuccessful in obtaining a Personnel Officer's post. He is later told that he was thought liable to experience communication difficulties if he had got the job as 'Asian people have a tendency to talk a lot without getting to the point'.

Activity 13

But we've always done it this way

Description

Often employees are blamed for their lack of commitment to change imposed by management, but sometimes the culture of an organization can suppress creativity in its workforce. It may be autocratic, or locked into traditional methods of working. This activity looks at motivation, and suggests ways managers can encourage initiative, innovation and imagi nation in their staff.

Objectives

By the end of this activity participants will:

• have looked at ways in which their own management style, departmental or organizational culture might suppress change
• have brainstormed ways in which initiative can be stifled
• be more aware of methods for encouraging innovative and creative
   thinking in their staff.

Participants

Number: Any
Type: Any supervisor or manager responsible for staff

Time

1 hour

Resources

• Flipchart sheets and markers for syndicate group work
• Sufficient floor/table-top space for groups to work independently
• Means of fixing flipchart sheets to wall
• Different colour marker for trainer use

Method

Step 1: Introduce the activity, explaining procedure and timings

This activity is called 'But we've always done it this way'. This is just one of the excuses given when an imaginative employee suggests an alternative way of working. The old way may be the best way, but then again new circumstances, market conditions, different personnel and so on may validate the need to look at new methods of working.

Participants will work in small groups to list as many ways as they can think of to suppress new ideas, imaginative solutions, enterprise, creativity and so on. They should consider previous companies worked for as well as looking to their present organizational culture. Ask them to remember managers with whom they have worked who were less than enthusiastic about suggestions for improvements. Consider your own staff. What reasons have they given/could they give for not pursuing suggestions for change made by their own staff? Have they failed to delegate recently for example? What justification did they have?

One person should act as scribe for each group. They should head each sheet of flipchart paper with 'But we've always done it this way' as a reminder of the task in hand. Syndicate groups will brainstorm why and how ideas for change are suppressed within a department/organization. Instruct them to be as creative, inventive, imaginative as they can!

Suggest that brainstormed ideas be recorded as simple statements, such as 'Pass the buck'. There will be an opportunity later, in plenary, to explain the statement more fully, eg 'By "Pass the buck" we meant something like "Talk to personnel about it – it's more their cup of tea."' Thoughts as well as actions can be included, eg (thinks) – 'It will mean more work for me.'

Half an hour will be allowed for this part of the exercise, after which time the group will reconvene for a general discussion.

Step 2: Divide group into syndicate groups of 3–5 people

Ensure that there is sufficient space for syndicate groups to spread out and write on flipchart sheets.

Step 3: Issue sheets of flipchart paper and a marker to each syndicate group; begin the activity

Circulate among groups to check that they understand and are implementing the brainstorming rules, ie any suggestion, however fantastic, should be recorded without censure. Try to ensure that ideas are recorded as simple statements (see step 1).

Step 4: After 30 minutes ask group to reconvene; fix flipchart sheets to the wall

Lead brief discussion of items included on lists. Ask for explanations from syndicate groups if necessary.

Step 5: Select a marker of different colour from one used by syndicate groups, and add the words 'DO NOT' to each list

If syndicate groups have written their lists as statements as requested, by adding the words 'do not', 'do not say', 'do not think', etc to each item listed, they have in fact produced a reminder of things they should not do, as line managers, if they wish to have a motivated and innovative workforce.

Step 6: Close the activity referring to the objectives

Activity 14

Coblocks

Description

In developing strategies for managing change at a functional level it is easy to overlook the corporate dimension – the degree to which the work environment (systems, politics and so on) contributes to the difficulties we have to cope with. The core of this activity is a questionnaire designed to help highlight problems in organizations where change may be needed. The nature of organizations, and the complex interactions of formal and informal systems, often results in difficulties of analysis. This activity provides one tool which can help to break down complexity and suggest avenues which may need to be tackled *at corporate level*.

Objectives

By the end of this activity participants will:

* be familiar with the Company Blockage Questionnaire
* be able to use the Questionnaire's results to analyse possible areas for action and change *at corporate level*.

Participants

Number: Maximum of 10
Type: Managers who see a need for change *at corporate level*. The activity works best if you can group together people from the same area/division/subsidiary and so on.

Time

1 hour 15 minutes

Resources

* One copy of Document 1 for each participant
* One copy of Document 2 for each participant
* One copy of Document 3 for each participant

Method

Step 1: Introduce the activity
Outline the main points contained in the introduction and objectives.

Step 2: Decide on your groupings
Groupings should reflect existing work teams if possible so that there is a common organizational perspective within each group.

Step 3: Issue Documents 1 and 2 to each participant and establish the small groups; ask all the groups to begin the exercise when they are ready
Allow 15 minutes for individual questionnaire completion. The documents are self-explanatory.

Step 4: Issue Document 3 and ask each person to transfer their scores to this document
Only a few moments will be required for this.

Step 5: Ask each group to analyse its scores and discuss the implications
Allow 15 minutes. Visit each group in turn.

Questions you might use:

- *Does the group agree with the suggested problem areas thrown up by the questionnaire?*
- *Are there any other areas of organizational problem that could be added to the list in Document 3 (eg new technology, attitudes towards the European Single Market/Europeans generally, and so on)?*
- *If so, what symptoms could there possibly be for those problems?*

Step 6: Re-form the main group. Ask each group to report its main findings
Allow 15 minutes. You can use some of the same questions from step 5, or raise and develop in the full group issues and questions you may have picked up during step 5.

Step 7: Canvass ideas for action from each group
Allow 15 minutes.

Questions you might use:

- *To what extent can you, as managers, influence problem x?*
- *Are there any easy solutions to any of the problems? If so, which and what?*
- *What other ideas might people have about how to tackle any of the identified problems?*
- *Whose responsibility is it to tackle corporate problems of this nature?*

- *What other problems might there be which are not included in the list? What symptoms would people look for?*

Step 8: Ask each group if it can discern any sort of action plan that might be open to it to tackle company blockages

Allow 10 minutes. This step will build upon the ideas generated in step 7 and will allow them to be put into some kind of cohesive framework.

Step 9: Close the activity by referring briefly to the objectives

Coblocks - Document 1

Company blockage questionnaire

There are always problems in any organization. Managers have to tackle them. Often the problems are complex and do not have single causes. Frequently they stem from the *company* or *organization* and it is often helpful to analyse problems from this perspective. This questionnaire will help you to do this.

You have 15 minutes, working on your own, to complete the questionnaire which follows. You should record your answers according to the instructions on Document 2. Apply the questions to your own company or organization. Be honest in your answers!

1   This company seems to take on idiots a lot of the time.
2   No-one knows exactly who is responsible for what.
3   We have lots of problems – but no-one really seems to know what causes them.
4   There are plenty of skilled people around – but people's skills rarely seem to match the demands of the job.
5   People don't seem *really* committed to their jobs; there are too many clock-watchers.
6   Good ideas are seldom taken seriously.
7   Each department or division seems to be a separate empire.
8   Managers seem to believe that people only come to work for the money.
9   There seems to be no clear succession planning for important posts.
10   We plan for tomorrow rather than for the future.
11   There is a lot of disagreement about rates of pay.
12   People make mistakes – but they don't seem to learn from them.
13   New people take far too long to reach an acceptable level of work performance.
14   Jobs are not clearly defined.
15   I don't see much evidence of delegation.
16   Managers don't have the time to train people.
17   Performance won't improve since there are no real incentives to do it.
18   Lateral thinking cuts no ice round here.
19   I wish groups would get together more in order to solve common problems.
20   Managers equate tight supervision and control with better output and results.
21   New managers are usually recruited externally.
22   I don't *really* know what's expected of me.
23   People often leave to earn more elsewhere.
24   People will avoid even constructive criticism.

25 The qualifications of job applicants seem to be getting lower every time.
26 Our internal organization definitely needs bringing into the 1990s.
27 Important decisions are exclusively the province of top management.
28 Training is valued highly by some departments and virtually ignored by others.
29 People are more likely to get chivvied and disciplined than praised or rewarded.
30 If only we took more risks. . . .
31 I just wish people would say what they *really* think.
32 Managers believe that people are fundamentally lazy.
33 There is no development plan for the future.
34 Staff are told one thing and then judged by another.
35 Not rocking the boat seems to bring the best rewards.
36 People are set in their ways and they seem comfortable with that.
37 New people don't stay.
38 The various parts of this organization all seem to be ploughing their own furrow.
39 There *is* talent around – but it's not channelled properly.
40 Skills tend to be picked up almost accidentally rather than being learnt properly.
41 People put in a lot of effort but the organization exploits that without rewarding them properly.
42 Innovation is not valued.
43 Under pressure, everyone looks after themselves first.
44 There's resentment by many managers at the passing of the 'good old days' when discipline really meant something.
45 Management feels threatened by potential high achievers and does nothing to develop them.
46 There is often a mismatch between corporate and individual objectives.
47 The pay structure is a real obstacle to better, more efficient work organization.
48 Time and energy are not channelled properly.
49 Many staff are only barely up to scratch.
50 The 'top dog' has so much on her/his plate that she/he cannot keep in touch with everything that's going on.
51 Our decision-making is hampered by lack of timely information.
52 Many managers feel that, as they had to learn things the hard way, so should others.
53 People do not feel that good performance is valued.
54 Other companies in the same business seem to have all the bright ideas.
55 Managers tend to look after their own areas and they do not welcome interference from others.
56 Managers seldom take the view that staff can make a significant contribution to the company's well-being/profitability.

57　People haven't got a clue what the company plans to do with them in the future.

58　People tend to be judged on their personality rather than their abilities and achievements.

59　Exceptional effort tends not to be rewarded.

60　When the going gets tough too many people opt out.

61　New people seem to get the better jobs; this causes resentment.

62　Some departments seem overstaffed in comparison to their contribution.

63　Old ideas carry the day.

64　Managers are just not up to training their staff.

65　If our company were in trouble, most managers would care little and do less.

66　Custom and practice are seldom challenged.

67　Meetings are generally unproductive, making minutes and wasting hours.

68　Management tends not to concern itself with whether or not staff are happy at work.

69　There are just too many variables in our company for succession planning to be effective.

70　The company's future plans are pretty feeble.

71　We just don't pay enough to attract really good staff.

72　Directness and openness are not concepts familiar to our senior management.

73　We just don't have the talent we need.

74　Important things either get done twice or not at all.

75　We just don't know what our labour turnover figures are.

76　If we had the skilled workforce we could increase productivity.

77　I feel like a lone crusader at times.

78　This company is living in the past.

79　We don't profit from the mistakes of others within this company.

80　We just don't do enough to try to make jobs interesting and meaningful.

81　We lose well-trained staff to other companies.

82　Corporate objectives, if expressed at all, are so vague as to be almost meaningless.

83　People are reliant on long working hours just to make up a decent pay packet.

84　We would all benefit if there was more challenge to the accepted order.

85　We seem to recruit people with little or no talent to do the job.

86　There's no balance in the workload managers have to carry; some are grossly overworked while others have an easy time.

87　We don't know how our pay compares with other companies because comparative figures are not available.

88　There's no encouragement to update skills.

89 People's commitment suffers because they don't get the chance to have a say and influence things.
90 People like to keep their heads down, by and large.
91 There's so much in-fighting that it's destructive.
92 Managers tend to feel that staff are not that interested in the quality of their working lives.
93 Senior management's collective experience is too narrow.
94 Priorities are far from clear.
95 People feel as if they work for a second-class organization.
96 Standards are just too low.
97 We get the chaff in with the wheat when new people are recruited.
98 The concept of reorganization is anathema.
99 Such management information as there is is not going to the right places.
100 If we had better quality staff we'd produce better quality output.
101 People are unhappy about their low pay levels in comparison with other organizations.
102 Managers are not alert or responsive enough to external change in the market-place.
103 People just don't care about others at work.
104 There's still a stiff formality about the way we deal with our managers here.
105 'Management education? What can it possibly teach me?' is a fairly common attitude among managers here.
106 Plans are cooked up in ivory towers.
107 Our total benefits package just doesn't stand comparison with similar firms.
108 Strong individuals are resented.
109 We don't have established recruitment procedures. It's left to individual managers.
110 Departments constantly snipe and put down the work of other groups.
111 Management just doesn't acknowledge the true cost of an unhappy member of staff.
112 The way people are treated here in their first few days – it's surprising they stay!
113 People would love more challenge in their work.
114 We push problems under the carpet, or discuss them covertly. Character assassination is rife.
115 Teams tend not to indulge in team-building activity.
116 Under the surface there's a lot of in-fighting between managers.
117 Managers are less than explicit about how they see the future prospects of their own staff.
118 Decisions are made *months* too late!
119 I know I'm underpaid.
120 No-one is stretched enough.

Coblocks - Document 2

Scoring chart

In the grid below there are 120 squares which correspond to the numbered questions. Put a circle around each statement which you think is generally true, or symptomatic, of your organization. If you think it's not generally true just leave it blank.

A	B	C	D	E	F	G	H	I	J	K	L
1	2	3	4	5	6	7	8	9	10	11	12
13	14	15	16	17	18	19	20	21	22	23	24
25	26	27	28	29	30	31	32	33	34	35	36
37	38	39	40	41	42	43	44	45	46	47	48
49	50	51	52	53	54	55	56	57	58	59	60
61	62	63	64	65	66	67	68	69	70	71	72
73	74	75	76	77	78	79	80	81	82	83	84
85	86	87	88	89	90	91	92	93	94	95	96
97	98	99	100	101	102	103	104	105	106	107	108
109	110	111	112	113	114	115	116	117	118	119	120

Now count the number of circled boxes in each column and enter the total in the box at the bottom.

Coblocks - Document 3

Questionnaire interpretation sheet

Transfer your totals from the scoring chart to the table below.

Totals

A		Inadequate recruitment policy/procedures
B		Confused organizational structure
C		Inadequate management control
D		Poor training
E		Low levels of motivation
F		Low levels of creativity
G		Poor teamwork
H		Management philosophy is causing problems
I		No succession planning or management development
J		Aims unclear
K		Reward system unfair
L		Personal stagnation

The blockages with the highest scores are those that need investigation and change. Do you agree?

Activity 15

Crossing the line

Description

This activity uses a simple visual technique which managers can use to assess the support for, and resistance to, change and to identify which areas to concentrate on in order to increase support. It is a less analytical, more intuitive alternative to Activity 20, 'Push-me-pull-you'.

Objectives

By the end of this activity participants will:

- be able to use a visual method of estimating supporting and resisting forces for change
- be able to use the technique to determine a strategy for increasing support for change
- be aware of the value of analysing change situations with others.

Participants

Number: Maximum of 12
Type: Managers who are confronting organizational change

Time

1 hour 15 minutes

Resources

Flipchart stand, paper and marker pens

Method

Step 1: Introduce the activity

When promoting change it is helpful to 'know one's enemy' as this will help to dictate the tactics to be adopted. This activity proposes a very simple way of mapping out the 'enemy' (those likely to be opposed to the change) and the 'allies' (those likely to be in favour). It also provides a means of identifying a way forward with least resistance.

Step 2: Discuss with the group, and get agreement on, an organizational change which will, or needs to, be tackled in the near future

This can be a change which will involve the whole group or it can be a small number of changes each of which affects two or three of the group. This will determine the groupings you will use for step 3. In the former example you would keep the group together. In the latter you would set-up up to four interest groups based on a common involvement in the change identified.

Step 3: The task is to identify all the interested groups and key individuals who will be either directly or indirectly affected by the change

Allow 10 minutes and use brainstorming as the technique; accept and write up all offerings without comment or discussion.

However, you may want to prompt the group to widen its horizons if they seem too narrow, especially when identifying the 'indirectly' affected groups and individuals. For example, the woman who brings the tea trolley round to the different departments may not be personally influenced by the proposed change – neither need she be consulted – but because she is at the heart of the informal grapevine of the organization, she could spread either enthusiasm or discontent and resistance. She is, therefore, a person of humble status within the organization, but one who could exert considerable influence, and she ought to be included for this reason.

If you are going to use the whole group to tackle one problem, ask a participant to do the flipcharting for you. If you have smaller syndicate groups ask each to prepare its own flipchart.

Step 4: Ask the group(s) whether they are absolutely sure that they have covered everybody likely to be involved

Step 5: Introduce the first part of the 'Speedometer' concept as set out in Figure 15.1 on p. 88

Allow two minutes. Flipchart the example as you go along.

Step 6: Again using a participant at the flipchart with the main group, or small groups working on their own, get the group(s) to break down their brainstormed lists into the various headings suggested by the 'Speedometer'

Allow up to 10 minutes.

Step 7: Introduce the second part of the 'Speedometer' concept as set out in Figure 15.2 on p. 88
Allow two minutes. Flipchart the example as you go along.

Step 8: Get the group(s) to re-draw the 'Neutral' line on their own flipchart; encourage discussion of how feasible it is to move the line in this way
Allow 15 minutes.

Questions you might use:

- *How could the parties on the immediate left of the old neutral line be encouraged to move across? What practical ideas are there for achieving this?*
- *If there are difficulties here, does the difficulty arise because a group should have been in a more extreme category?*
- *What practical strategies could there be for shifting even further the promoting forces already on the right-hand side of the neutral line?*
- *Is there an argument not just for tackling the parties on the immediate left of the initial neutral line, but for trying to move all groups to the right?*
- *Is there an argument for encouraging the most extreme parties on the left-hand side of the neutral line to become even more extreme, on the basis that they become more polarized and isolated?*

Step 9: Encourage the group(s) to draw up an action plan based on the 'Speedometer' model
Allow 10 minutes.

Questions you might use:

- *What specific steps need to be taken now? By whom? With whom?*
- *What is the timescale?*
- *Is the action to be overt or covert?*
- *Is the action reliant on formal or informal systems/relationships in the organization?*
- *How will you know if you have been successful in shifting opinions in the way suggested?*

Step 10: Allow some time to reflect on the group process and its value in an activity like this
We suggest you allow 15 minutes. Most participants gain much from having the luxury of 'unpacking' problems with a peer group. In the workplace, individuals often feel isolated, and in times of change, the 'them' in 'them and us'! Often too, it must be admitted, the most profitable sessions in a training programme are those where participants have responsibility for small-group self-help.

If the main group was broken down into smaller groups, ask if any syndicate group would like to share any part of their discussions which would be useful to the whole group. A discussion of action-plans can be especially helpful. Explain that, although it is recognized that time for such analysis is seen as a luxury in the workplace, it is time well spent to use methods like this in order to clarify thinking and to see, diagrammatically, areas which need the most work in order to smooth the pathway to change and to identify where support can be expected, a most valuable, and too often neglected, facet of change management.

Step 11: Close the activity by referring briefly to the objectives

Trainer's notes

The 'Speedometer' is shown in Figure 15.1. This represents the various shades of resistance and support for a specific change which is planned. The example given relates to a local authority issue, but the tool works well with any proposal for change.

In Figure 15.2 the 'speedometer' is re-drawn to represent the minimum attitude shift which must occur if the change is to be successful.

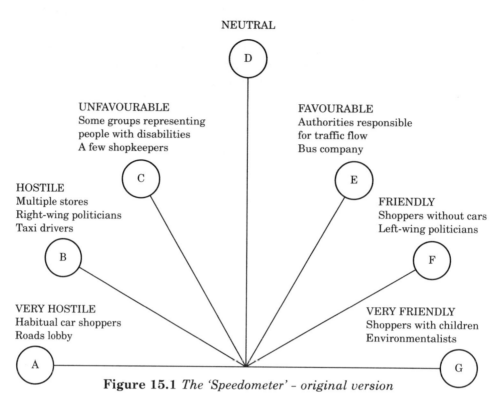

Figure 15.1 *The 'Speedometer' – original version*

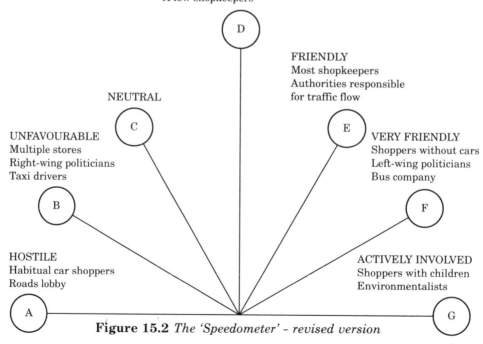

Figure 15.2 *The 'Speedometer' – revised version*

Activity 16

Cynic's guide to change

Description

This activity is not meant to be taken seriously, but it *does* have a serious message. Many of the activities in this volume treat the subject of managing change as a serious organizational issue – which it is – and various straightforward techniques are suggested. However, sometimes complete honesty and straightforwardness is not matched by other people. This activity focuses on that and suggests ways in which people are devious – and how to counteract such deviousness. For example, it is common for people to have good ideas – thank goodness – and for their good ideas to be (apparently) well received with encouraging 'noises' from superiors, peers and subordinates. Far too often, however, these encouragements do not bear fruit when it comes to delivering the good idea. We hope, through this activity, to promote a certain healthy cynicism so that people with good ideas recognize that they should not necessarily take responses to their good idea at face value. It is a high-speed and often amusing activity which is best used as an antidote to more cerebral material on managing change!

Objectives

By the end of this activity participants will:

- be aware of some of the more devious practices which people adopt when they want to resist change
- be aware of some of the more devious practices which people adopt when they want to introduce change.

Participants

Number: Maximum of 10
Type: Managers involved in managing change

Time

15 minutes (maximum)

Resources

- One copy of Document 1 for each participant
- Ten mini-scripts as described in the trainer's notes
- 'Cynic's Guide' board as specified in the trainer's notes
- Furniture arrangements as specified in the trainer's notes

Method

Step 1: Introduce the activity

Don't waste much time on this. We suggest you enlist the group's help in re-arranging the furniture as shown in Figure 16.1 on p. 93.

Step 2: Sit all participants down in the semi-circle (the two chairs at the table should be empty); issue the mini-scripts (as specified in the Trainer's Notes) in their envelopes to each participant; ask them not to open the envelopes until they are sitting at the table; outline the activity

Don't take more than a minute to do this; if this activity becomes too serious or laboured it loses its point and spontaneity. Simply explain that:

1 *The group represents the Editorial Board of a new publication called* A Cynic's Guide to Managing Change.
2 *The Board is observing some day-to-day exchanges between two managers in a typical organization to gather material for the new publication.*
3 *You (the trainer) will play the part of the person with The Great New Idea which is going to change the face of The Organization, not to say the world.*
4 *Each member of The Board will in turn play the part of a senior manager in The Organization. Each has a 'mini-script' and, when their turn comes, they will sit at the table and interview the manager with The Great New Idea, reading from their mini-script.*
5 *At an early stage you will stop the interview and ask The Board to offer the cynic's interpretation of what has been said by the senior manager. This should not just be couched in terms of the opposite to what the senior manager said, but should offer some healthy, cynical opinions as well as advice to the manager with The Great New Idea. (For example, if a senior manager were to say 'That's a terrific idea' it is not enough to just say the opposite, which would be something like 'That's a lousy idea'.) All members of The Board can contribute by simply calling out their views and advice.*
6 *The manager with The Great New Idea will then move to the next senior manager's office and see what advice they have to offer. In practice this means the first script-reader will vacate their chair. The next reader will replace her/him and The Board will each move along one chair so that the returning reader sits at the far end. (The diagram in the trainer's notes should make this clear!)*

7   *The exercise proceeds until all mini-scripts have been acted out. (In a group of fewer than 10 some people get a second 'go'; this is not a problem.)*

Step 3: Invite the first senior manager to take their place and to open their script in readiness to interview you; run the activity in accordance with the notes for step 2 and the suggestions above

While the senior manager is taking their place and is opening their mini-script, you should march briskly round the perimeter of the room, or whichever is the longest path to the desk and chair, muttering audibly 'I've got a Great New Idea'. Knock on the desk and sit down. Wait for the senior manager to read out the mini-script and respond with an Appropriately Grateful Response. These are suggested in the trainer's notes. Stop the interview after the Appropriately Grateful Response, hold up the 'Cynic's Guide' board (see Figure 16.2 on p. 93) and wait for The Board to suggest one or two cynical views. Drumming your fingers on the table and fixing the senior manager with a glassy stare helps the 'fun' atmosphere to develop at this point.

When you've had a few seconds of responses, put the 'Cynic's Guide' board down on the desk, say 'Next manager please', leave the chair and do another brisk perimeter 'march and mutter' while the others change seats and the next senior manager takes over. Continue in this vein until all the mini-scripts have been used.

The whole of this activity should be carried out at breakneck speed and with barely more than a few seconds of interview and responses.

Step 4: Issue Document 1 to each participant; get some brief response to the idea behind the activity

Don't spend more than five minutes on this.

Questions you might use:

- *How useful is a dash of cynicism as a tool in a manager's armoury?*
- *Do people feel the statements in Document 1 are unnecessarily cynical?*
- *Have people ever used any of the suggested techniques for getting change accepted?*

Step 5: Close the activity by referring briefly to the objectives

Trainer's notes

Before running the activity you will need to prepare the following 10 mini-scripts. We suggest you write them on postcards and seal them in envelopes.

1 'I think your idea should be taken to the top. Why don't you ask the MD for an interview?'
2 'Welcome to the team! We're really looking forward to the new ideas you've got for us!'
3 'Tell me about your new idea! We all speak the same language here so I'm sure it'll be something we can support 100 per cent!'
4 'I like your idea very much. It's very similar to a scheme I dreamed up myself recently. Let me tell you about it.'
5 'The big meeting is next week. Your idea will be floated then. I suggest you keep quiet about it in the meantime.'
6 'This idea is so good you ought to be shouting it from the rooftops! I'd like to see lots of enthusiasm – get out there – jump up and down and really sell it to them!'
7 'When we get to the meeting I think you should hit them between the eyes with this new idea of yours. Don't waste any time. Get in there and gobsmack them!'
8 'This new idea of yours. . . Keep this to yourself while you develop it. It's your baby.'
9 'This is a really radical idea. People will just love it!'
10 'You know that Alfie is dead against this whole new idea! Of course, everybody loathes him but I suggest you try to win him around as he'll be a real pain otherwise.'

Your Grateful Responses to these (See step 3) should be spontaneous but could be along these lines:

1 'Thank you very much. I will!'
2 'You're so kind!'
3 'Great! Well, it's like this. . .'
4 'Er . . . yes, of course.'
5 'Right!'
6 'OK! I'll get to it!'
7 'Terrific!'
8 'You really think I should?'
9 'That's really reassuring! Thank you.'
10 'I'd been wondering about him!'

The furniture should be arranged as follows shown in Figure 16.1. The Cynic's guide board (step 3) should be made from some card with a handle attached. Tape some white paper to the front with 'CYNIC'S GUIDE SHOULD SAY' in lurid marker pen colours at the top, as shown in Figure 16.2.

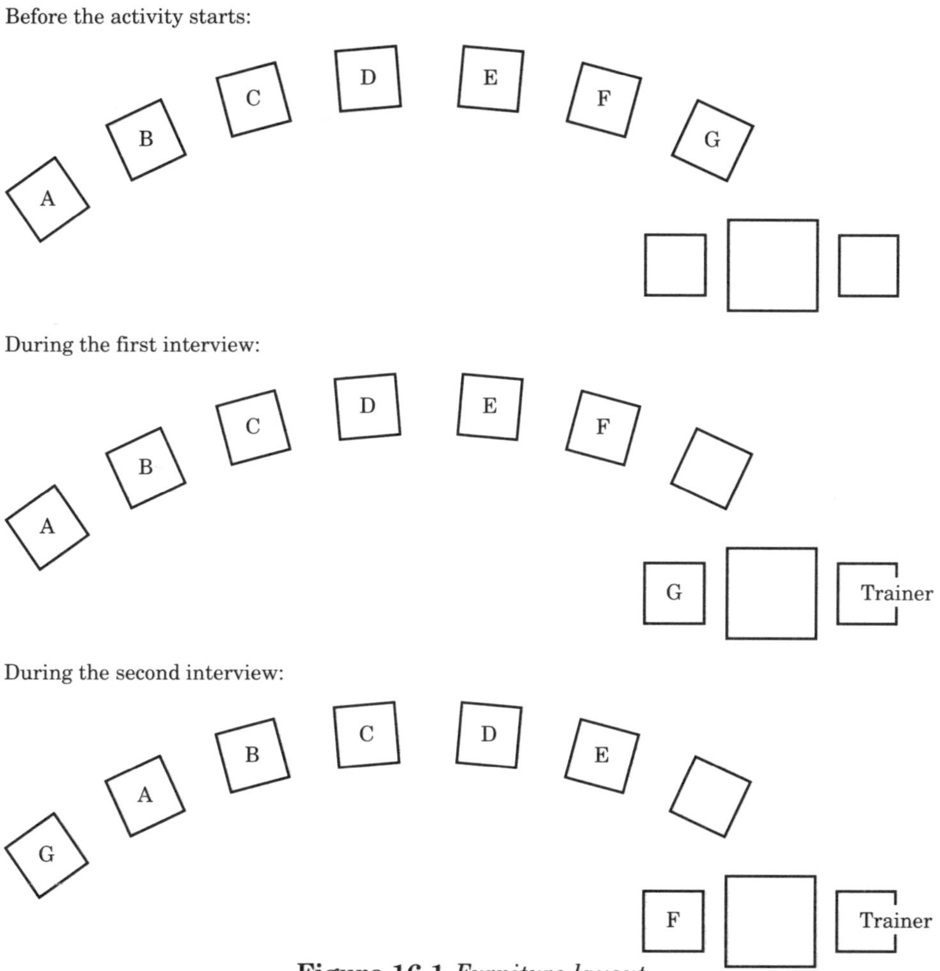
Before the activity starts:
A
B
C
D
E
F
G
During the first interview:
A
B
C
D
E
F
G
Trainer
During the second interview:
G
A
B
C
D
E
F
Trainer

Figure 16.1 *Furniture layout*

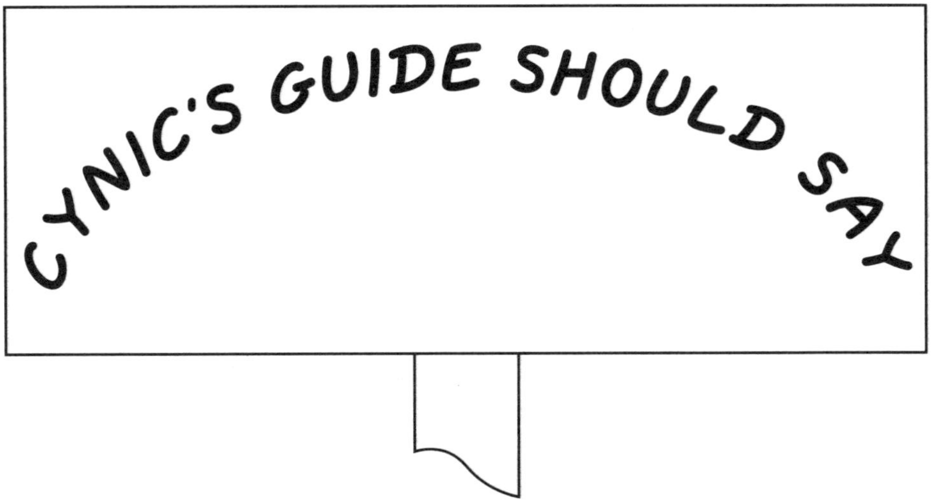
CYNIC'S GUIDE SHOULD SAY

Figure 16.2 *Cynic's guide board*

A cynic's guide to managing change - Document 1

We've all had great ideas at one time or another; but getting those ideas accepted and, worse, getting them translated into action, all too often means negotiating an organizational minefield.

People are often entrenched. Anything which undermines the status quo undermines them. You may have a wonderful new idea, but perhaps you don't have the special skills required to sell that idea effectively. There are some little tricks that you can use. . .

- If someone says you should go and talk to someone in higher authority, they are setting you up because they know that the 'higher authority' is as entrenched as they are – but they can inflict permanent damage on your career.
- If people say they want change assume they want something which looks like change but which actually changes nothing. Something cosmetic is probably as far as they'll willingly go.
- Don't think people think the same way you do. If they did, they would have come up with the same idea. You will probably find a chasm of non-understanding when you come to share your new idea.
- You'll probably have to decide which is more important to you – to get your idea *accepted* or to *receive the credit for it*. You're unlikely to achieve both.
- Try to get approval to anything new *before* any meeting to discuss it. If there are objections try and establish what they are before the meeting so that you can counter them before the critical time.
- Stay relaxed! If you appear not to care if your idea is taken up or not you will greatly reduce people's pleasure in shooting the idea out of the water.
- Do let other people in on your idea. Active participation in its development and introduction gives others a sense of achievement and involvement.
- You might like to think about some 'decoy' ideas, or sacrificial lambs. Let people savage them and get the steam let off before you introduce the *real* new idea.
- The more original or far-reaching your idea, the less you should emphasize it. Give people time to get used to it so that they feel less threatened by it.
- Try and get an unpopular person to oppose it; this can win you no end of allies. Or try suggesting that it's only a matter of time before the competition does it.

Activity 17

Handling redundancy

Description

One of the less congenial aspects of organizational change may be the need to make staff redundant. This activity is designed to assist managers who have to conduct termination interviews to undertake the task efficiently but with sensitivity.

Objectives

By the end of the activity participants will:

- be able to schedule both organizational and individual announcements of redundancy in a manner which reduces to a minimum the negative corporate and personal impact
- be able to conduct a professional yet sensitive termination interview
- be able to predict common questions asked by staff who have just been made redundant.

Participants

Number: Minimum of 4, maximum of 8
Type: Senior managers who may be required to handle termination interviews or who may be otherwise involved in 'down-sizing' of a company or organization

Time

2 hours 30 minutes

Resources

- In addition to the course room, sufficient small rooms will be needed to accommodate up to four pairs for individual role-plays
- Up to four copies of Document 1
- Up to four copies of Document 2

- One copy of each of Documents 3, 4, 5 and 6
- One copy of each of Documents 7, 8, 9 and 10
- Up to eight copies of Documents 11, 12 and 13
- Flipchart stand, paper and marker pens
- Paper and pens for individual notes to be made

Method

Step 1: Introduce the activity

Organizations seldom prepare themselves or their managers for the difficult task of handling redundancies. It is worth noting that the impact at both corporate and individual levels is bound to be negative, however sensitively handled. However, a professional approach will reduce short-term distress and help to bolster longer-term corporate morale. Decisions to reduce the size of the workforce are normally taken for the overall good of the company and should be seen as such.

Step 2: Divide the group (maximum of eight) into two smaller groups, maximum of four in each; assign one group to be the Senior Managers' Group and the other to be the Site Managers' Group

Settle the two groups in different rooms and give out the relevant briefing sheets to each group, copies of Document 1 to each member of the Senior Managers' Group and copies of Document 2 to each of the Site Managers' Group. Allow both groups a few minutes to read their briefings and then check their understanding of the task.

Each group should be evenly matched, ie 2 and 2, 3 and 3 or 4 and 4. If there is an odd number you could assign one person to be an observer during steps 3 and 7, asking them to make notes on the process that they have been watching. If you wish, you can of course draw up your own briefings based on the local situation, or, if this activity is being used to prepare managers for a known, real termination situation, you may change the parameters to reflect local reality.

Step 3: Begin the exercise as described in the Briefing Sheets (1 and 2), and note the starting time

Stop the exercise after exactly 60 minutes, unless it finishes earlier. Move between the two groups occasionally and observe the discussions. Alternatively, assign the observer to monitor one group while you monitor the other. If necessary, after 40 minutes, remind the Senior Managers' Group that they do need to brief the Site Managers before the hour is up. Ask both groups to keep any notes they may have made for later on.

While this is proceeding decide on the 'pairings' for step 4. Fill in the bottom sections of Documents 3–10 accordingly, but do ensure that real-life managers are not paired up with real-life subordinates, or the exercise could be too close to reality for comfort.

Step 4: Separate the two groups once again; issue the individual role play briefings (Documents 3–6) to individual members of the Senior Managers' Group

Explain that the Senior Managers' Group members are now being asked to come out of their first role and, at step 6, act out new roles of staff about to be told of redundancy. They should be briefed to assimilate their roles and to act in the interview as they think they would given the role description assigned to them. Ask them not to compare notes with the other group during the break (step 6).

Step 5: Explain to the Site Managers that they will shortly each be asked to role play a termination interview with a colleague details of which you are providing; give out copies of Documents 7, 8, 9 and 10 to the appropriate people (See step 3). Explain that you expect them to keep to any agreements made with the Senior Managers' Group and to observe the guidelines they may have agreed during step 3

Ask them not to compare notes with the other group during the break (step 6).

Step 6: Take a 15 minute break

This will not only add some realism but will also serve to heighten anxiety levels somewhat! It is important to keep the two groups apart. Coffee or tea could be served and individuals should use the time to prepare for the role plays which follow.

Step 7: Start the role plays as specified in the Briefing Sheets, allowing the Site Managers' Group to implement any strategies devised during step 3

Make sure each pair has its own room to operate in. Allow no more than 10 minutes for the interviews. Briefly observe each pair during the role plays (or divide the task between yourself and the observer).

Step 8: Bring the whole group back together. Process the activity in accordance with the guidelines provided below, your aim being to draw up and issue a working guide for managers on how to handle terminations and termination interviews. Issue Documents 11 and 12 as the discussion progresses, getting the group to add in any extra items to these checklists which have emerged in the discussion and which do not appear on the checklists. Finally, issue Document 13 which is self-explanatory and which needs discussion only if time allows

Allow 45 minutes. First of all you will need to spend a short while 'unpacking' how people felt about the role-plays. Acknowledge the strength of feeling engendered by the experience of confronting redundancy, not just to the recipient but to those who have the difficult task of conducting the interview. Next, flipchart the strategy which the Senior Managers' Group identified (step 3) by way of a strategy for dealing with redundancy. Compare it with Document 11 and inject any missing ideas. Issue Document 11 and allow people to add in any new ideas.

Next, take the ideas which the Site Managers' group identified as guidelines for conducting a good interview (step 3) and flipchart them. Consider each in turn and check to what extent the pairs felt the guidelines were observed during the role-play interviews. Bring in your own (and observer's, if applicable) observations once the pairs have given their views. Compare the flipchart list with Document 12. Look for any omissions and ask the group what they think about the missing ideas or suggestions. When Document 12 has been distributed, allow the group time to add in new items not already covered.

Issue Document 13 and, if you have time, see if any of these questions actually arose in the role-plays. Ask how they were dealt with – did people have the necessary information and, if not, how did this affect the professionalism of the interview?

Step 9: Close the activity by referring briefly to the objectives

Handling redundancy - Document 1

Briefing sheet for Senior Managers' Group.
It is a Thursday morning. You are a group of senior managers in a service company. You have just been told by your company's Chief Executive that a Board-level decision has been made to reduce the workforce by a total of three people in each of your divisions. This represents a 10 per cent reduction for each of you. The reductions must be implemented no later than Friday of next week, and it is company policy to operate on a 'Last In, First Out' basis. This is *not* negotiable. The Company is not able to use Outplacement Consultants to assist in the process.

You are disappointed by the decision but not surprised. It results from a very sluggish market and the company's need to remain in profit, which it will do – just – if the staffing cuts are implemented immediately.

Each of your divisions operates on a different site but all are within the same town. All operate on a 7-day, 24-hour shift-work basis. There are line managers on each of the sites who will clearly be responsible for conducting individual termination interviews.

The company is well-advanced in terms of IT, and most staff have individual computer terminals on their desks with a password-based access security system. Your company's computerized database contains sensitive information on members of the public (eg credit ratings, details of accounts and so on) and you will need to protect the integrity of this system during the period of terminations.

Four weeks' pay in lieu of notice will be given in addition to statutory redundancy payments which are to be enhanced by the company to make reasonably attractive packages. Anyone possessing a company car will be required to return it on or by their last day of service, which may be different from their last day at work. All affected staff have at least two years' service so all will qualify for redundancy payments.

The Group Personnel Department is responsible for drawing up the paperwork and they will provide your Site Managers with documentation and cheques for each individual together with guidance on pension fund implications if required by individuals.

You want to limit the damage as much as possible both to the company and to individual members of the workforce by planning the exercise with care.

Your should therefore determine how to implement the announcement of redundancy to the workforce. You will need to meet with your Site Managers, as a group, in order to (a) tell them of the redundancies and (b) agree with them how the process is to be managed. Although you should make it clear that these managers are to be responsible for telling those individuals selected for termination, you may negotiate any other tasks with them.

Your specific tasks
1 Decide on what day the terminations should be carried out.
2 Draw up and write down a list of steps, in *chronological order*, which you would wish to see taken on the announcement day.
3 Call in, and brief, the Site Managers.

You have 60 minutes to carry out all three tasks. Your trainer's or observer's role is purely that of observer. She or he cannot give you any additional information but you are free to make any assumptions that you feel are reasonable in the circumstances and which do not infringe company policy as set down in this briefing note.

Handling redundancy - Document 2

Briefing Sheet for Site Managers' Group

You are a group of Site Managers for a service company. You are each responsible for a different site within the same town. You each head a team of some 30 people, all of whom have workstations with individual computer terminals, accessing a sensitive database containing credit ratings and account details for members of the public. Access to the system is via individualized passwords. Each site operates a 24-hour, 7-day a week shift pattern.

It is a Thursday morning and you have been summoned as a group to meet collectively with your respective Divisional Managers who will call you in within the next hour.

You have strong suspicions that the meeting is about recent company performance in a very sluggish market. You suspect redundancies may be on the cards. You hope that it won't be your own jobs that are to go. As a group you are agreed that slimming down is the likely reason for this meeting and, as you await your summons to the meeting, you begin to exchange ideas about how a redundancy interview should be handled, as you feel that this responsibility may fall on your shoulders before too long.

Your specific task

While you are waiting to see your Divisional Managers, discuss together and prepare a list of 'Do's and Don'ts' for conducting a professional termination interview and which you could make good use of if the need arose. Note down the points which you think you would need to cover. Each of you should make a personal copy of the list as it emerges in discussion.

When called into the meeting with your Divisional Managers, make any notes during the meeting which you feel may be necessary.

If, during the meeting with your Divisional Managers, you or they do not possess a piece of information, make a reasonable assumption which does not conflict with company policy (of which the Divisional Managers can be expected to be aware!). You cannot use the trainer or observer as a source of extra information.

Handling redundancy – Document 3

Briefing for Hilary Brindley

You are aged 32 and have worked for the company for four years. You are directly involved in dealing with enquiries from the public by telephone and you use the company's IT system constantly. You have done similar work before for two other companies, and you know that you are good at what you do.

You have a family at home, partner and two children, and you are the main provider of the repayments on the substantial mortgage you have on your home. You earn more than your partner does. Your main perk with the company is private medical insurance.

There are rumours at work that, with business being quiet, there may be lay-offs soon. As one of the more recent arrivals (staff turnover has been very low in the last three years) you feel vulnerable and are not happy to have been summoned during your night shift to meet your manager this morning, especially as both she/he and her/his secretary have both been very secretive about the purpose of the meeting.

You are now awaiting the meeting with some trepidation. You tend not to get on with your shift supervisor. You are tired and feel that you may get quite angry if the rumours turn out to have some substance.

(To be completed by the trainer)

Participant's name ....

Your Manager will be role-played by ....

Handling redundancy – Document 4

Briefing for Kim Callander

You are aged 28 and have worked for the company for just over two years. You are directly involved in dealing with enquiries from the public by telephone and you use the company's IT system constantly. Before that you worked in a variety of jobs in the fast-food industry, but you do have a university degree and aspirations to do something better with your life.

You live at home with ageing parents who are to some extent dependent on you financially. You pay them rent for your accommodation. Your main perk with the company is private medical insurance.

There are rumours at work that, with business being quiet, there may be lay-offs soon. As one of the more recent arrivals (staff turnover has been very low in the last three years) you feel vulnerable and were thus not too surprised to have been summoned, late yesterday, to meet your manager this morning. You have not been given any clues as to the reason for the meeting and you have found out that one or two colleagues have also received similar summonses. You are already putting two and two together. . .

If it turned out that you were to be made redundant, you feel that this might actually be a chance to go for something better, especially if you get a reasonable pay-off. Doing this job has been 'OK' but has prevented you from doing much about going on to something else. You are concerned about the possible impact of unemployment on your responsibilities to your parents, though, and you'd be a bit surprised if you were proved right since your manager was instrumental in getting you this job originally; you met through a mutual acquaintance.

You are now awaiting the meeting.

(To be completed by the trainer)

Participant's name ....

Your Manager will be role-played by ....

Handling redundancy - Document 5

Briefing for Chris Sutherland

You are a shift supervisor in the company. You have been in the job nearly four years and you absolutely hate it! It's only the money (good) and the poor job market that has prevented you from leaving. In addition to the perk of private medical insurance the company also provides a car for you in view of the night shifts and to ensure you can travel between sites on a regular basis.

Rumour has it that redundancies are in the offing. Since you are aged 25, single, with no family responsibilities and living fairly cheaply in rented accommodation close to work, you fervently hope you will get the chance of redundancy, with some money to speed you on your way. You may travel for a year and then maybe try for a place on a course at a University or College.

You have been summoned yesterday to attend this morning's meeting, as have two of your colleagues on your shift (though they are coming in later on). You have promised to ring them afterwards and let them know what is happening to you, since they both live just round the corner from work.

You have a reputation for being a somewhat fiery character, which stems from your general feelings about the job, but, if you are offered redundancy, you would be thrilled!

(To be completed by the trainer)

Participant's name ....

Your Manager will be role-played by ....

Handling redundancy - Document 6

Briefing for Pat Dobson

You are a shift supervisor for the company. Aged 56 you have only been in the job just over two years having worked for nearly 15 years before that in insurance. That job ended in redundancy and it took you some months to secure your present job. Your present perks extend to private medical insurance and you have a company car in view of the night shifts and the need for you to travel to the other sites frequently.

You are married with grown up children. Your mortgage has another four years to run although it is not financially crippling. Your partner is unwell and cannot work but does not need looking after on a daily basis. You certainly cannot afford to be without a job, and you dread the mysterious meeting you were told about yesterday – no reasons given for it – with your manager today. There has not been much business lately and there are rumours of cutbacks.

You are waiting for your manager to call you in. You count your manager as a family friend and you are terrified you will break down emotionally if you get the news you expect, as you also feel unsure how you will cope with it all again so soon after the last experience. You also feel your age is against you.

(To be completed by the trainer)

Participant's name ....

Your Manager will be role-played by ....

Handling redundancy – Document 7

Briefing for Hilary Brindley's manager

You are to tell Hilary that she or he is to be made redundant, using the information and strategy you have put together during this activity so far.

Hilary is aged 32, has worked for the company for four years and is directly involved in dealing with enquiries from the public by telephone, using the company's IT system constantly. Hilary did a similar job for two other companies before joining yours and is a good worker; you would not, if it had not been for the 'LIFO' policy have chosen Hilary for redundancy, even though the two of you do not 'get on' too well.

You know that Hilary has a family at home, a partner and two children, and is the main provider of the repayments on a big mortgage. Hilary's only perk is private medical insurance.

You are seeing Hilary at the end of a busy night shift.

(To be completed by the trainer)

Hilary Brindley will be role-played by...

Handling redundancy - Document 8

Briefing for Kim Callander's manager

You are to tell Kim that she or he is to be made redundant, using the information and strategy you have put together during this activity so far.

Kim is aged 28, has worked for the company for just over two years and is directly involved in dealing with enquiries from the public by telephone, using the company's IT system constantly. Before that Kim worked in a variety of jobs in the fast-food industry. Kim is bright and you are going to be genuinely sorry to part company.

Kim lives at home with ageing parents, and considers the main perk of working for the company to be private medical insurance.

You don't anticipate any great emotional difficulty with this interview although you feel some responsibility since you were instrumental in helping Kim get the job originally, having met through a mutual acquaintance.

(To be completed by the trainer)

Kim Callander will be role-played by..

Handling redundancy – Document 9

Briefing for Chris Sutherland's manager
You are to tell Chris that she or he is to be made redundant, using the information and strategy you have put together during this activity so far.

Chris is a shift supervisor and has been doing the job in a competent, if unexciting, way for 4 years. There is a lack of energy which surprises you in a 25-year-old. As far as you know Chris has no burdensome family responsibilities, being single. Chris's package, apart from salary, includes private medical insurance and a company car.

Chris has a reputation for being a bit of a noisy troublemaker. Although you like Chris as a person you are concerned that this interview could degenerate into a shouting match.

(To be completed by the trainer)

Chris Sutherland will be role-played by ....

Handling redundancy - Document 10

Briefing for Pat Dobson's manager
You are to tell Pat that she or he is to be made redundant, using the information and strategy you have put together during this activity so far.

Pat is a shift supervisor aged 56, has been with the company for just over two years and joined on the back of redundancy after 15 years in insurance and a very difficult, lengthy job-search campaign. Pat has to cope with a permanently unwell partner and, as you know, cannot afford to be without a job. If it hadn't been for the 'LIFO' policy you would certainly not have identified Pat's post for redundancy.

In addition to basic salary, Pat's package includes private medical insurance and a company car.

Pat is a friend as well as an employee and is very easy to get on with. You know the family well and you meet socially.

A competent supervisor and no fool, Pat is well liked by all. You are confident that Pat would be aware of the general decline in business and would also be aware of rumours which you have reason to believe are buzzing around.

(To be completed by the trainer)

Pat Dobson will be role-played by ....

Handling redundancy - Document 11

Checklist for stage managing redundancy announcements
- Decide when the announcements are to be made, trying to avoid Fridays, before Bank Holidays and 'busy' work days.
- Liaise with Personnel Department and take advice on procedures.
- Brief all managers who are to be involved at least a day before (and train them if there is time!).
- Ensure that only those with a 'need to know' actually know before the announcement is made formally.
- Ensure that adequate, private accommodation is available.
- Timetable interviews with care, being sensitive to grades (see senior staff first), identifying anyone known to be on leave, abroad or just out on that day. You may prefer to prepare the ground in advance by a general statement issued through managers about 'An important statement will be made tomorrow on the company's future direction' or you may prefer that no advance warning is given. General advice is impossible here. Ensure that all staff give priority to the redundancy interview and instruct people to attend where necessary. Do not divulge, or even hint, at the reason for the interview in advance when arranging a time for an interview.
- Have contingency plans for dealing with staff timetabled but who go sick or are absent for some other known or unknown reason. Is it reasonable to telephone them, or even visit them at home? Know clearly how you will deal with people once seen. If they are to return to their desks how will you deal with other people in the section who are also affected and who have yet to be seen?
- If people are terminating immediately can you make arrangements for evening or weekend access for them to clear their desks?
- Are there any security issues, eg computer access passwords which should be deleted to avoid vengeful and wilful damage? What about security passes and access generally?
- Be clear with Personnel what the packages are to be and ensure you know where their role in the process starts and finishes.
- If an outplacement firm is to be used, who is the link person in your company for liaison purposes and what briefing is to be given to the company? When will referrals take place – immediately after the interview or at some other time? (Immediately after is to be preferred.)
- Finally, ensure that you have a clear strategy for informing those who still have jobs what has happened and what the future holds (as far as you can see). This should be done immediately after the individual terminations are complete and it is essential to counteract and damp-down the rumours which will have, by that stage, already have spread like a bush-fire.

Additional notes In the space below add any additional notes which you may wish to make.

Handling redundancy - Document 12

Checklist for handling a termination interview

Location: Private. Absolutely no interruptions.

When: Try to avoid Fridays, or just before Bank Holidays. Also avoid known birthdays or anniversaries if you can. Check on people's diaries and make sure they can give priority to your meeting with them.

Time: For everyone's sake, keep it short. Around 10 minutes maximum, but normally at least 5 minutes.

Plan: Have a structure for the meeting, knowing the points you want to cover and in what order.

Style: Efficient, professional but not cold, unkind or uncaring. Explain clearly but don't justify or get involved in recriminations. Don't blame others. Above all, don't stress 'How difficult it is for you'.

Points to cover:

- How events have led to the decision.
- Decision is final and irreversible. There is no appeal.
- Any possibilities of internal transfers all exhausted.
- Clarify last day of service and last day at work.
- Outline main details of package (have severance letter, cheque, etc to hand) and ensure person is clear about return of company car etc.
- Policy on references.
- Policy on safeguarding company secrets (if any).
- How the decision will be announced within the company as a whole.
- Who else knows about it.
- What is to happen about handing over duties and responsibilities.
- What happens when the person finishes this interview: where do they go, who do they see? What about collecting personal belongings?'
- Any other points:
  -
  -
  -
  -

Closing the interview: Give the person the opportunity to ask questions. Be quite sure in your own mind she or he knows the decision is irreversible; they must not leave 'hoping' that it will all come right tomorrow or the next day. (If the company is using outplacement facilities this would be the time to hand the person on to the consultant.)

After the interview: Write a brief report on the interview, its content and outcome in case matters need following up, or there needs to be a referral of queries (eg to Personnel) or there is any possibility of subsequent Industrial Tribunal investigations.

Additional Notes In the space below add any additional notes which you may wish to make.

Handling redundancy - Document 13

Some questions which redundant staff may ask either in the interview or later and to which answers need to be ready

- Why pick on me?
- What about transferring to another job/division/whatever?
- Are these figures open to discussion?
- Do I have any appeal rights?
- Am I required to work my notice?
- When do I finish?
- What is my last day of service?
- What about the company car?
- What about . . . (other aspects of any package, eg preferential rate mortgage etc)?
- How is my pension affected?
- What is the position on references?
- Can I take some time to find another job during the firm's time?
- Can I use the firm's facilities to start my job search, eg photocopier, phone, secretarial help and so on? (Can arise before or after last day at work.)
- Supposing another job came up in the company later; would you consider me as a serious applicant?
- Am I the only one?
- Can I return to my desk now?
- Do my colleagues know?
- Can I tell my own staff yet?

And finally, be prepared for reactions along the lines of. . .

'You'll be hearing from my solicitor.'

'You've never liked me, have you?'

'Why don't you get rid of that other so and so everyone's complaining about?'

'This is totally unfair'!

'You can stuff your job!'

. . .and so on.

These are common, human reactions to difficult, stressful circumstances and can happen even when the termination interview has been very sensitively handled. If you experience these, don't take them personally or assume you have failed to do the job properly.

Activity 18

How am I doing?

Description

A self-evaluation post-course activity, which gives individuals a means of monitoring progress in chosen areas for development.

Objectives

By the end of this activity participants will:

- have the means to appraise aims and achievements
- be able to assess progress within their chosen areas for change
- have undergone self-reflection and self-observation in the context of personal progress.

Participants

Number: Any
Type: Any

Time

A few minutes, daily, for weeks/months depending on nature and complexity of change pursued

Resources

One copy of sample rating chart, Document 1, for each participant

Method

Step 1: Introduce the activity

It is usual to leave a training course fired with enthusiasm, convinced that the learning which has taken place will be acted upon, and that progress will be steady – even rapid. It is important to recognize that there may be unforeseen obstacles. Often change is best consolidated if achieved slowly and thoroughly. It is also important to keep an objective oversight of progress, because once caught up in the issues of your everyday working life, it is easy to let good intentions slip.

This is an optional post-course activity offering a means to monitor progress in whatever areas of change it is wished to pursue.

Step 2: *Issue a copy of the rating chart, Document 1, to participants*

This rating chart can be duplicated and used for as many individual areas of change as are required. Each horizontal column has an opening section to identify a problem for solution or desired objective. For convenience it is headed 'aim'. Ensure that the aim recorded is realistic and specific.

Beyond the 'aim' block are boxes, each square representing one day of the week. On a daily basis, participants should look at their aim, and record any progress (or lack of it!) by plotting a point on the grid. The middle line represents no change, or stasis; the line below represents regression and the line above, progression. See from the example given how to plot progress towards the given aim.

Step 3: *Explain how to monitor, assess and develop progress*

Participants should be told to keep the chart with them – in wallet or diary – as a reminder, particularly of their aims and, once a week, to assess the graph they have created. If it shows a downward trend, they must try to understand why this is, listing the factors which hindered the aim, what they tried to do about them, and the outcome. Problem areas should be highlighted and focused on. If the graph gives a 'no change' picture, the learning points of the training course should be reviewed to see where these can be applied more rigidly. If not as successful as had been hoped, participants should consider whether their initial aim was perhaps too high or too general. They may have to begin more slowly.

If all is proceeding well, a note should be made of factors which helped progress and how these can be capitalized on. This is a continuing process of self-knowledge, so making a mental note of key learning points will be useful.

Over the weeks, aims may change, or need to be modified to meet new situations or circumstances. New problems may present themselves which would benefit from monitoring in this way, or participants may wish to pursue present objectives in more detail. Point out that critical and honest self-observation is one of the major keys to successful change management.

Step 4: *Close the activity referring back to the objectives*

Note: *It may not be appropriate, in some instances, to keep a daily record; weekly plotting on the chart may suffice with monthly assessments of progress*

How am I doing? - Document 1

DATE							
AIM							
DATE							
AIM							
DATE							
AIM							
DATE							
AIM							
DATE							
AIM							
DATE							
AIM							

Activity 19

Learn to love it

Description

We felt we could not put together a volume on the management of change without including in it reference to the work and writings of Tom Peters. His *In Search of Excellence* (Peters and Waterman, 1992) and *A Passion for Excellence* (Peters and Astin, 1986) were best sellers and he locates a love of, indeed passion for, change at the heart of his book *Thriving on Chaos*.

The activity which follows provides a structure for considering radical change which will allow participants at least to begin to explore what some will see as being a completely radical approach. Peters himself would freely allow that his approach *is* radical. It has to be if it is to succeed.

We cannot hope to give processing notes with this activity which fully reflect the flavour of Peters's work. Before embarking on this activity with managers we therefore *very strongly* urge you to: (a) read *Thriving on Chaos*: it is full of challenging, thought-provoking ideas on change, (b) believe in those ideas. Both processes are necessary, we believe, if the activity is to have any value, since you, as trainer, will be sucked into debate and argument throughout and you need to be clear about where you stand and why!

Objectives

By the end of this activity participants will:

- have been made aware of a radical approach to change in business
- have begun to consider alternative strategies for business which embrace, and thrive on, change.

Participants

Number: Maximum of 12
Type: Senior managers who are able to influence organizational strategy

Time

2 hours 30 minutes

Resources

- Two overhead projector (OHP) transparencies prepared as shown on pp. 120–21
- OHP and screen
- One copy of Document 1 for each participant
- Flipchart stand, paper and marker pens for use if required

Method

Step 1: Introduce the activity

You may wish to suggest to participants that they read Thriving on Chaos *before they attend the programme, or at least before they undertake this activity. In any event, cover the main points raised in the introduction and objectives.*

Step 2: Outline Peters's two basic leadership tenets

Allow five minutes. Reveal OHP transparency 1.

Peters offers, in his book, 45 prescriptions for organizations to cope with the shattering pace of change which is now, he argues, the norm. The leadership implications of these are:

Love change: *People have somehow to be shifted from resisting change to loving it. Love of it has to become the driving force rather than the restraining force of resistance. Otherwise the organization will sink under the weight of change in the world or market in which it strives to succeed.*

Apparent anarchy can be controlled: *Love of change can be seen to result in apparent anarchy as the ground rules constantly shift and new ways of thinking and doing things have no time to become the old ways.*

(For further elaboration of these two themes, see Thriving on Chaos, *Chapter 2.)*

Step 3: Outline the 'Our World Turned On Its Head' scenario (see Document 1)

Allow 10 minutes. Use OHP transparency 2. Refer to trainer's notes on p. 123 for further guidance on your presentation of this material.

Step 4: Divide your group into two or three smaller groups; the basis for the grouping should reflect one or more of the 10 items presented at Step 3

For example, one group might have a particular interest in marketing, another in leadership and so on. You should limit the topics to three altogether, but each group could tackle the same topic if this seems appropriate to their needs.

Step 5: Issue Document 1 to each syndicate group; Ask them to read the instructions

The instructions are self-explanatory.

Step 6: Ask each syndicate group to commence its task
Allow 60 minutes.

Step 7: Re-form the main group and ask each syndicate group in turn to present its findings; discuss the results
Allow 60 minutes. We suggest you use the questions posed in the document as a framework for 'quizzing' each syndicate group on its findings.

Step 8: Draw together any threads which have emerged; you may like to note them down and issue them, after the activity has ended, by way of a handout
Allow five minutes. Look for practical strategies. Get some reactions to the Peters concepts and, finally, and if you feel it is appropriate with the group, challenge them if you feel they are espousing change but actually finding reasons to resist it. To Peters such behaviour is a classic example of what business does not need if it is to survive, let alone thrive, in the twenty-first century.

Step 9: Close the activity by referring briefly to the objectives

1:   LEARN TO LOVE CHANGE!

2:   CONTROLLING ANARCHY?

What does this love for change mean for. . .

* MARKETING?

* INTERNATIONAL ASPECTS OF OUR BUSINESS?

* MANUFACTURING?

* SALES AND SERVICE?

* OUR CREATIVE EFFORT?

* OUR PEOPLE?

* OUR STRUCTURE?

* OUR LEADERSHIP STYLE?

* OUR MANAGEMENT INFORMATION SYSTEMS?

* OUR FINANCIAL MANAGEMENT SYSTEMS?

Trainer's notes - OHP 2

For each of these functions you should present a snapshot of how it (probably) is now and how, according to Peters, it needs to be in future.

These twin perspectives are set out in Document 1 and you should elaborate/discuss these as you make your presentation.

Learn to love it - Document 1

Group task: Our world turned on its head

You have just been presented with 10 different business functions together with Peters' view of what must happen in each if business is to survive in a world full of major change.

These perspectives were:

Marketing	*Now*: Geared to mass markets, mass advertising, big campaigns to gain minor competitive advantage.	*Must be*: About creating markets, focusing on developing a market niche, closeness to the market leading to responsive innovation, welcoming of market fragmentation and differentiation.
International	*Now*: For 'big' corporate organizations only!	*Must be*: Essential part of *every* firm's strategy, regardless of size. All market and product development to have an international dimension to it from the word 'go'.
Manufacturing	*Now*: All about volume, cost, equipment, technology.	*Must be*: A main constituent of the marketing function as it becomes a source of quality management, responsive to the market and innovation. Must be part of any new product design from the start, concentrating on how it can produce short, low-volume runs, be flexible and use automation to support the business rather than drive it.
Sales and service	*Now*: 'The Pits'.	*Must be*: 'The Angels'. Managing customer relationships, prime source of new ideas for products as they listen to the customer.
Creative effort	*Now*: Mainly the province of a central Research and	*Must be*: Small and widespread. Drive must be to satisfy the customer. New ideas are *everyone's* business.

	Development group. Big projects dominate. Pure science rather than customer driven. Clever rather than functional design. Only work on new products.	
People	*Now*: Must be kept on a tight rein. Specialists given enhanced status.	*Must be*: Prime source of value. About moving people away from specialisms and more towards broad competencies. Constant training and involvement. Financial stake in good business outcomes.
Structure	*Now*: Bureaucratic, hierarchical.	*Must be*: Flat, devoid of functional barriers, full of self-managed teams (rather than lots of line supervisors) with middle managers as facilitators rather than whip-crackers.
Leadership	*Now*: Remote, uninvolved, analytical, concerned with strategic affairs.	*Must be*: Lovers of change, able to articulate a sense of vision and shared values, strategy driven from the bottom of the business.
Management information systems	*Now*: Centralized, geared to internal needs.	*Must be*: Decentralized with emphasis on facilitating customer satisfaction and identifying paths for new strategic development.
Financial management systems	*Now*: Centralized and basically a policing system.	*Must be*: Decentralized, with 'business members' integrated into teams. Much devolment of spending authority down the line.

Your task, for which you have 60 minutes, is to take the function you have agreed to work on, and to discuss it with reference to your own organization.

The basic questions you should address:

1 Is the 'Now' scenario true of our chosen function in our organization?
2 Do we accept the 'Must be' scenario as good for our organization? Why? Or why not?
3 What are the problems for us in getting from the 'Now' to the 'Must Be' scenario? Are they organizational/resource based or attitudinal?
4 If we are defining them as problems – can we ever become the 'lovers of change' espoused by Peters?

and then the most critical question of all

Can you map out a strategy for moving your chosen functional area towards the 'Must be'?

You may find the following ideas helpful in discussing this:

Strategic issues for our business:

- How can we create a climate where *total* customer responsiveness is the driving force?
- How can we nurture and promote constant innovation and creativity?
- How can we place the utmost value on our people resource so that *we* get flexibility and *our people* get a true sense that the business's success is their success?
- Can we ever learn to love change?
- What are the implications of all this for our leadership style and people?
- What are the implications of all this for our systems?
- Well, we're doing this together with our peers, on this course but who should we *really* be doing this with?
- What can we build into our strategy to ensure it – and the business – stays flexible and responsive? Can we be sure the strategy *itself* will not become out of date, redundant, a 'white elephant', 'tablets of stone' and similar clichés?

Activity 20

Push-me-pull-you

Description

This is an activity which is intended for use with groups of people who constitute some kind of workplace management team and who need to face change.

Rather than provide an artificial case study to which to apply the principles included in the activity, the maximum benefit with this particular approach is to be derived from using a real-life situation. It could be adapted by using a case study if desired but the experience will be less valuable.

The activity is intellectually fairly demanding and it would normally be appropriate for use with more senior managers. *Before embarking on this activity it is strongly recommended that you familiarize yourself with the example in the trainer's notes on pp. 130–34.*

Objectives

By the end of this activity participants will:

- be able to analyse the factors affecting a situation undergoing - or needing to undergo - change
- be able to determine a change strategy which has maximum chance of success.

Participants

Number: Between 2 and 10
Type: A team of senior managers confronting change.

Time

Anything from 1 to 4 hours

Resources

- Overhead projector (OHP) and screen

- Pre-prepared OHP transparencies as shown on pages 000–000
- Table for group to work on
- Pads of lined A4 paper and pens

Method

Step 1: Introduce the activity

The activity is based upon a technique known as Force Field Analysis *and it stems from the work of Kurt Lewin in his book* Field Theory in Social Science *(1951). It is also based on the development of that theory by Pedler, Burgoyne and Boydell in their book* A Manager's Guide to Self Development *(1986). The main aim of the activity is to consider the analytical tool called Force Field Analysis and then to apply it to a real-life situation confronting the team. The final element will be the determination of a strategy for moving the desired change forward.*

Step 2: Display OHP transparency 1 (see p. 130); explain the basic principle involved in Force Field Analysis

Allow 10 minutes. Lewin's basic idea is that any situation can be seen as being in temporary equilibrium. Forces acting for change in a situation are counter-balanced by forces acting to resist the change. Change managers need to recognize this in order to calculate the extent of resistance to change and/or to minimize it.

Carrying out a Force Field Analysis can often help to focus on what might at first appear to be a complex mess and to suggest ways in which the situation may be influenced, or pushed, in a desired direction.

Step 3: Reveal OHP transparency 2 step by step and present the associated ideas

There are 7 stages:

Stage 1:   *Select the problem where change is desired*

Stage 2:   *Define the problem clearly. Who is involved in it? How big is the problem? What factors have some bearing on it?*

Stage 3:   *How do you want the situation to be changed? Can you define the desired change clearly? Is it quantifiable? The advantage of saying 'Yes' will be that some kind of measurable target can be set.*

Stage 4:   *Define the* pushing *forces and the* restraining *forces.*

Stage 5:   *Determine which forces are of low, medium and high power, both pushing and restraining.*

Stage 6:   *Draw a diagram of the situation.*

Stage 7:   *Use the diagram to suggest and develop a strategy for taking the desired change forward with minimum resistance.*

Step 4: Work through the seven steps with the team, acting as a facilitator/consultant

This may take quite some time, depending on the scale and size of the problem identified. Anything up to a half-day would be reasonable.

A worked example of the technique in action is given in section 3 of the trainer's totes on p. 132.

As you act as facilitator/consultant be clear throughout in your own mind which stage the group has reached and that it is asking questions appropriate to that stage.

Step 5: End the activity by determining that there is a clear strategy based on rational choices

This does not need to be a formal closure. You should be ensuring that this target is being worked towards as the activity progresses, especially throughout stage 7.

Trainer's notes

These notes consist of three sections: *Section 1* is the material for OHP transparency 1; *Section 2* is the material for OHP transparency 2; *Section 3* is the worked example referred to in Step 4 of the activity.

Section 1

Material for OHP transparency 1:

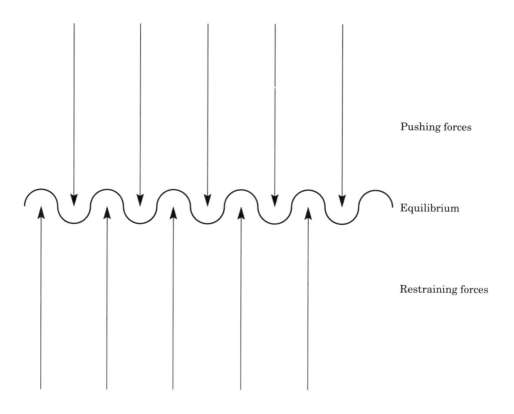

Pushing forces

Equilibrium

Restraining forces

Material for OHP transparency 2:

Stage 1
Select the problem

Stage 2
Define the problem

Stage 3
What change do you want?

Stage 4
Pushing forces vs restraining forces

Stage 5
How powerful are these forces?

Stage 6
Diagram

Stage 7
Strategy

Section 3

An example

You should note that this is a very simple example. It has been so designed to aid quick reading and assimilation. The technique works just as well on much more complex, less easily definable problems.

Stage 1: Select the problem   As a manager I'm concerned about the high and growing absentee rate amongst my staff.

Stage 2: Define the problem   Staff sickness is running at about 8 per cent per person per year with signs that it will increase to around 10 per cent before long. Morale seems poor yet the demands on the team from the company are relentless. Staff turnover has fallen off because of an economic recession but many would have moved on if they had the chance to do so. A new supervisor seems to be having trouble adjusting to her role.

Stage 3:   I want to reduce the absentee rate to 5 per cent or less. This is a measurable target and I will know how close I am getting to it.

Stage 4:   What are the *pushing forces* that might help me move to reduce absentee rate? They could include:
  (a) My own determination to lower the absentee rate
  (b) The company's concern at poor performance of team
  (c) Low staff turnover
  (d) General employee unhappiness at present situation
  (e) Possibility of office relocation to quieter premises later in the year.

What are the *restraining forces* that might tend to continue pushing up the absentee rate? They could include:
  (a) Same pattern of behaviour by new supervisor
  (b) Staff frustration at being unable to move jobs
  (c) Relentless company demands
  (d) Lack of team spirit showing in unwillingness to cover for colleagues' absences
  (e) Persistent Union sniping at management.

Stage 5. How powerful are these forces?
Pushing forces: High: (a), (d); Medium: (b); Low: (c), (e).

Restraining forces: High: (a), (c); Medium: (b), (d); Low: (e).

Stage 6. See Figure 20.1 on p. 133.

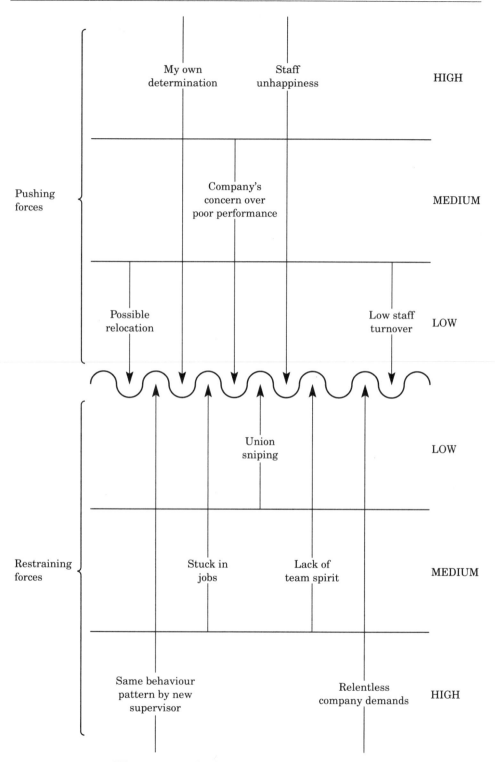

Figure 20.1 *Pushing and restraining forces*

© Sue Bishop and David Taylor 1994, published by Kogan Page

Stage 7. Strategy.
Two points to remember:

- The harder you push the greater resistance you often meet.
- The easiest change to manage is that which causes least hassle.

Some questions to pose:

- Have you identified all the pushing forces? Can you find any new ones?
- Can you actually reduce any of the restraining forces without compromising the push for change?
- Can you push in any way but without increasing the resistance?
- Can you sideline any of the restraining forces so that they focus on new targets? (This may not sound very professional, but perhaps there are parts of your organization better equipped to deal with them?)
- Are you pushing too hard? If you were to 'let up' in one direction would the resistance decrease?

A strategy which takes into account a Force Field Analysis should:

- Be clear about its targets; what they are, with timings and measures to know when they have been successfully achieved.
- Be broken down into achievable sub-strategies, especially if the original problem is large and nebulous.
- Identify the key resources and allies which can be brought to bear.

Activity 21

So far, so . . . good?

Description

An activity to be run during a course to check on progress so far, and whether the sessions are meeting participants' needs. It is also a useful means of consolidating learning.

A note of caution; you will have to be flexible and prepared to change sessions - within the remit of the overall course objectives - to meet negotiated needs.

Objectives

By the end of this activity participants will:

- have discussed in small groups the effectiveness of the course so far; of learning gained; of changes they intend to put into practice back at the workplace and of changes they would like to see to the course better to meet their needs
- have been given the opportunity to negotiate any reasonable changes to the remainder of the course within the remit of course objectives.

Participants

Number: Any
Type: Any

Time

1-2 hours

Resources

- Notepaper and pencils/pens if required
- Flipchart stand, paper and marker pens
- Copies of the course programme if available

Method

Step 1: Introduce activity and explain procedures

This activity is intended as an appraisal of the course so far. Participants will discuss, in small groups, the sessions and activities and evaluate their effectiveness. What has each learnt from the various sessions? What changes will they wish to make back at the workplace as a result of the training so far? How will they implement these – do they foresee any problems? How might these be overcome? This can be seen as a mutual support session where individuals can offer advice and counselling to each other.

Finally participants will look at their own training needs in relation to the course objectives, and assess whether these are being, or are likely to be, met. If there are key areas which are unlikely to be covered, but which are within the remit of the course objectives, participants should discuss, in their groups, ways in which they would like to see the remaining sessions modified. Suggestions will be examined by the whole group in a plenary session.

Step 2: Divide group into two or three syndicate groups (any more and the processing could get unwieldy); issue paper and writing materials should groups wish to make notes; inform groups that a time check will be taken after 20 minutes

Seating should be arranged so that syndicate groups can sit in circles and discuss issues without interrupting the other group(s).

You may wish to issue copies of the programme, if available, for group reference; or to write on flipchart paper the issues the syndicate groups are to discuss (as outlined in step 1).

Step 3: Check progress after 20 minutes and negotiate more time if required

Each group will differ. Some may be happy with the course so far and see no difficulties in putting learning into practice back at work. Other groups may be very analytical and will wish to probe all aspects of the course. The latter type of group will obviously need more time.

Step 4: Reconvene whole group; ask for a spokesperson from each group to report on the discussions

Offer guidance, if appropriate, on effecting any changes back at the workplace. It would be wise to take notes of any suggestions regarding a restructuring of the remainder of the course. Ensure that recommendations are pertinent, specific, practical and remain within the overall course objectives.

Step 5: Thank group for its hard work and useful recommendations which will be considered and accommodated if possible; close the activity referring to the objectives

Activity 22

Who manages IT?

Description

This activity is for senior managers who wish to make a success of introducing Information Technology (IT). The focus of the activity is at the macro (corporate) level as opposed to the micro (departmental or sectional) level.

Note this activity is *not* targeted at IT specialists – although they could benefit – but at managers who see IT as a tool.

Objectives

By the end of this activity participants will understand some prerequisites for the satisfactory introduction of organizational change based on Information Technology.

Participants

Number: Maximum of 6
Type: The nature of the activity is such that it is most likely to appeal to those at a senior management level who have organizational policymaking responsibilities

Time

1 hour 30 minutes

Resources

- Flipchart stand, paper and marker pens
- A4 Paper and pens for participants to make notes on
- Two copies of Document 1 (three if a triad is used at step 3)
- Two copies of Document 2
- Two copies of Document 3

Method

Step 1: Introduce the activity
Cover the points made in the introduction and objectives above.

Step 2: Get the group to identify an IT application in their organization with which they are familiar and which is not as satisfactory as it could be
Allow 10 minutes. Flipchart the name of the system and identify the perceived problems. (It is assumed that all managers are working for the same organization and would thus be able to identify a system which would be familiar to all. If this is not the case it is possible to identify more than one system, to have it described briefly and to have the problems highlighted. In this case, you should flipchart the names of the systems and the perceived problems.)

Questions you might use:
- *How long has the system been in use?*
- *Who was responsible for introducing it?*
- *How was it introduced?*
- *Who experiences problems?*
- *What, precisely, are the problems?*
- *Can anything be done to remedy the situation?*

Step 3: Divide the group into pairs (or pairs and one triad if an odd number); issue two copies of Case Study A (Document 1) to the first pair, two copies of Case Study B (Document 2) to the second pair and two copies of Case Study C (Document 3) to the third pair (each case study has a full set of instructions with it)
Allow 30 minutes.

Step 4: Re-form the group; ask each pair to present its findings; flipchart them
Allow each group two minutes to present its findings.

Step 5: Identify common features and non-common features; draw up a strategy for the successful introduction of IT into an organization based on the features identified
Allow 30 minutes. You should be aiming for the following as a basic strategy: all of these points can be deduced or inferred from one or more of given case studies.
- *The existence of a senior person in the organization who was able to articulate a vision of what could be achieved.*
- *Long-term commitment to making things happen; not devolved to operational level.*
- *An 'end-point' or ultimate target may be inappropriate; there is unlikely ever to be a final stasis in terms of process, organization and technology.*

- *No IT system can ever be specified that will prepare an organization for every eventuality. But constant vigilance for new opportunities as they arise can be achieved.*
- *Measures need to be devised to check whether an organization is moving towards the original vision, not simply a test of whether or not it has moved from where it was. (Beware strictly financial tests which tend to be slanted towards the latter.)*
- *It is unrealistic to 'change the world' in one fell swoop. Recognize that the change process in any organization will be constrained by others who may not share the same vision, or who do not want the changes at all.*
- *Even where everyone is excited by the process, it may take time for the constituent parts of the organization to accommodate it and adjust to new working practices.*
- *Planning IT should not be left to the IT people; the evidence in the case studies reveals changes in tasks and working practices beyond that originally envisaged – in other words, the systems which govern working practices in general and not just the IT system. IT changes cannot be regarded as an isolated sub-system of the organization.*

  'Leaving it to the IT people' in any case just reinforces 'technophobia', a regrettably common phenomenon at high levels of management in British industry.
- *Many benefits don't become apparent until implementation and will often not be perceived as part of the original vision. This is normal.*

Step 6: Reflect with the group on the IT system identified earlier
Allow 20 minutes. Use the following questions:
  Can any of the problems identified be attributed to a failure to observe the basic strategy formulated during step 5? Which? How could things have been improved? Be specific.

Step 7: Close the activity by referring briefly to the objectives

Who manages IT? - Document 1

Case study A: West Midlands Fire Brigade
Please read these instructions first.

This document consists of a case study in which Information Technology has been recognized as crucial to the development of a business. The case study refers to the *successful* introduction of IT.

The company and the circumstances described are real. The material has been reproduced (with permission) from: *Managing IT for Competitive Advantage: Case Studies of Organizations in Japan, USA and Europe* edited by Mark Helme (1991).

Please take a few minutes to read through the case study. You are asked to identify, and then to discuss and agree with your colleague, *the factors that you think made the project concerned a success*. Please list them and have them ready to discuss with the main group later.

There are three case studies in total; you have just one to consider. You have 30 minutes altogether to carry out this task.

Introduction

The West Midlands Fire Brigade has a wide range of responsibilities in protecting the community from loss of life and property due to fire and other hazards. A large proportion of its annual budget of £54m is spent on the staff and equipment spread across forty-one fire stations and two headquarters. Organised in five divisions on a geopgraphical basis, the stations are able to deploy 110 appliances which include both fire fighting and support units and 80 officers in cars. The majority of the 2400 staff are uniformed firemen, a disciplined force with clear rank structures and career paths.

Responding to incidents involving fire, chemicals or other hazards forms the core of the Brigade's operational activities. Some 80,000 incidents per year are reported, which range enormously in scale and complexity. For example, fire on a grass verge may be simple to deal with and pose relatively little immediate danger to life or property, but major fires or incidents in airports or inner cities require a complex response.

In most cases, speed of response is essential if incidents are to be dealt with safely and with minimal risk to the lives of the public and the fire fighters themselves. Fires in commercial sites cause damage at a rate of tens of thousands of pounds per minute and beyond a certain point in a fire's development, containment is the only option.

The 'proposal' for a response consists of the nature and number of appliances to be despatched. Special circumstances, such as tall buildings, large scale incidents, special hazards, risk to nearby premises containing people, property or combustible or dangersous chemicals, all have a bearing on the scale and nature of proposal. 'Overkill' responses to minor incidents reduce the available cover in the short term and in the longer term lead to increases either in risks or costs to the public.

The Fire Service has always been a heavy user of communications and regard rapid communication as intrinsic to their success. As a result, they are accustomed to infrastructure investment, although I/T has in the past had little impact on the actual fire fighting part of their operations. Up to 1984, the local council provided I/T support to the Fire Service, the focus of their technical organisation being on administrative systems such as payroll and accounting.

As reliability and speed of response to incidents are paramount, the Brigade is very cautious in evolving the operational procedures that underpin their activities. Since 1984, the communications and computing group has been a part of the Fire Service, led by a management team of fire officers who rotate from other career appointments. This approach was adopted to enable the Brigade to innovate successfully in the high risk area of operations.

Trigger

The Brigade covers an area of over 30,000 streets, and responding to major incidents often involves appliances from more than one station. As a result, crew knowledge of the local geography and hazards cannot be guaranteed. Initial mobilisation was carried out using a private voice telephone network, with subsequent information being passed to the moving appliances by radio. The average time taken to receive a call, identify the destination, create the proposal and mobilise the units was 75 seconds.

Voice briefing by telephone or radio was time consuming, error prone and only a fraction of the available knowledge about the site of the fire and special hazards could be passed to the crews. The location and status of appliances was tracked through a system of 'button boxes' which firemen used to transmit simple codes from the appliances using the radio equipment. The number of codes was very restricted, so location could only be expressed in terms of broad geographical area, to confirm arrival at an incident or return to base.

The Chief Officer of West Midlands Fire Brigade had a wide knowledge of the service in having been an adviser to the Home Office, and served on numerous Fire Service Committees. He was also aware that Fire Services in America and Europe were attempting to tackle the problems of rapid mobilisation and saw opportunities to use Information Technology to support their operation.

The Chief Officer set up a small project team of fire officers with a very open ended brief: to identify how to make a substantial improvement in mobilisation time using technology that was currently available and robust and reliable enough for the operational environment.

The approach
The original method of command and control involved a number of staff handling different aspects of a call, from the conversation with the caller, through to the mobilisation messages to stations and their confirmation. This process could be considered as two main phases; the assembly of the 'proposal' for responding to the incident and the subsequent mobilisation of the units. Several aspects of these phases were critical:
- unambiguously identifying the site of the incident,
- identifying the nature of the incident and what resources might be required,
- ensuring that the incident has not already been reported and units mobilised,
- deciding what resources are available and suitable to send,

- sending clear mobilising messages to the stations at which the units are based,
- confirming receipt of messages and the current status and location of invididual units.

The diversity of information required to respond to a call and the reliance on local knowledge intensified the need to share the process between staff in the fire control room. However, the 'handoffs' between staff carrying out different tasks and the short time frame increased the possibility of error.

The project team began work on the prime objective of reducing the time taken to accurately develop and communicate proposals. The only constraints were that human validation of the proposal was required, that nearly all reports came by telephone and that mobilisation messages would be addressed to stations. A number of out side resources were called on to help them tackle the problem. The Local Authority provided an analyst to support the team although their staff had no experience with this kind of system. Bradford University played a major role in advising on available technology. The Directorate of Telecommunications was also involved in providing basic information on current practices standards applying in government and civil service.

Visiting the US and Germany to look at the ways which other service were achieving speed and efficiency in their operations, the experienced fire officers on the team were very much aware of the importance of the practicalities of changing operational procedures and the risk to human life if the response to a single incident was compromised, either during implementation or thereafter.

They therefore very carefully analysed the logical processes that needed to occur in the preparation of a proposal and its subsequent communication. It became evident that, theoretically, a single person could handle all aspects of a call, from receipt to confirmation of despatch of the appliances. What was needed was a way of supporting each operator with the information needed to carry out the whole process, closely integrated with the way that they would need to handle the caller. This meant a fundamental change from applying local geographical knowledge to acquiring the skill of simultaneously talking to a caller and using the computer to help gain the data to develop a proposal.

As the callers reporting an incident could come from a variety of backgrounds and situations, experience showed that a wide range of information was used in identifying the location. For example, the general public might refer to the location of a fire by the name of the nearest road or major building, but on railway premises or embankments, railway staff could only refer to the number of the nearest gantry. These locations had to be translated into a map reference to brief the crews of appliances.

Also, callers are often excited or distraught, and it is not always possible to get them to *answer* precise questions. Operators often had to prompt callers with information during the call, and they would need to continue to be able to do this without having to spend valuable time following a structured response pattern. Features like 'soundex' coding would be required to ensure that orally received place names could be typed in as they sounded and possible matches identified automatically for the operator. As all the calls for one area would no longer be routed to a single individual, any new system would have to warn operators of any potential repeat reports within a kilometre.

Once the site of the incident had been established, the number and type of appliances proposed needed to be decided. The proposal could be generated by taking account of the nature of the area, overridden by the nature of the incident, any special requirements of the premises and then the closest available appliances identified and despatched.

Information about the current status of appliances was already transmitted using the button boxes, but the 'fixed' information required to support the new way of working had to be assembled in a useable database. The gazetteer of important features of the region included map references of junctions, bridges, major buildings, railway gantries and telephone kiosks. Other important information about access to sites of major risks was also identified, such as one way streets. The assembly of this data took more than two years, carried out in parallel with the subsequent detailed design work on the system.

The team spent 12 months attempting to develop a description of 'what' they wanted the system to do, rather than exactly 'how' it was to do it. A software house which had some experience in developing Command and Control systems was engaged to produce a turn-key system. Although this company had experience of communications and radio using current 'button box' technology, the system as a whole was very different from their previous developments in Command and Control and there were substantial problems in the interpretation of the specification.

The project team needed to work closely with the software house, ensuring that the specifications were correctly interpreted and documenting any variations as they were agreed. In these circumstances, the practical knowledge and experience of the team members as firemen and the support of the Chief Fire Officer proved essential.

Acceptance testing was vigorous and took nine months, performance being a critical issue. At first, the software house tried to gain sign-offs for meeting performance criteria one by one, not realising that they were *all* meant to be met simultaneously.

The resulting system was based on 'action verbs' which the operators used to gain the necessary information to identify the site of the incident (assisting the caller if necessary), and to develop and despatch the proposal. Apart from basic keyboard skills, the operators had to learn the 120 different 'action verbs' and how to use them. When dealing with a call, the operator could use the system flexibly in helping to identify the location. For example, when a caller identifies the location of a fire by saying 'there's a fire in a shop ', the operator could immediately check to see if there were more than one branch and check which one. If a named site is selected, any special circumstances which override the normal response in the area will be reflected in the proposal. The same incident might be reported by another caller as 'a fire in the High Street', with the operator prompting the caller for the name of the area or town.

Training the operators to work this way took 15 months, due to the high level of skill and practice required. Staff found the new way of working very satisfying, as it gave them a chance to exercise their skills in using the system to best effect and also to see the whole process through from call to despatch.

In comparison to the effort expended in training and implementation, the hardware requirements for the system were relatively modest; fourteen VDU screens attached to a minicomputer, with communication links to printers in the stations and two HQ locations. A second, 'hot standby' minicomputer was also installed.

Conclusions

The main target benefit was achieved; the time from receipt of a call to mobilisation was reduced from an average of 75 seconds to 12–15 seconds. The focus on the objective of speed of response to calls led to a performance advantage over other command and control systems that is still being maintained. Other services specified Management Information Systems as part of the Command and Control functionality, but West Midlands designed this as a separate module that received downloads of data every 10 minutes.

Although the system involved major changes to working practices, it was popular with staff in the fire control room. Other benefits were hard to quantify as there was little hard information before, but it was felt that there was substantial improvement in the accuracy of proposals, identification of the most suitable resources to mobilise and the number of errors in communication.

The success with the Command and Control System is now leading to further developments and a project to consolidate existing systems to provide a strategic operational focus. Supporting two way communication had always been a part of the long term vision, and Mobile Data Terminals (MDTs) are currently being tested in the cabs of appliances, which will allow the two-way transfer of text. Appliances will be able to be mobilised when they are away from the stations, enabling response times to be equalized through the dynamic positioning of appliances on standby. More detailed feedback on status and location will also be possible.

The potential of providing crews with further information once mobilised is also being examined. Vast amounts of information are collected already, in the form of maps, surveys for fire certificates, water main overlays and special hazards. The possibility of communication of information to the crews within an operational timeframe has led the Brigade to reappraise the way in which its base of information is handled and stored, and to reconsider its value.

Who manages IT? - Document 2

Case study B: Yamato Transportation Co
Please read these instructions first.

This document consists of a case study in which Information Technology has been recognized as crucial to the development of a business. The case study refers to the *successful* introduction of IT.

The company and the circumstances described are real. The material has been reproduced (with permission) from: *Managing I/T for Competitive Advantage: Case Studies of Organizations in Japan, USA and Europe* Edited by Mark Helme (1991).

Please take a few minutes to read through the case study. You are asked to identify, and then to discuss and agree with your colleague, *the factors that you think made the project concerned a success.* Please list them and have them ready to discuss with the main group later.

There are three case studies in total; you have just one to consider. You have 30 minutes altogether to carry out this task.

Introduction

Yamato Transport is the pioneer of the private parcel delivery business in Japan. Yamato's parcel delivery, known in Japan as *Takkyubin*, began 14 years ago. Before 1976 when Yamato entered the parcel package business, Yamato's business was largely running regular routes for specific consignors. Accordingly, Yamato's main customer was one of the largest department stores. In entering the new business Yamato stopped serving the department store because Yamato's top management realised the private parcel business required an entirely different way of doing business. Moreover, Yamato was threatened by the oil crisis which reduced the number of packages being sent. Since then business has grown consistently, allowing Yamato to produce double figure revenue growth for more than 10 consecutive years.

In the past, parcel service was seen as a time-consuming, inefficient and unprofitable business. The new approach Yamato has adopted keeps deliveries moving quickly, enhances business efficiency, and thus increases profitability.

Today, Yamato is the largest private parcel delivery business in Japan, with a market share approaching 40%. In 1988, Yamato further upgraded their services when they introduced refrigerated deliveries with a newly outfitted fleet of refrigerated trucks capable of carrying goods at three different temperatures. Japan has a major gift season in July when fresh fish, fruits and other delicacies have long been popular gift items, but whose practicality has in the past been limited by Japan's hot and humid summer. Yamato's new 'Cool Takkyubin' service greatly increased the popularity of such perishable gifts. In addition to every day parcel deliveries, Yamato Transport offers many distinctive, and, even unique services. Japan is a nation where the trains are still the main form of transportation. Their ski and golf delivery services now carry equipment to the slopes or the course, allowing people to travel easily and to get the most out of their free time.

The speed, reliability, and diversity of Yamato Transport services grew out of their national network. Customers can conveniently leave their packages at any of their 200,000 subagents – local retail outlets such as grocery stores distributed throughout small neighbourhoods within Japanese cities. To speed up parcels on their way to virtually anywhere in the archipelago, Yamato operate 770 processing centres which serve as focal points for parcel interchange. To deliver parcels as fast as possible (more than 90% are overnight deliveries) Yamato owns a fleet of about 16,000 trucks, employs 15,000 truck drivers and 4,000 other staff to pack, manage and direct more than 293 million parcels annually.

The approach

In 1973, Yamato split its systems functions from head office and set up Yamato Systems Development (YSD), mainly by recruiting experienced technical people. Since then, YSD has taken charge of all information systems work. In 1981 Yamato established a Task Improvement Department (TID) at its head office, recruiting people with extensive business experience, because they realised the importance of establishing a central I/T planning group. This organisational change was closely related to a change of attitude amongst senior executives towards I/T. They had previously seen I/T as a means of cost reduction rather than as a means of influencing and changing current business practices.

The Task Improvement Department

develops initial systems requirements which are then given to YSD to take charge of detailed design, programme development and implementation. Underlying this organisational change is Yamato's strong belief that it is nowadays impossible to think of new services independently of I/T, so much so that every management strategy has an associated I/T strategy.

At the same time Yamato created the position of Chief Information Officer; the first appointee to this position was Mr Miyauchi, one of whose main responsibilities was TID. When ideas for new services are agreed at the strategic management meeting held every week, each related department is asked to develop the scheme in detail: Mr Miyauchi as CIO takes charge of five departments including the Task Improvement Department, to co-ordinate the departmental interests. Mr Miyauchi attends the weekly strategic management meeting, and helps examine information systems considerations when looking at new business requirements. After a project gets the go ahead, he manages and leads the design and implementation. Top management at Yamato now realise that the introduction of a new service may require a change in methods of sales and distribution as well as those of the development of I/T.

Yamato also puts some emphasis on bottom-up management to increase the technology awareness of every employee. For instance, a Systems Manager leads OA at branch level, which aims at establishing the needs for I/T, and delivering the benefits of I/T at the lowest level of the organisation. Statistics showing the degree of overnight delivery achieving are available to every operating office daily. As every employee can freely access this information, employee participation has increased and morale has improved.

The first system was not specially concerned with Takkyubin but with the provision of a general fixed route service. Terminals in each operating office were connected with the head office's host computer via private lines, enabling central control and storage of package information. However, in 1980 the second system was designed and tailored to fit specific needs of the Takkyubin business. Until then, Yamato had not been concerned to build systems specifically for Takkyubin because its package fee is standardised and the process is quite simple. However, payments from customers and vouchers were often misplaced in the busy season, and this urged Yamato to develop the new system.

The new Takkyubin system was designed to be as customer oriented as possible; the vision of *service first* is the underlying principle of the Takkyubin business. The concept was simple: To provide positive tracking of every package each time it changes hands and direction. Yamato realised the value of information to the customer and so conceived a system on which the customer could rely.

The objective of scanning every package at the point of pickup and delivery is to be able to reply to customer enquiries concerning the whereabout of his or her package. In fact, relatively few people do ask where their packets are, and the number of lost packages should be below 0.005%. The system has been built to cope with these rare cases in order to uphold the service first philosophy. Yamato can access up to the minute information on the whereabouts of the parcels from 1,600 workstations within three seconds, so a customer can be told where the package is in less than a minute by just making a phone inquiry. This requires parcel data to be input constantly – which in turn means that staff have to check parcels regularly, which also improves Yamato's accuracy of delivery.

Yamato also developed their own POS terminals to make data input by couriers simple and easy. Bar code printing machines were not available at that time in Japan, so Yamato had to import one from Germany, asking Matsushita to manufacture a bar code reader. Yamato therefore became a pioneer with the new technology, which was subsequently used by United Parcel Service. Before this system was developed it was time consuming to input data, and as the business volumes went up, tracking the movement of packages became more difficult.

Attitudes and technological awareness had changed so much since the second system that I/T came to be regarded as an essential means to differentiate Yamato's service in the eyes of the customer. A third system, implemented in 1982, enabled sales drivers and couriers to input information at the time of pickup and delivery using portable POS terminals, improving the timeliness of information along with the method of input itself. In 1983, Yamato equipped their trucks with private automobile network equipment and printers, which enabled Yamato to advise the sales drivers of pickups and deliveries even when absent from their trucks.

In addtion, Yamato connected this pickup system to their customer database, containing names, addresses, and phone numbers of customers, enabling Yamato to give pickup data to drivers right away, shortly after a customer phones in his or her order together with their phone number. This has increased the speed of pickup and a simpler ordering process has resulted. The database now includes almost half a million customers.

Not content there, in 1987 Yamato developed a system to identify the traffic situation on the extremely busy highway between Tokyo and Kobe, enabling Yamato to poinpoint the trucks and provide accurate information of delays or road hazards. Yamato intends to extend this system to other highways to meet the just-in-time requirements of customers.

Conclusions

The system has produced a steady stream of benefits and has helped Yamato maintain industry leadership. This kind of responsiveness and attitude to the detailed needs of customers has allowed Yamato to make major inroads into new business like home moving, catalogue delivery etc.

Mr Miyauchi explains that whenever Yamato plans a new service, they think how they can use I/T to gain competitive advantage; I/T is used to differentiate Yamato from its competitors and deliver more customer-oriented services.

This positioning of Yamato has reaped enormous competitive benefits. In February 1989, the largest convenience store in Japan, Seven Eleven, agreed to act as Yamato's agent, switching from Nitsu Transportation, Yamato's main rival in the parcel delivery business. The increase in business from Seven Eleven amounts to 4 million parcels a year, a volume equal to that handled by the tenth largest transportation company.

The reason for this switch was due to Yamato's reliability, accuracy and speed of pickup and delivery. Convenience stores have to think of accuracy and speed because they have little space to store parcels. In order to accommodate this requirement, Yamato uses the third system developed in 1983. Yamato sales drivers know where to go and when, within ten minutes of an operating office receiving a request from a customer or agent. Yamato was able to add value not only to its direct customers, but also to agents through the provision of this information.

In this case, I/T made Yamato more competitive in its speed and efficiency, accommodating just-in-time requests from agents. Agents, like convenience stores, have a need for just-in-time delivery. Such service to agents is a key success factor in increasing the market share in the Takkyubin business.

Yamato's top management realised that they couldn't expect benefits to happen without changing the way they did business. By the time of the second system, they thought of I/T as an enabler and as such decided to get technology into the Takkyubin business. From once regarding computing expenditure as an expense, Yamato came to view I/T in a more strategic context.

Competitors like Nitsu Trannsportation copied the system developed by Yamato, developing a similar system two years later.

Yamato believes that thinking of I/T as an integrated and integrating part of their business has prevented their compeitors from catching up, and they continue to invest repeatedly in this area.

Who manages IT? - Document 3

Case study C: Flashkit
Please read these instructions first.

This document consists of a case study in which Information Technology has been recognized as crucial to the development of a business. The case study refers to the *successful* introduction of IT.

The company and the circumstances described are real. The material has been reproduced (with permission) from *Managing I/T for Competitive Advantage: Case Studies of Organizations in Japan, USA and Europe* edited by Mark Helme (1991).

Please take a few minutes to read through the case study. You are asked to identify, and then to discuss and agree with your colleague, *the factors that you think made the project concerned a success*. Please list them and have them ready to discuss with the main group later.

There are three case studies in total; you have just one to consider. You have 30 minutes altogether to carry out this task.

'Flashkit' - A UK Clothing Manufacturer*

Introduction

The Flashkit company is a publicly quoted manufacturer of clothing for major UK High Street retailers. It has a turnover in excess of £100m and employs over 3,500 personnel in 5 sites in Northern and Southern England. It is currently engaged in an aggressive plan to increase its market share and plans to grow at between 10% and 15% per annum, particularly focusing on increasing its share of supply to two or three major retailers.

Flashkit automated much of its manufacturing process during the early 1980's and feels itself to be competitively positioned in terms of both flexibility of response and cost-effectiveness. There was, however, an awareness that there were a number of information technology driven opportunities to improve the process by which designs were presented to the prospective buying departments of the target retailers.

The company employed a design team of 10–15 specialists, who were engaged in developing ideas for fabric patterns, presenting them to buyers and refining them to a final design. This was a laborious process that involved hand drawing and colouring of patterns and the use of external artwork services to produce sample sheets on paper and 'artists impressions' of finished garments. Much of the designers' time was spent on laborious production of drawings and little was devoted to actually thinking. Redrawing designs could often take up to a day and a half.

The trigger

The chief design executive, Mary Pont, had been monitoring the market since 1986/87 and had been keeping senior management abreast of the potential for the business in this area. She had been aware that developments in IT could have a significant impact on the quality of the design process and presented the following opportunities:

- modelling modifications to artwork could be made without having to get the artwork redone from scratch
- significantly more complex designs could be presented to buyers
- the quality of the presentations made to buyers could be improved
- the quality of design work could be improved by increasing the 'thinking time' available to the design team by reducing the design production effort.

In addition to these major opportunities, there were also believed to be some other longer term implications for changing the design presentation process, which included:

- reducing the cost of sample production by conditioning buyers to do their initial sample selection direct from a high-quality graphics system. This allowed the buyers to reduce the range of colours that they would want to see actually made-up into a garment, thus significantly reducing cost and time.
- allowing buyers direct access to the manufacturer's design system so that they could model aspects of the design for themselves
- linking-up the design departments in the North and South of the Country, so that they could share designs in a 'real-time' sense, rather than relying on postal systems and the recreation of designs in separate locations.

* The name, dates and some details in this study have been changed to disguise the organisation, at its own request.

The approach

In 1988, Mary Pont had gone as far as having a demonstration system from a leading supplier sited in the Flashkit design office. At that time, however, she was not convinced that the techology had been completely proved and, indeed, still showed significant weaknesses in a number of key areas, especially the quality of the colour graphics produced by the printer. In mid 1989, Mary Pont visited the Three Letter Acronym (TLA) computer design company in the USA and was convinced that their system was now sufficiently developed to enable Flashkit to remain competitive over the next few years.

The system was based around TLA proprietory software, using a computer physically small enough to be unobstructive in an office environment. A single high quality graphics screen and a Canon colour printer were attached and the total cost of software, hardware and printer was in the region of £95,000.

The software was designed in a modular fashion and allowed Mary to select only those modules that were directly relevant to pattern design such as supporting the manipulation of colour schema on scanned-in designs.

All aspects of software development, maintenance and support remained the property of TLA, with Flashkit taking no technical responsibility for the support of the system, beyond the recruitment of an appropriately trained technical operator. However, the processes of software selection and implementation were led throughout by Mary, who ensured that this operator was in place from day one, so that the system was always available to be used and the many technical barriers that may have existed in introducing the system into the design team's work habits were rapidly overcome. Three of Mary's design team were also trained by TLA in using the system.

Conclusions

The system has had a significant impact on the way the print design process works, especially in removing the need to get patterns redrawn from scratch if colour changes or minor amendments need to be made. Redrawing could take between half and one day before the system was implemented; it now takes only one or two hours.

The designers themselves have taken to the system extremely enthusiastically, with one of the more experienced designers comparing it to her first washing machine, saying 'I can't see how we ever got on without one'.

Another potential impact on the design process is currently on trial with one of the company's major buyers. The buyer has also invested in the same sort of TLA system and Mary is now transmitting some designs directly from the screen in her office to the buyer's screen. In the long term Mary believes that the buyer will become converted to a toally screen-based presentation culture, but believes that it will take some time to overcome some deep-rooted suspicion of computer technology amongst many of the buyers.

This system has, however, presented a couple of problems. Firstly, its use has had to be managed; because everybody wants access to it and is available only on a single workstation, Mary has had to take on an extra management role in taking bookings for work to be done on it and in prioritising those not infrequent 'rush jobs', which are endemic in the design business.

Secondly the system has led to problems because of the way buyers have responded to the increased responsiveness and flexibility this system has given to the company. Buyers will now request more changes to be made to designs at much shorter notice and have also shown a tendency to request extra, often frivolous, additional designs to be presented to them. Mary is having to be quite forthright in addressing these buyer-led problems, which often reflect the fact that buyers are simply not thinking through their requirements.

Mary is a member of the TLA user group which liaises actively with TLA with suggestions and recommendations about future developments and modifications to the system and is monitoring developments in those modules of the software that her company has not taken, in particular the facility for three dimensions representation.

The quality of output that can be achieved using the technology was an important factor throughout. As technologies become more reliable and cost effective, they are being considered. For example:

- the purchase of a higher quality A3 colour printer. This technology is evolving rapidly and the quality of the final printed output must be extremely good if the system is to really prove its worth. This investment would cost around £10,000 and should take place by the end of the year.
- leasing or purchasing a colour photocopier. In the long term this would be extremely desirable, especially if colour photocopying costs continue to fall, as multiple copies of prints are often required. In the short term outside copying bureaux wil be used.
- the purchase of a personal computer to host the TLA software and possibly one extra full workstation. The requirement for an extra workstation has been proved beyond doubt as the system has become an integral part of the

design team's working practice.
- communication links with the design teams in the North of the country are also being investigated by the in-house IT operation. This would allow design ideas to be shared more rapidly across all the designers in the company.

In Mary's opinion, there has been an improvement in the quality of the design work itself. This is probably a consequence of designers being able to spend more time on thinking about designs, rather than on the mechanics of producing designs. Presentations have a far more professional finish and work is done faster.

In addition to this, there has been some reduction in the costs of using outside people to redraw designs. This is, however, not that significant when set against the costs of buying and running the system.

The application of information technology to the design process is relatively new in the clothing industry. In the long-term, it is expected that other benefits may also be achieved as the market begins to appreciate the benefits of transferring information between suppliers and customers. For example, the costs of the design, sample production and presentation process will fall as buyers become educated in modelling and selecting designs direct from screens and closer relations with leading buyers are developed through the on-line transfer of designs between Flashkit and buyer systems. Buyer expectations are already changing in terms of the time taken to amend designs and the inclusion of minor changes to patterns.

Activity 23

Worldly wise

Description

An activity to test managers' ability to work effectively under stress. It has the additional optional spin-off of opening discussion on the importance of international awareness.

Objectives

By the end of this activity participants will:

- recognize the importance of preparation before action
- be more aware of the personal stress involved when meeting deadlines and/or encountering something 'new'
- have discussed the impact of stress induced by time pressures, recognizing personal limitations and so on, and methods of dealing with these stressors
- have had the opportunity to examine their own awareness of international business, compared with other group members, and the advantages of developing less parochial attitudes to management (optional).

Participants

Number: Any
Type: Any

Time

1 hour

Resources

- One copy of Document 1 for each participant
- One copy of Document 2 for each participant
- Pencil/pen for each participant
- Clipboard or table space for each participant
- Flipchart stand, paper and marker pens

Note: You should familiarize yourself with the test, Document 1, before reading the method and notes; it is not what it first appears! The questions and answers set were relevant and correct at the time of writing (1993), but may require amendment in the light of future changes.

Method

Step 1: Introduce the activity, making no reference to the objectives

This activity should come early in a course, perhaps after the ice-breaker. Explain to participants that you will issue a short, simple test, which will be collected for assessment by you. It is to help you establish individuals' awareness of international markets, in preparation for a (hypothetical) exercise later in the course. (You could give further reasons to justify the test, depending on the group, such as 'importance of a global approach in times of rapid growth and change', 'to test top management potential', 'necessity of knowledge of foreign markets approaching the twenty-first century', etc.)

Do not tell participants that the main purpose of the activity is to ascertain whether individuals take the time to prepare/read instructions fully, before embarking on a task – especially when pressure and time limits are involved. The exercise which you will issue states clearly 'Read all of this paper carefully before answering the following questions'. Many participants will, however, plough straight into the test although the penultimate instruction is 'Now that you have read through most of this paper, obey only the first instruction, ie to print your name, title and place of work in the box at the top of the sheet. Do not answer any of the questions set'.

Step 2: Explain the procedure and timing

Give each participant a pen/pencil and their copy of the test which they should keep face down until instructed to begin. Participants will have exactly 10 minutes to complete the test. A time check will be given at five minutes, and two minutes before completion time. After 10 minutes, participants should stop writing whether or not they have finished.

Step 3: Issue clipboards, or ensure that every participant has table space in which to work

If possible arrange seating so that no participant can see another's work.

Step 4: Issue pens/pencils and test sheets, face down

Remind participants that they should not look at the test until instructed to do so.

Step 5: Begin the exercise

Instruct participants to turn over their sheets; they now have 10 minutes to complete the test.

Step 6: Give time checks at 5 minutes and at 8 minutes

Step 7: Close the exercise
Instruct participants to stop working. Do not collect the test sheets.

Step 8: Ask for reactions to the test
Most, if not all, will be aware of the 'catch' by now. Ascertain how many realized immediately, either by following the instructions fully, or because of prior knowledge of similar exercises. Ask if, nevertheless, the imposition of examination-like conditions had an effect on performance or stress levels.

Discuss how pressures such as these – examination conditions, time constraints or deadlines, external pressures – can affect performance.

Questions you might use:

- *How many saw through the exercise at once?*
- *Who didn't follow instructions and immediately started to attempt the questions?*
- *Why did you do this?*
- *Did the fact that one of the questions on the first page was visual (and to most, immediately attemptable) have any bearing on the fact you didn't read the paper through first as instructed?*
- *How often does this happen in the workplace – either making errors through cutting corners, or seizing on the attractive/easy task rather than the tedious/important/difficult? (How many times have you, or people you know, tried to assemble a piece of equipment in the home without fully reading the instructions, and wasted more time putting things right afterwards. Everyone will have an anecdote!)*
- *Can anyone share a work situation where failure to follow instructions caused problems?*
- *How did you react to the first minutes of the exercise, when examination conditions were introduced?*
- *Why did you react in this way?*
- *Can you think of situations in your working life where similar pressures were imposed either on you, or by you?*
- *What was the outcome/are the implications?*

Step 9: Give answers to test
Explain that you will not be collecting the tests; participants may keep them. For the sake of those who completed the test, and for general interest, either go through the questions giving answers, or issue Document 2 which can be given as a handout to accompany the test sheet.

Step 10: (Optional) If appropriate, lead a short discussion on the importance of an international approach to management today
It may not be necessary for participants to know the answers to the

questions posed on the sheet. However, as we move towards the twenty-first century, inter-country dealing and co-operation is a fact of life. Changes in our way of thinking, working and our concept of corporate culture have to be encompassed.

Questions you might use:

- *Is it necessary for anyone but senior management to have a knowledge of, say, languages other than English?*
- *If so, at what level, and to what extent should there be a knowledge of languages other than English?*
- *Do you think it important for receptionists to know courtesy expressions in languages other than English, for example (see question 6)? . . . and so on, depending on the composition of the group, type of course etc.*

Step 11: Close the activity

Worldly wise - Document 1

Wordly wise test

NAME   TITLE

PLACE OF WORK

Read all of this paper carefully before answering the following questions:

1 Fill in the gap in the following statement:

    Nikkei is to Japan what _____ is to the USA

2 Identify the European Community member countries on the following map

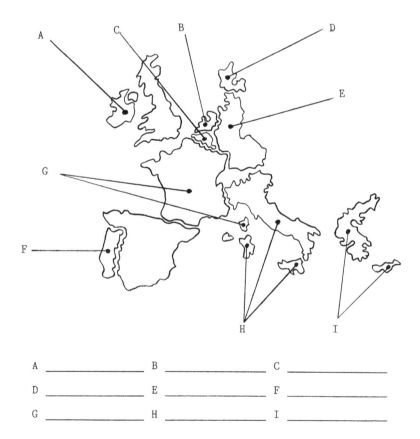

A _____   B _____   C _____

D _____   E _____   F _____

G _____   H _____   I _____

3 What is the name of the Federal Bank of Germany?

4 If the *bestuurder* was visiting your company from the Netherlands, who would you be expecting: the Accountant, the Marketing Director, or the Managing Director?

5 Name six of the OPEC countries

....

....

....

....

....

....

6 What do the following Spanish phrases mean?

Buenos dias

....

Le presento al Senor. . .

....

No entiendo el espanol

....

Sientese por favor

....

Salud

....

7 Two Japanese top executives, the chief finance officer, and the manager in charge of human resource development, are visiting your company. Who is the senior of the executives?

8 What does the acronym GATT stand for?

....

9 If an international deputation were to visit your organization, comprising members of a German *Vorstand*, a Portuguese *Conselho de Administracio*, and a Danish *Bestyrelsen*, who would these people be?

....

....

....

10 The International Bank for Reconstruction and Development is an institution set up to assist countries to develop their economies by the provision of economic aid in the forms of loans and technical assistance. It is more commonly known as

....

11 Now that you have read through most of this paper, obey only the first instruction, ie to print your name, title and place of work in the box at the top of the sheet. Do not fill in any of the answers to the questions set.

....

12 If you have read this entire paper before attempting the questions, as instructed, and are now aware of the 'catch', do not give the exercise away by comment or exclamation. Please be patient, and spend the time considering how you would have answered the questions had you been asked to do so!

....

Worldly wise – Document 2

Answer sheet

1 Dow-Jones is to the USA what the Nikkei index is to Japan. The Financial Times 30 share index, the 100 share index, and the all-share index are used to measure the value of ordinary shares quoted in the UK stock market. A similar role is played in the USA by the Dow-Jones index, and in Japan by the Nikkei index.

2 The countries are:

A	Republic of Ireland
B	The Netherlands
C	Belgium
D	Denmark
E	Germany
F	Portugal
G	France
H	Italy
I	Greece

3 The Federal Bank of Germany is called the Bundesbank.

4 Managing Director.

5 Any six from the following list: Algeria, Bahrain, Egypt, Iraq, Kuwait, Libya, Quatar, Saudi Arabia, Syria, or the United Arab Emirates. (Tunisia ceased to be a member in 1987.)

6 The phrases mean:

Buenos dias – Good morning
Le presento al Senor – This is Mr
No entiendo el espanol – I don't understand Spanish
Sientese por favor – Please sit down
Salud – Your good health!

7 The manager responsible for human resource development. In the USA and Britain, it is usual for the chief finance officer to have seniority over personnel executives. However, the reverse is true in Japan where human resource development is given much greater credence. It is usual for the human resource development officer to be junior only to the chief executive in organizational structures.

8 GATT – General Agreement on Tariffs and Trade. Formed in 1948, this organization was established as a multilateral treaty aiming to liber-

alize world trade and place it on a secure basis. At the time of writing, over 100 parties apply the rules to their commercial policy.

9 They would be members of the Board of Directors.

10 The International Bank for Reconstruction and Development is better known as The World Bank.

SECTION 3

HELPING OTHERS TO MANAGE CHANGE

Activity 24

Acronym

Description

Run this activity early in the course – after introductions and ice-breakers. It is intended to focus participants' minds on general issues about, and attitudes to, change.

Objectives

By the end of this activity participants will:

- have discussed positive and negative attitudes to change
- be focused on some of the issues surrounding change in readiness for more detailed activities to follow.

Participants

Number: Any
Type: Any

Time

60–90 minutes

Resources

- Notepaper and pencil/pen for each participant
- Tables/clipboards or facility for lap-top writing
- Flipchart stand, paper and marker pens
- Dictionary for each syndicate group (optional)
- Copy of Trainer's notes (p. 167) for reference

Method

Step 1: Introduce the activity, explaining procedure and timings

This activity is a fairly simple method of getting participants to look at the impact of change on individuals and organizations. Working in small groups, participants will think of as many words as possible, starting with the initial letters C-H-A-N-G-E, explicitly and implicitly connected with the concept of change. Any aspect of change can be considered. For example, under C could be 'challenge', or 'calculating' (do instigators of change have to be calculating?) or 'colour' (how does the colour of our clothes change the way we feel, or how others perceive us?). Under H could be 'helpful' or 'horrid'; under A could be 'ambition' or 'antibiosis' (dictionary definition: 'Condition of antagonism between organisms'!) and so on.

Groups will be allowed 20–30 minutes for this part of the exercise, and will then be asked to report back to the main group. A spokesperson from each group should be elected.

At the end of the allocated time a combined list of words suggested by the groups will be written onto a flipchart and reasons for each word's inclusion briefly discussed.

Step 2: Arrange the group into syndicate groups of three to five people; issue notepaper and pencils (and dictionaries if to be used); begin exercise

Each syndicate group should have sufficient space to work uninterrupted. Suggest that one person act as scribe. This does not necessarily have to be the spokesperson. Leave groups to work alone, but be available to answer questions about procedure.

Note: *Some groups will find the activity more beneficial if a dictionary is available. If dictionaries are to be used, however, the exercise could take longer than the 20–30 minutes suggested.*

The trainer's notes giving approximately 100 words beginning with C which could have change implications, may be a useful crib. You could offer suggestions from this list to groups who have difficulty getting started.

Step 3: Check progress after 20 minutes; negotiate more time if necessary; at the end of the agreed time, stop the exercise and reconvene the group; ask each spokesperson in turn to read out their syndicate group's list

Record each word on flipchart paper. Suggest that other syndicate groups strike out words from their list which duplicate. Do not discuss reasons for the inclusion of the words at this stage. Repeat the process with other syndicate groups until a complete list has been drawn up.

Step 4: Discuss each word in turn; why it was included; what implications there are in the context of change

The spokespersons can lead on this, but it is also an opportunity, early in the course, to encourage whole-group involvement.

Step 5: Do a word count; how many words listed, associated with change, have negative or have positive connotations (some will be neutral)

Invariably there will be more words listed which have negative implications. If this is the case, ask why this should be? Could it be that this is a reflection of participants' own attitudes?

Assure participants that this is quite normal; most individuals see change as a threat to be avoided rather than as a challenge to be enjoyed – or will be somewhere on the left of that spectrum. At best, the status quo is preferable to movement, however beneficial that movement may turn out to be.

Step 6: Close the activity referring to the objectives

Participants should now be 'tuned in' to the idea of change with all its implications, and ready for a more detailed look at more specific areas of change management.

Trainer's notes

Some examples of words which may appear on participants' lists have been given within the activity (step 1). Here are some more, obtained with the help of a pocket dictionary. Some are more obvious than others, but a few seconds' thought should be enough to see why each was included.

For brevity, only the letter C has been covered:

cajole • calamity • calculating • calibre • callous • calmness • camouflage • campaign • candid • canker • can • cannot • cant • capable • capitulate • caprice • captious • care • career • careful • cascade • castigate • castrate • catastrophe • causal • caution • cavil • ceaseless • censure • cerebral chagrin • challenge • chancy • chaos • character • chary • choice • circumvent • clarify • clash • coax • coerce • cogency • cogitate • coherent • colour • combat • compel • communication • commute • compete • competition • complain • complicate • comply • conciliate • conduce • confidence • confusion • conquer • consequence • constrict • consult • contempt • contend • contest • contort • contradict • contravene • contrive • control • contumacy • convention • converge • convert • convince • co-operate • coordinate • cope • corner • cosmetic • counsel • coup • courage • course • courtesy • cowardice • creative • credible • crisis • criterion • critical • criticism • crucial • cruel • cunning • cure • current • curse • curtail • cut • cynical

Activity 25

Back to the real world

Description

This is a useful end-of-course activity which can help people to reflect on what techniques they can call on to help others confront change which may require the acquisition, development or modification of knowledge, skills and attitudes. It is basic training stuff; but often less than obvious to those who have not been trained as trainers or change agents. It can help people to reflect on techniques they have used already, or to suggest and consider new ones.

Objectives

By the end of this activity participants will:

- understand a model commonly used in training needs analysis
- be able to select appropriate techniques to use as trainers or as change agents.

Participants

Number: Any
Type: Managers responsible for training or for managing change

Time

45 minutes

Resources

- Flipchart stand, paper and marker pen
- 1 copy of Document 1 for each participant
- 1 copy of Document 2 for each participant

Method

Step 1: Introduce (or refresh people's memories on) a basic model used in training needs analysis and which is useful for

*any manager who needs to analyze what her/his staff might
need to help them confront change in the work environment*
*Allow five minutes. A model frequently used in training needs analysis is
to break down a job or task into those parts that require:*

- *specific **knowledge***
- *specific **skills***
- *specific **attitudes***

*on the part of the job-holder for that job to be carried out effectively.
Flipchart these and leave them on display. Obviously, organizational
change can require change in a job, or its disappearance, or the creation of
a new one. People who are staying need to be equipped to cope with the
changing demands made upon them. They will worry about whether or
not they know enough, whether or not they have the right skills. They will
worry about whether or not they can ever acquire new knowledge and
skills.*

*Managers will worry over whether or not their staff have the right attitude
to confront change and deal with it effectively. The good manager will
recognize these anxieties and provide support on all three fronts.*

*This exercise is designed to help managers to increase their awareness of
the techniques they can call on but also to be able to recognize the
limitations of each technique as well.*

Step 2: Divide the group into small syndicate groups of three or four; issue one copy of Document 1 to each person; check that each group is clear on its task
*The task is specified on the Document. There are three blank lines at the
end of the Document so that you, or the group, can add any missing
techniques that may be appropriate to, or used within, a very particular
environment. Brainwashing, for example, has been omitted but in certain
firms. . . who knows?!*

Step 3: Start the exercise
Allow 20 minutes for the groups to complete the task.

Step 4: Re-form the whole group; discuss the results with a view to arriving at agreement on each item
*Allow 15 minutes. Use Document 2 yourself as a checklist. It's not
necessary to get each small group to give its responses though you might
want a group to justify its position if it's at variance with the general view.*

Questions you might use:

- *Why do you feel that technique is/is not appropriate?*
- *Could that technique ever be appropriate for. . ..?*
- *If the technique is agreed as useful, are there any problems or
limitations in using it effectively?*
- *Why does your group take a different view on that?*

Step 5: Close the activity by issuing a copy of Document 2 to each participant; refer briefly to the activity's objectives

Document 2 is, effectively, the 'answer' sheet to the exercise. The group can mark on it any variances identified during steps 3 and 4.

Back to the real world - Document 1

In this exercise you are asked to look at each technique listed below. The list represents most of the commonly used approaches to training and change. You are asked to discuss in your group, and agree, which of the three basic needs (Acquisition of Knowledge, Development of Skills, Change or Modification of Attitude) each technique could be used with to good effect.

The first has been worked for you by way of an example.

Use a '?' to indicate uncertainty, or to indicate 'in some circumstances'. Otherwise use a tick (appropriate) or a cross (not appropriate).

TECHNIQUE	ACQUISITION OF KNOWLEDGE	DEVELOP-MENT OF SKILLS	ATTITUDE CHANGE
Listening to a lecture	✓	X	X
Sitting next to Nellie			
Watching a demonstration			
Reading a text book			
Group discussion/staff meetings			
Case studies			
Interactive video			
Role playing			
Group projects			
Watching a film/video			
Listening to an audiocassette			
Practical exercises/games			
Field activities			
Technical manual			
Directed study			
Exchange visits			
Open or distance learning			
Computer assisted learning			
Individual research projects			
Sensitivity training (eg T-Groups, Encounter Groups)			
Secondments			
Involvement in consultation over change			

Back to the real world – Document 2

TECHNIQUE	ACQUIISI-TION OF KNOWLEDGE	DEVELOP-MENT OF SKILLS	ATTITUDE CHANGE
Listening to a lecture	✓	X	X
Sitting next to Nellie	?	✓	X
Watching a demonstration	✓	?	X
Reading a text book	✓	X	X
Group discussion/staff meetings	?	X	✓
Case studies	?	✓	✓
Interactive video	✓	?	X
Role playing	X	✓	✓
Group projects	✓	✓	✓
Watching a film/video	✓	?	X
Listening to an audiocassette	✓	X	X
Practical exercises/games	X	✓	?
Field activities	✓	✓	✓
Technical manual	✓	X	X
Directed study	✓	✓	?
Exchange visits	✓	?	✓
Open or distance learning	✓	✓	✓
Computer assisted learning	✓	✓	X
Individual research projects	✓	✓	✓
Sensitivity training (eg T-Groups, Encounter Groups)	X	✓	✓
Secondments	✓	✓	✓
Involvement in consultation over changes	?	X	✓

Activity 26

Flavour of the month

Description

This activity is essentially a competitive game which is meant to be fun. It can be used as an ice-breaker or as an antidote to cerebral hard work. But it works best as a course closure since it contains some cautionary advice about implementing change. It tends to be most effective with more junior levels of management.

Objectives

By the end of this activity participants will be aware of techniques of change management which should be avoided.

Participants

Number: Maximum of 10
Type: Junior managers or supervisors who may have to play a part in introducing change into their area of responsibility

Time

30 minutes

Resources

- Square or round table with sufficient room on it for 20 A5-size cards to be placed face down without overlap.
- 1 copy of Document 1 for each participant
- Set of 20 A5 cards prepared as set out in the trainer's notes on p. 176 of this activity
- Flipchart stand, paper and marker pen for recording scores
- A token 'prize' for the winning team (optional)

Method

Step 1: Introduce the activity
Avoid mentioning the introduction and objectives. Simply say that you

are going to play a simple competitive game about change-management techniques.

Step 2: Divide the group into two teams; explain the rules of the game

1 *The teams are in competition. The highest scoring team at the end wins. You (the trainer) will keep score.*
2 *There are 20 cards on the table. 10 of these cards have 'labels' on them and these are matched by 10 cards which describe the change management technique which the label refers to.*
3 *The purpose of the game is to match labels with descriptions. The first match will score 10 for the team concerned, the next 9 and so on.*
4 *Each team takes it in turn to turn over and display just two cards for all members of both teams to see. If the team considers that there is a match (consultation is allowed) then the cards are handed to the trainer. If it is a match the trainer records the score for that team on the flipchart and takes the two cards out of play. The winning team then has another go immediately. If a claimed match is incorrect then the cards are returned to the table in the same position and the team is awarded a score of 'minus' 5. If no match is claimed then the two cards are replaced in the same position.*
5 *All team members should take turns to reveal cards.*
6 *The winning team is likely to be the one which can remember the location of cards as the game progresses.*

Take any questions about the rules.

Step 3: Run the game; judge any matches, retain correct match cards, keep score

The game should only take around five to eight minutes to complete. It is not meant to be taken too seriously! Record scores (10 for the first match, 9 for the next and so on, with scores of -5 for incorrect matches). Keep a copy of Document 1 handy to check claimed matches.

Step 4: Total the scores and award a small token prize to the winning team

A bar of chocolate? A bag of crisps?

Step 5: Issue Document 1 which summarizes all the approaches; ask for comment

Allow 20 minutes.

Questions you might use:

- *Can people give any examples of the techniques from their own experience? (Best asked with a smile and ensure people aren't set up with a view to knocking them down, since this activity is meant to be light-hearted!)*
- *What exactly is wrong with these techniques?'*

- *Why* do *people use them?*

Step 6: *Close the activity by referring briefly to the objectives*

Trainer's notes

First, prepare 10 A5 cards each with a label written on it (in marker pen) as shown on Document 1. (eg one card with 'Cascade' written on it, one card with 'Volcano' and so on).

Then prepare 10 A5 cards with a definition written on it (in marker pen) as shown in Document 1. (eg one card with 'Concentrating entirely on managers and hoping the changes will filter down eventually' written on it and so on).

Note: Ensure that the cards are not so thin that the marker pen ink is visible on the back when the card is face down on the table or the whole point of the activity will be lost!

Finally, before the activity begins set the cards out, face down, on the table.

Flavour of the month – Document 1

Change management techniques to be avoided!

Cascade	Concentrating the responsibility for change entirely on managers or senior staff and hoping change will filter down eventually.
Volcano	Working on brighter/younger staff in the hope that they will erupt from underneath and force changes at higher levels where management or staff are stuck in a rut.
Flower show	Promoting the image of, and favouring, already outstanding people in the team so that they become very visible 'models' for change.
Prize giving	Awarding the 'goodies' of change – new equipment/office/favourable rosters/working methods as a reward to those in post longest and who will be the most resistant to change.
Dive bombing	Driving ineffective staff away by putting them on complex training programmes which you know they won't cope with.
Muesli	Providing lots of 'bitty' training – relevant to change but without coherence or clear overall plan.
Respray	Calling something everyone knows perfectly well by a new name, necessitating major re-training throughout the whole department.
Flavour of the month	Training for all staff immediately and at regular intervals in quite different and theoretically incompatible methods of work which they are expected to implement at once.
Arcade games	Instant introduction of complex, powerful new technology systems on the basis that it has to be a more efficient way of doing things and everyone else is doing it anyway.
Magic dust	Change managers are frequently asked for this. It involves: • changing people's personalities overnight • training people to do things that are quite beyond them • making pigs fly.

Activity 27

Games

Description

This activity considers creativity, often a vital element in planning and managing change effectively.

Objectives

By the end of this activity participants will:

- have experience of the need to be creative under pressure
- be able to identify certain conditions which must exist if creativity is to be maximized

Participants

Number: Up to 18
Type: Managers or professionals

Time

2 hours

Resources

- As many rooms as there are syndicates (up to 4)
- One copy of Document 1 for each participant
- One copy of Document 2 for each participant (but be sure to separate the documents - see p. 180)
- Depending on the number of syndicate groups, sufficient sets of items and furniture as listed in Document 2
- Flipchart stand, paper and marker pens

Method

Step 1: Introduce the activity
Explain that the activity will be looking at aspects of creativity.

Step 2: Allocate participants to syndicate groups of between four and six

Use any method that seems appropriate.

Step 3: Assign syndicate groups to their separate rooms and issue Document 1: Task One, after ensuring you have separated it from Document 2; start the exercise

Half an hour is allowed for the completion of Task One. Observe and monitor the syndicate groups during this phase.

Step 4: After 30 minutes, issue the items listed in Document 2 (Task Two), together with copies of Document 2 to each syndicate group; start Task Two

Half an hour is allowed for this. Observe and monitor the syndicate groups during this phase.

Step 5: Each syndicate group tries out the game it created as Task Two

Allow 10 minutes for this. A group may try out its Task One game if practicable and if it wants to, but the nature of this activity is such that the Task Two game is likely to be the most playable!

Step 6: Re-convene the full group. Discuss the two tasks, drawing out any differences between them in terms of:

- creativity
- motivation
- group and individual performance

Allow up to 45 minutes for this.

Questions you might use:

- *Were your reactions to the two tasks different? If so, why?'*
- *Can you define creativity?*
- *Under what conditions can creativity best be encouraged? (Flipchart these – you could consider turning the flipchart into a handout for issue later.)*
- *What stifles creativity?*
- *Are some people naturally more creative than others?*
- *Do creative people present any particular problems for managers?*
- *How important is creativity to planning and implementing change? Can you think of any examples?*

Step 7: Close the activity, referring to the objectives

Games - Document 1

Briefing notes to group

Task One: Create a game that people will enjoy playing. You have 30 minutes to complete this task.

- - - - - - - - - - - - - - - - -

NB - BE SURE TO SEPARATE THE TWO BRIEFINGS

✂ - - - - - - - - - - - - - - ✂

Games - Document 2

Briefing notes to group

Task Two: Your task is to create a game which can be played *indoors*, by *four people*, which lasts for about *10 minutes* and which makes use of *any three* of the supplied items (no more, no fewer). No other items may be used.

Your trainer will make available the following items:

- A table
- A jug of water
- A towel
- A tray
- A piece of string, 12″ long
- A wristwatch
- A pack of drinking straws
- Six chairs
- A potato
- A ruler
- A sunhat

At the end of this activity you will have a chance to play this game within your own syndicate group.

Activity 28

Jargoner's question time

Description

Most managers use computers in their work. Many feel they could not do their jobs without them. But at least one survey has revealed that a staggering 92 per cent of managers are uncomfortable with the technology. The aversion of many senior managers is strong enough to have resulted in a new word entering the language: 'Technophobia'.

The aim of this light-hearted activity is to try to break down just a little of the jargon barrier and to encourage people who have so far avoided the computer to take their first, small step. The activity focuses on the everyday use of the office PC (of the IBM-compatible type running MS-DOS).

Objectives

By the end of this activity participants will:

- have tested their own knowledge of the (IBM compatible PC) computing field
- (if already expert or competent) be aware of the perils of using jargon with beginners
- (if not already expert or competent) be less inhibited about tackling the computer
- (if not already expert or competent) be aware of the meaning of some of the more familiar computer jargon.

Participants

Number: Any
Type: Managers or senior managers who feel they may suffer from technophobia but who need to confront their fears.

Time

30 minutes

Resources

- One copy of Document 1 for each participant
- One copy of Document 2 for each participant

Method

Step 1: Introduce the activity

Cover the points in the introduction. It's important that managers who feel 'left behind' by the technology recognize they are not alone. This activity is a fun piece of nonsense with a serious purpose. Stress that no-one will be made a fool of or made to feel inadequate. The activity can only be a beginning; the two problems at the root of the situation are: (a) lack of training and (b) jargon. This activity seeks to encourage people to think about training as a way forward and it also seeks to crack the pedestal upon which jargon sits.

Step 2: Issue Document 1; stress that you want honest answers!

Allow 5 minutes for people to complete the questionnaire.

Step 3: Get some reactions to the questionnaire

Allow 5 minutes.

Questions you might use:

- *Should we make fun of this important management tool, the computer?*
- *Was anyone completely and* honestly *unable to answer 'Yes' to any question? (This would be most unusual!)*
- *What percentage of the questions do people feel relate to the use of the PC* as a tool *and what percentage to its* technicalities? *(The answer is: 25 per cent to its use as a tool, 75 per cent to its technicalities.)*
- *Does most computer literature (magazines, sales pamphlets etc) concentrate on what the computer can do to help management or does it concentrate on the technicalities? (We feel it's the latter.)*
- *Is there an analogy between driving a car and using a computer?*
- *Does a car driver actually* need *to know what goes on under the bonnet in order to drive it safely from A to B?*
- *Does a manager need to understand all the technical jargon in order to use a PC?*

Step 4: Issue Document 2; ask people to score their questionnaires

Allow five minutes. It should not be taken too seriously! Encourage laughter and flippancy; it all helps to remove some of the perceived threat.

Step 5: Draw conclusions

Allow 10 minutes.

Questions you might use:

- *How accurate are the results?*
- *Do people agree that it is jargon and a lack of training that prevents people from maximizing the use of the PC?*
- *If people are competent, or even expert, how have they got that far?*
- *Are they essentially self-taught with an aptitude of some kind, either mathematical, technical or analytical?*
- *What do the jargon experts need to do in order to open up their world?*
- *Do the jargon experts ever create the impression that they do not actually want their world opened up?*
- *What is the price that industry will pay if management cannot get to grips with computer technology?*

Step 6: *Close the activity by referring briefly to the objectives*

Jargoner's question time - Document 1

Twenty questions about the PC in your office
(Do answer *honestly*! There is nothing to be gained by cheating and you will not be asked to divulge your marks to anyone else!)

Circle your answer in one of the two right hand columns.

Do you know. . .

1	what the letters 'PC' actually stand for	Yes	No
2	whether, if you had to buy a new PC, you should choose a 386 machine or a 486 machine to meet your office's needs?	Yes	No
3	what WYSIWYG means?	Yes	No
4	why WISIWYGs have a liking for dahlias and chrysanthemums?	Yes	No
5	what a printer does?	Yes	No
6	why you should not wait in the rain for a 16-bit bus?	Yes	No
7	what a VDU (or monitor) is for?	Yes	No
8	what a word-processor does?	Yes	No
9	what RAMs do (the sort that don't stand around in a field all day)?	Yes	No
10	where you would stick a modem (seriously, though)?	Yes	No
11	the difference between software and hardware?	Yes	No
12	why PCs often attract mice?	Yes	No
13	if databases existed before computers did?	Yes	No
14	that there are at least two ways of storing data permanently for use with a PC, on *floppy* disks and on *hard* disks?	Yes	No
15	the difference between EGA, VGA and the CIA?	Yes	No
16	why the diet of an autoexec bat consists mainly of insects?	Yes	No
17	why a PC needs regular booting?	Yes	No
18	how a PC can catch a virus?	Yes	No
19	why systemic chemical treatment will not affect program bugs (but may possibly affect your PC)?	Yes	No
20	the difference between a program download and a jargon overload?	Yes	No

Jargoner's question time - Document 2

Scoring sheet

Circle the scores which match with your marking of the questionnaire.

Question	Yes		No	
1	100k	RAM	–	
2	2	MHz	10k	RAM
3	2	MHz	10k	RAM
4	–		–	
5	100k	RAM	–	
6	2	MHz	10k	RAM
7	100k	RAM	–	
8	100k	RAM	–	
9	2	MH	10k	RAM
10	2	MHz	10k	RAM
11	2	MHz	10k	RAM
12	2	MHz	10k	RAM
13	100k	RAM	–	
14	100k	RAM	–	
15	2	MHz	10k	RAM
16	–		–	
17	2	MHz	10k	RAM
18	2	MHz	10k	RAM
19	2	MHz	10k	RAM
20	2	MHz	10k	RAM

Now total your MHz scores: _____

Now total your RAM scores: _____

If you scored 0 MHz write 0 in this box:
If you scored 2–8 MHz inclusive write 20 in this box:
If you scored 10–18 MHz inclusive write 40 in this box:
If you scored 20–24 MHz inclusive write 60 in this box:

If you scored 0k–100k RAM write 0 in this box:
If you scored 110k–300k RAM inclusive write 15 in this box:
If you scored 310k–720k RAM inclusive write 25 in this box:

Now add the totals in the two boxes together and write the answer in here:

Now interpret your scores as shown below:

Score Comment

0–10   Your problem is not with computers but with numeracy! It is impossible to score 10 or less on this questionnaire! . . .

15–25   There is no earthly reason why you should not work perfectly well with computers! Maybe you learned once to drive a car or ride a bike? You will have stalled the car, been embarrassed, fallen off the bike and bruised yourself. . . but did you give up? You may know all about carburettors and pistons and fuel injections systems – but you don't actually *need* to in order to drive a car. Likewise, you don't actually *need* to understand 75 per cent of the questions on this exercise – but you can still use the computer as a valuable tool.

35–55   Chances are you are already using a computer with a fair degree of confidence. You probably curse it when it goes wrong, but you blame the machine rather than yourself. You can probably deal with simple problems but you don't want to concern yourself with the inner working of the machine, although you do understand something of the jargon.

65–85   You are probably an expert PC user! You know the jargon and you are probably endlessly fascinated and challenged by the sorts of operating problems which people can encounter. You can probably impress people by your ability to type in miracle-working spells from the keyboard. But you just *may* be partly responsible for some of the problems which people have in improving their own knowledge and conquering their own fears. Could this be true? If not, then you probably answered 'Yes' to question 20, *and really meant it*!

This next section is for the really pedantic, who want to know the answers.

1 PC stands for Personal Computer

2 A 486 machine (the number refers to the type of processor) will be more powerful and able to handle complex demands such as multi-tasking (or running more than one program at a time) more efficiently than would a 386. However, a 486 will be more expensive, and a 386 is (in 1992) the industry standard and capable of performing most office

tasks perfectly well. As prices drop, though, the 486 is becoming much more commonplace.

3 WYSIWYG is an acronym for What You See Is What You Get and it refers to the ability of some programs to show you, on screen, exactly what you will get when you print something off. Most word-processors do not do this automatically, for example.

4 A daft question!

5 A printer prints. Jargon-lovers would say it produces hard copy. There is a variety of printers around, from the simplest (9-pin dot matrix) to the more complex and sophisticated (ink-jet, bubble jet, laser). It all depends on what you want it to do and how much money you're prepared to pay. You don't need to understand the technical differences involved.

6 A bus is another bit of computer jargon and it relates to the movement of electronic data around the computer's internal workings. Strictly for the specialists.

7 A VDU or monitor is the TV-like box which displays what the computer is currently doing for you.

8 A word-processor is a commonly-used piece of business software which has largely replaced the process of typing directly onto paper.

9 RAM is measured in kilobytes (k) and is the part of the computer's memory which does most of the work when a program is being run. The basic amount of RAM on a PC is usually (in 1992) 640k, often extended to 1000k (or 1 MegaByte – 1MB) though machines are available with 8MB RAM and more. A word-processor would normally require around 500k of RAM to be available before it would work properly. (MHz – or MegaHertz – (by the way) tells the specialists something about the speed at which your computer runs).

10 A modem is a device which enables computers to speak to each other over telephone lines. They have to be installed by people who know something about what they are doing, and a modem would either sit inside the PC (a modem card) or in a box with flashing lights on the desk.

11 Hardware is the stuff you can physically touch. Software is coded program data stored on disks. A floppy disk is thus *not* software but hardware. But the code for a word-processor program, stored on a floppy disk, *is* software. (Confused?)

12 A mouse is a device used to move a cursor (or pointer) around on a VDU screen. The mouse is used most commonly with programs that involve drawing (such as Desk Top Publishing) or graphics (such as Computer Aided Design and MS Windows) or games, and it has a ball underneath which rolls around on the desk surface. The computer works out relative positions and the cursor on the screen reflects the mouse's movement. Buttons on a mouse are used to select things on screen, such as 'icons' (or pictures which represent certain functions that will be carried out if 'clicked' over).

13 Anything which holds data so that the data is organized is a database. So, a filing cabinet with alphabetically organized files is a database. The word has been rather hijacked by the computer industry, since computer power can be harnessed into a very efficient, high-speed means of keeping databases well organized, up-to-date and instantly accessible.

14 Floppy disks and hard disks just store data. Floppy disks can be carried about while hard disks sit inside the PC permanently. Hard disks work much faster than floppy disks and hold much more data. But both are the same in principle, ie they store data. This could be a program to run a word-processor or a set of files which could be letters or reports produced by a word-processor. An analogy is with a cassette-tape which stores electronic data and which needs a special machine to interpret it in a form we can understand. (Indeed, early mass-market PCs often used audio cassette tapes for data and program storage rather than disks.) The PC just interprets data stored on a disk in a form we can understand – well, some of the time. . .

15 EGA and VGA (and CGA and SVGA etc) are fairly technical terms which relate to graphics and how well a VDU will display pictures, diagrams etc, together with the colour range available. Best left to the experts but VGA is, in 1992, the standard with SuperVGA on the horizon. (The CIA is the Central Intelligence Agency of America.)

16 Same answer as question 4 – although autoexec.bat *does* have a serious application in a PC. However, as it relates to operating systems we do not propose to go into detail here!

17 Booting is another bit of jargon. It's what a computer does every time it is switched on or re-set. It has to run a series of checks and load some preliminary programs before you can start to work with it. This process can often take up to 30 seconds.

18 Viruses are a big problem for IT departments in business. They are simply computer programs written by morons. They are destructive and they can 'infect' PC's by being hidden away on floppy disks or on computers with which you may link up and transfer files. They may lay dormant and then do things like wipe all the files on a hard disk when a computer's internal calendar registers 'Friday the 13th'. They do not harm a computer physically but they can, and do, cause loss or corruption of data and they are thus very worrying for businesses dependent on accurate, volume data. Anti-virus software is now available so that checks can be made, but the best insurance for an individual PC user is *never* to import files by telephone from another computer you know little about, and *never* to use pirated or illicit copies of software.

19 Bugs in programs are things that go wrong. Usually some kind of illogicality has been missed when the program was designed or written, or a possibility was not anticipated. This makes the program do

strange things. Generally it is wise to avoid the first releases of new software programs which may have been rushed out in a competitive market and which may contain irritating bugs. They are not viruses, just 'glitches' which are usually impossible to remedy locally.

20 Downloading means transferring data or programs from one computer to another, or from a computer's memory to a device such as a floppy disk or printer. *If you know what jargon overload is you can work wonders with the 92 per cent of managers in that survey!*

Activity 29

Mobiles

Description

Activity 32 – 'Towers of strength' – focuses on some important inter-group issues, notably those of communication and motivation. This activity is more modest in scope, concentrating on the differences between written and oral forms of communication.

Faced with change, and getting people to undertake new tasks or do things differently, managers can choose between explaining/training or setting things down in new procedures to be followed. Of course, in reality both methods are used, but this activity tries to expose the relative strengths and weaknesses of each method so that participants are aware of the limitations.

Objectives

By the end of this activity participants will:

- be able to identify the advantages and disadvantages of giving oral instructions on new or unfamiliar procedures
- be able to identify the advantages and disadvantages of giving written instructions on new or unfamiliar procedures
- be able to identify simple communication issues in planning and conveying new ideas to others.

Participants

Number: Between 6 and 20
Type: Managers and supervisors

Time

1 hour 15 minutes

Resources

- Sufficient syndicate rooms for each syndicate to work independently from the others

- One copy of Document 1 for each participant
- Material as specified in the trainer's notes on p. 192
- Flipchart stand, paper and marker pens
- Easy access to speedy photocopying facilities

Method

Step 1: Introduce the activity

It is suggested that you concentrate on the third learning objective. The others will surface as the activity proceeds.

Step 2: Allocate participants to syndicate groups of between three and six

Any method will do.

Step 3: Allocate syndicate groups to their rooms and issue Document 1, Briefing notes, to each participant; start the exercise

Allow 30 minutes. Monitor the progress of the syndicate groups, making sure they understand that written instructions are required at the end of the first period.

Step 4: Terminate the planning phase and collect up the written instructions for duplication; make sufficient copies of the instructions for ALL participants (ie the full group) to have a copy, plus yourself

Ensure that syndicate groups do not talk to each other while this is being done. Try to minimize the time taken for this copying stage.

Step 5: Move to the mobile construction phase, as described in Document 1

Make sure each syndicate group has sufficient stocks of material. Check that any material used for practice is not visible or available. Allow 10 minutes and monitor each group, making a note of any problems they encounter. Do not attempt to answer any questions or clarify any instructions.

Step 6: Stop the construction phase and re-convene the main group; ensure all participants have copies of each syndicate's instruction sets; invite each syndicate group to display its mobile

Allow five minutes.

Step 7: Discuss the merits of the various (un)finished mobiles and establish what went wrong, if anything

Allow 5 minutes.

Questions you might use:

- *Why could your syndicate not complete its task?*
- *What went wrong, and why did this happen?*
- *Were the instructions too complex?*
- *Can the planning syndicate offer any comment on any problems experienced by the production syndicate?*

Step 8: Compare the merits of written versus oral instructions and procedures

Allow 15 minutes. Flipchart the issues as they arise, using two flipchart sheets. One should be used to identify the pros and cons of written instructions, the other to identify the pros and cons of oral instructions.

Questions you might use:

- *How would mobile production have been affected if the instructions had been provided orally?*
- *What are the advantages/disadvantages of exclusively written instructions to communicate new ideas and procedures?*
- *What are the advantages/disadvantages of exclusively oral instructions to communicate new ideas and procedures?*

By way of guidance, the following are likely to arise. These suggestions are not exhaustive but they may help get the discussion going:

Written

Pros	•	*Unambiguous (or should be)*
	•	*Can be referred to repeatedly*
	•	*Ensures that everyone receives the same instructions*
Cons	•	*Don't allow for questions or clarification*
	•	*What about people who can't read?*
	•	*Can be intimidating*

Oral

Pros	•	*Allow for questions and clarification*
	•	*Can be paced to individual ability*
	•	*Feedback can be gained on learner problems*
	•	*Practical demonstration can be given*
Cons	•	*Potential for non-standard instruction and operation*
	•	*No written record for the future*

Step 9: Close the activity by referring to the objectives

Trainer's notes

You will need to collect together the following in advance of this exercise:

For each syndicate group:

- Reel of cotton

- Thin string or cord – about 4 metres for each group
- Card of fuse wire – varying thicknesses
- Coloured card or paper: four different colours, at least 2 sheets of each
- Scissors
- Glue
- Sellotape
- A4 paper and pen (for instructions)

Note: Ensure you have spare stocks of string and coloured paper as, in many cases, each mobile may be constructed twice from each set of materials.

Mobiles - Document 1

Briefing notes for group

The task

Your task is to design and plan the production of a mobile. This mobile should consist of four different items made from the materials available. The mobile should be capable of being made by another team within 10 minutes.

Requirements

You have *30 minutes* to:

- design a mobile
- draw up a plan for its construction
- write out a set of detailed instructions for its construction, using a new set of materials.* These will be followed (to the letter) by another team later. They will have just 10 minutes to read your instructions and to construct the mobile. You will not be able to guide or assist them in any way once your written instructions are complete.

Issue of instructions

At the end of this 30-minute period, your instructions will be collected by your trainer and duplicated. Your instructions will be issued to another team who will then attempt to construct the mobile. (Your syndicate will attempt to construct another team's design.) Each syndicate group has identical materials.

Construction

When you receive the instructions from another design group, you have 10 minutes to:

- follow their instructions *to the letter*: no more, no less. Do *not* assume anything you have not been explicitly told
- produce a finished mobile according to those instructions

*Don't do **anything** which is not in the instructions.*

---

* If you decide to practise your mobile's construction as part of your design phase, please ensure that there is sufficient material left for another group to attempt its construction later on - you will NOT be allowed to give practice materials to the other team to use! Your trainer can supply you with spare material if required.

Activity 30

Perspectives

Description

An activity which looks at how problem solving might differ depending on the perspective of the protagonists, ie looked at from a manager's point of view or from the workforce's viewpoint. It also examines the effect on group discussion when the composition of that group changes.

Objectives

By the end of this activity participants will:

- have had the opportunity to contribute to a team exercise in problem solving
- have experienced or observed the effect of altered group membership on group dynamics
- have discussed ways in which communication changes depending on how we perceive other people
- have looked at ways to minimize negativity to, and maximize the use of, new input to group discussions.

Participants

Number: Up to 12
Type: Those working within the same or similar type and size of organization

Time

1 hour 30 minutes

Resources

- One copy of Document 1 for half the participants
- One copy of Document 2 for half the participants
- Sufficient space for two syndicate groups to work independently – separate rooms if possible

Method

Step 1: Introduce the activity without, at this stage, referring to the objectives

The group will be split into two syndicate groups who will work independently on the same task. Group A will role-play employees - the workforce of an organization, and group B will represent the management of the same organization. For 30 minutes the two groups will discuss an issue which could be relevant to every participant - that of cutbacks and the development of flatter organizational structures. A brief will be issued.

Step 2: Divide the group into two syndicate groups; nominate a leader for each syndicate group

The leaders' task will be to chair the discussion, and to report back to the main group later, in a plenary session.

Step 3: Arrange seating so that each group can work independently; issue a copy of Document 1 or 2 to each participant; begin activity

Check to see that everyone understands the task. Leave syndicate groups to work without interruption, but observe the process of discussion.

Step 4: After 15 minutes, visit Group A and nominate one of the group to act as their representative to join the managers in Group B

The representative should not be the nominated leader, but someone who, from your observations, could articulate her or his group's views.

Step 5: Take the nominee from Group A to Group B and explain that this person - an employee - is to join their discussion from this point; nominate one of Group B, using the same criterion as above, to represent the managers in the employee's discussion

Stress that the new members of the groups keep their original role identities as 'worker' or 'manager'. Introduce the manager to the employees, and explain that she or he will be joining their discussion from this point.

Step 6: After 30 minutes in total have elapsed, re-convene the main group; ask the leaders from each group to report on the progress of their groups, and what recommendations they intend to make to the Board of Directors

Ensure that the leaders' reports represent the view of the whole group, ie allow other participants to contribute should they wish to do so.

Step 7: Process the activity, bringing out the learning points

There are two aspects to this activity. First, problems are often seen very differently depending on the perspective of those trying to find the *solutions. Self interest plays a large part in any discussion. That is human nature, and needs to be acknowledged. Second, the way we communicate is often governed by how we perceive other people. One might argue that this shouldn't be the case, but it is a fact of life nevertheless. This activity explored both issues.*

Questions you might use:

- *Do you feel positive about the end result of your discussions? Why, or why not?*
- *During the first part of the activity, with the original groupings, what strategies did you use to assess the problem and come up with possible solutions?*
- *Did your group consider organizational, as well as self-interests?*
- *Did everyone feel they had an equal input to the discussions?*
- *In what way, if at all, did the dynamics of the group change after the 'manager'/'worker' joined the discussion?*
- *If there was a change, why was this?*
- *What new ideas/angles/suggestions did the new member bring to the group? How were these suggestions received?*
- *Did these new suggestions change the original thinking of the group?*
- *If the transfer had been another 'worker' to Group A and another 'manager' to Group B, do you think this would have made a difference? Why?*
- *How did the transfer of a manager to the workers' group and vice versa affect the leaders' roles?*
- *If it did, can you see analogies with communications at your place of work?*
- *Did the transferred 'worker' and 'manager' feel that their presence in the new group changed the group's approach to the task in any way?*
- *In what way does this activity give insights into the positive and negative affects a newcomer can have to a group or team?*
- *How can this learning be applied to your own teams at work?*
- *If, during the activity, the introduction of a new member to the group produced a negative affect, how could these negative elements be eliminated or reduced in the workplace?*

Step 8: Close the activity referring to the objectives

Perspectives - Document 1

Employees' brief

Your organization has announced that because of market conditions/ reduction in government grants, there will have to be savings of 30 per cent in the next financial year.

You are a member of the workforce, and are attending this meeting to discuss ways in which these savings could be achieved. You have 30 minutes to compose a proposal to put to management which they, in turn, will present to the Board of Directors for their consideration.

Perspectives – Document 2

Managers' brief

Your organization has announced that because of market conditions/ reduction in government grants, there will have to be savings of 30 per cent in the next financial year.

You are a one of the management team and are attending this meeting to discuss ways in which these savings could be achieved. You have 30 minutes to compose a proposal to present to the Board of Directors for their consideration.

Activity 31

Tell me about it

Description

One of the major skills which any manager can bring to bear in situations involving change is that of counselling others who are experiencing problems of transition. This activity sets out to explore counselling styles.

Objectives

By the end of this activity participants will:

- know a definition of counselling
- know their most natural counselling style
- know how to adopt a style appropriate to situations of change.

Participants

Number: Maximum of 10
Type: Managers who are involved in managing people experiencing change

Time

1 hour

Resources

- One copy of Document 1 for each participant
- One copy of Document 2 for each participant
- One copy of Document 3 for each participant
- Either a pre-prepared flipchart sheet or an overhead projector (OHP) transparency prepared in accordance with the notes for step 4
- Either a flipchart stand or an OHP and screen

Method

Step 1: Introduce the activity
Counselling may be defined as 'listening and helping'. When people are

undergoing change this is clearly a useful skill. This activity is designed to help managers determine what their own preferred counselling style is, and to consider whether it, or others, are appropriate to situations involving change. The activity is based on the work of Carl Rogers (1951), one of the foremost writers on counselling.

Step 2: Issue Document 1; ask people to complete it, working on their own
Ten minutes will be required for this. The document is self-explanatory.

Step 3: When all participants have finished, issue Document 2 and ask them to complete the scoring
Allow 5 minutes.

Step 4: Present a short input on the 5 counselling styles represented in Document 2 by the five letters 'E', 'T', 'S', 'P' and 'U'
Allow five minutes. You should either use a prepared flipchart for this or an OHP. Simply place on it the five styles and explain them in accordance with the information given in Document 3. Stress that no one style is any better or worse than any other, but you may wish to suggest that some styles are more appropriate in change situations *than others. Don't at this stage mention the most and least used styles (information which is also included in Document 3).*

Step 5: Ask for people's reactions to the styles
Allow 20 minutes. You might need to explain why some of the answers are as they are, so you do need to have a grasp of this yourself beforehand!

Questions you might use:

- *Do people recognize themselves from their scores?*
- *Can people relate the responses to the styles?*
- *If we* tend *towards a style – but don't use it exclusively – will people nevertheless assume that is always our style?'*
- *Which style would people assume is the most common? Why? (Evaluative)*
- *Which style would people assume is the least common? Why? (Understanding)*
- *What are the pros and cons of the various styles?*

Step 6: Try and get a consensus as to which may be the most appropriate styles to adopt for helping people cope with change and transition, and tease out reasons why this might be so
Allow 10 minutes. The essential point to draw out is that people need to confront change with a degree of confidence and with some sense of commitment to the way they propose to tackle the change or the problems

they are encountering. People tend to be more committed to solutions they have developed themselves, and so those styles which encourage reflection and problem solving through analysis are likely to be the most useful. Therefore the Interpretive, Probing and Understanding styles may be the most useful in transition, although there will be a place for the others too at an appropriate time. Good counselling is not about solving others' problems for them, but facilitating the problem-solving process within that person.

Questions you might use:

- *Why might an evaluative or supportive response be less valuable in helping a person in transition or confronting change?*
- *Conversely, what are the strengths of the other three in this situation?*
- *How easy would it be to adapt to a style other than one's preferred style?*

Step 7: This activity could usefully be followed by some role-play where the group pairs off and acts out statements and responses

The trainer's notes below give three examples of scenarios you could use, but you can of course develop your own. Participants should try practising responses they may be unfamiliar with.

Step 8: Issue Document 3

Step 9: Close the activity by referring briefly to the objectives

Trainer's notes

Suggested scenarios for the optional step 7.

1 A new supervisor, promoted just 2 weeks ago into the job, comes to see you, his manager. He is 23.
   I really can't cope with this job. I'm too young to handle all these older staff – they just run rings around me. I want to go back to my old job, please.

2 A friend, a man aged 38, has called round to see you. He is very upset.
   Daphne asked me for a divorce last week. I thought she was joking but she's just told me she was serious. I must be a hopeless husband and father if it comes to this.

3 A fellow manager, a woman aged 36, has just rung you up in your office.
   I've got to make Sam Brown redundant tomorrow. I know it's going to be awful. It's the first time I've ever had to do anything like this but it's certainly not going to be the last. Whatever am I going to say? I'm a friend of his for goodness sake!

Tell me about it - Document 1

My counselling style

Read through the eight short scenarios which follow and decide which of the five example responses given in each case sound most like the kind of response you think you would probably give as your initial comment. Do be honest, as there are no right or wrong answers on this exercise.

Scenario 1: A new colleague, male, aged 28, a manager, at the same level as you, and just settling in as head of his own department, is chatting to you in the pub at the end of his first day.

> *Hard work doesn't frighten me. I can take any number of knocks and I don't really mind if I trample on a few lesser mortals in order to get where and what I want. I have to prove myself in this job as it's the springboard to much better things.*

Choose just *one* of the following possible responses as the one you think you would give and tick it in the right-hand box:

1 **So you're a very ambitious man?** ☐
2 **You feel you just have to be out on top whatever it may do to others?** ☐
3 **What's behind this strong ambition to come out on top?** ☐
4 **With that sort of drive the world's your oyster! Have you ever thought of doing some psychometric tests to see what would suit you best?** ☐
5 **Are you really sure about all this trampling stuff? The bosses here are not too keen on that sort of approach.** ☐

Scenario 2: Your new deputy, a woman aged 24, is chatting to you at the end of her first week in the job. She was appointed after doing very well in her first junior management post in another division of the company.

> *My MBA has really equipped me to be a professional manager. Of course, I had to compete with the men all the time and I now truly believe that, now I've got this far, I'm as good as any man. Mind you, if they want to keep me, this company is going to have to buck its ideas up and take my own career needs into account more.*

Choose just *one* of the following possible responses as the one you think you would give and tick it in the right-hand box:

1 **Do you honestly think that a business degree actually makes you a good manager? If you ask me, you have to learn the hard way!** ☐
2 **What difficulties do you think you will have in succeeding as a woman in this company?** ☐

3 I've no doubt you're absolutely right! Let's talk again on
   Monday about how you can pack in as much experience as
   possible into your time in this department.   ☐
4 So you're saying, are you, that you expect respect from the
   organization for the managerial professionalism that you
   feel your degree gives you?   ☐
5 It strikes me that you feel you may not be accorded the
   status you think you deserve?   ☐

Scenario 3: A subordinate, a man aged 52, has been giving you concern as
you feel his performance has not been as good recently as you know it can
be. You call him into your office one morning to discuss this.

> *I used to be very ambitious, of course, but as time goes by other things
> become more important. I may not have been a success as far as this
> company is concerned but I've realized recently just how important my
> family is to me, and that is making me really happy and contented.*

Choose just *one* of the following possible responses as the one you think
you would give and tick it in the right-hand box:

1 I can't fault that and, after all, we can't all reach the top,
   can we? Is there any way I can help?   ☐
2 So you reached a point when you began to feel that your
   family was more important than your career - but do you
   feel there is something missing, perhaps?   ☐
3 I envy you! Why keep in the rat race when nobody really
   gives a damn! I'd love to do the same myself.   ☐
4 You're saying that, as you have got older, you have found
   increasing fulfilment with your family?   ☐
5 I'm not sure why you feel you weren't a success with the
   company? How do you define success?   ☐

Scenario 4: You meet an old friend from long ago, a woman in her mid-
forties, who took a new job with a local firm about six months ago. This
meant she had to move from London to a rural location.

> *When I moved here I had no doubts about my ability to make new
> friends. Living on my own I had never had any trouble making a social
> life for myself in London. But it's just not working out. It's not the job -
> that's fine - but the people around here seem insular and not really
> interested in socializing. I think it must be me; I'm getting old!*

Choose just *one* of the following possible responses as the one you think
you would give and tick it in the right-hand box:

1 How do you set about making friends? Have you made any
   recent efforts to meet more people?   ☐

2 So you're saying that living alone is no problem provided you have lots of friends to stop you getting lonely? ☐
3 It looks as though you may be worried that, having lived alone for so long, you've got out of the habit of getting close to people. ☐
4 Well, you'll just have to get out and about even more. It can't be *that* bad, surely? ☐
5 Well, I've got a few ideas. I run the local amateur dramatic society and there's the Christmas party for the old folks just down the road; I know they're looking for an organizer, and of course you could. . . ☐

Scenario 5: A junior colleague, a man aged 32, has come to see you about his supervisor, Snodgrass, who is responsible to you for running a small section within the department.

Look, I'm telling you! That guy Snodgrass has really got it in for me. I was highly thought of around this office until he arrived last year – you know that. He just hates my guts and he's going to put the boot in, come hell or high water!

Choose just *one* of the following possible responses as the one you think you would give and tick it in the right-hand box:

1 It seems to me you're getting paranoid about Snodgrass. Are you not working out your anger about not getting that promotion last month? ☐
2 I know he can be a difficult bloke at times, but your own attitude isn't helping. ☐
3 When, specifically, has he tried to undermine you? ☐
4 If I understand you correctly, you feel persecuted by Snodgrass and think he intends to wreck your reputation? ☐
5 Well, you should protect yourself. Have you joined the Union yet? ☐

Scenario 6: Your department is about to be reorganized. The new structure is not yet clear and there are rumours of redundancy. It will be at least three months before it's all resolved, and the rumours have been flying around for another three. A junior manager in your department, a married man, aged 27 has come to see you.

I've really decided I must go for another job and not wait around here for the chop. It's been difficult because I spent four years on day release and the company has been good to me. But I think I really do have to do something positive; the rumours are getting me down.

Choose just *one* of the following possible responses as the one you think you would give and tick it in the right-hand box:

1 You feel you'd be a lot happier just getting out and getting on with your life, is that it? □
2 Who can say if that's the right thing to do, but it's good that you have the confidence now to think seriously about this as a course of action? □
3 It seems a shame to throw up everything you've worked on so far? Isn't there some middle way? □
4 So you're committed to that course of action? □
5 Have you investigated the job prospects out there at the moment? □

Scenario 7: You meet by chance, on a train, a business acquaintance who you don't know well. He is aged 35.

Of course, starting up on my own is the chance of a lifetime. All I need is imagination, common sense and a smidgen of courage. I've got what it takes – and if I could only get hold of the cash the firm wouldn't see me for dust!

Choose just *one* of the following possible responses as the one you think you would give and tick it in the right-hand box:

1 Would you like the name of this really good financial adviser I know? □
2 Sounds like you're on the right track. You've got to believe in yourself to make running your own business a success. Good luck to you! □
3 So if you could get the cash you feel sure you could make a go of it? □
4 You feel you can make a go of it because you can see clearly what is involved? I can see why you're confident. □
5 Have you considered the risks? □

Scenario 8: A friend, a man aged 48, has just lost his job through redundancy after 24 years with the same company.

You'd think, wouldn't you, that after all that time, and with my loyal service, they wouldn't just throw me on the scrapheap like this. I don't know what I shall do. Who will want me when I've only worked for this lot most of my working life?

Choose just *one* of the following possible responses as the one you think you would give and tick it in the right-hand box:

1 So you feel bitter that it happened to you and you're not sure how useful your skills and experience will be on the job market? □
2 You must have done something to upset them. It's certainly

not going to be easy for you - they're a pretty unique
company after all.   ☐

3 I can recommend an excellent recruitment agency if you
   like. And you must contact Bill Knight - he will be able to
   suggest some good contacts for you.   ☐

4 Are you maybe thinking of taking early retirement?   ☐

5 Have you ever analysed your skills? Surely you must
   believe you have something to offer another employer?   ☐

Tell me about it - Document 2

Scoring grid
Circle your responses to the eight scenarios you have just considered, then add up the number in each column.

	E	I	S	P	U
Scenario 1	5	2	4	3	1
Scenario 2	1	5	3	2	4
Scenario 3	3	2	1	5	4
Scenario 4	4	3	5	1	2
Scenario 5	2	1	5	3	4
Scenario 6	3	1	2	5	4
Scenario 7	2	4	1	5	3
Scenario 8	2	4	3	5	1
Total					

Tell me about it - Document 3

Counselling styles

Carl Rogers identified five counselling styles based on his observations of two-way communications. The categories he suggested are:

Evaluative
: When responding with this style you are making judgements.

Interpretive
: When responding with this style you are interpreting what you have heard and are probably 'reading between the lines', perhaps being able to discern what people are not actually saying.

Supportive
: When responding with this style you are offering tangible help of either a practical or a psychological nature, tending to back up what people have been saying/are feeling.

Probing
: When responding with this style you are pushing the other person to provide more information, or to think more about what they have been saying.

Understanding
: When responding with this style you are reflecting back what the speaker has said in a non-evaluative way. You are not seeking to influence but to gain understanding of their thinking.

Rogers found that the responses were used as follows, with the most commonly used at the top and the least commonly used at the bottom:

- Evaluative
- Interpretive
- Supportive
- Probing
- Understanding

Rogers does not ascribe value to the styles: they are neither good nor bad, but they are each more (or less) appropriate in particular situations.

Activity 32

Towers of strength

Description

A competitive, hands-on activity to explore the effectiveness of planning and implementation working in tandem when introducing a new concept and managing change.

Objectives

By the end of this activity participants will:

- understand the difference between work groups and teams
- have experienced the planning and/or implementation of a task as part of a team function
- recognize that the content and process of a task, if performed in parallel, can be more effective than when units work in isolation
- have discussed the pros and cons of open system thinking in the effective management of change
- have experienced the possible conflict and lack of commitment to a task, if there is not adequate consultation and communication at all stages
- see how lack of information and lack of participative involvement in a task can be a demotivating factor.

Participants

Number: 16–20
Type: Any

Time

90–120 minutes

Resources

- At least two rooms (preferably three or four)
- Tables and chairs in main room(s) at which 'planners' can work. The table must be large enough to hold the materials available, and for

team members to work on their construction
- Chairs for the implementers in the waiting room(s)
- Paper, pencils and magazines or newspapers should be available in the waiting room(s)
- Four sets of construction materials to include:
  - 20 sheets of A4 paper
  - Roll of Sellotape
  - 8 paper cups
  - Scissors
  - Tape measure
- Spare sheets of A4 paper for planning teams
- One copy of Document 1 for each participant
- One copy of Document 2 for each participant
- One copy of Document 3 for each observer

Method

Step 1: Introduce the activity; do not refer to the objectives at this point

This activity is about teamwork. It is competitive. Participants will be divided into two teams, then each team will be sub-divided into planners, implementers and observers (or thinkers, doers and watchers!). The objective is for each team to design and build a structure using the resources provided. The challenge is which team can devise the tallest structure in the allotted time. The final constructions must be free-standing, and must stay upright until the judging is complete. The trainer will measure each team's efforts. Her/his decision will be final!

Step 2: Explain the procedure and timings

(Ideally) the two sets of planners will be in separate rooms. If this is not possible, they should work in opposite corners of the main training room. Their 'implementers' will be in another room(s). Planners have up to 30 minutes to devise a structure which will be as tall as possible. They should record exactly how it was constructed, because at the end of this time they must put their prototype 'tower' out of sight. It is then the task of the implementers to construct a 'tower' to the exact design of the planners' prototype, according to their instructions, written or oral. *Planners will* not *be allowed to help physically in the reconstruction. Implementers will* not *be allowed to 'interpret' or change the planners' design in any way at the time of reconstruction. The implementers will have 15 minutes to complete the task. At the end of this time, all construction work will end. 'Towers' will be compared with the original, and measured in order to declare the winning team.*

Observers will move between rooms during the whole process, taking notes according to instructions on their sheet. They must not communicate with planners or implementers, or assist in the design or construction of the 'towers'.

Step 3: Decide on team membership

Use any arbitrary method to divide the whole group into two teams. Let them decide who is going to be the observer (one only per team), which members are going to be planners and which implementers – a 50/50 split if numbers allow this.

Step 4: Issue Team Briefs (Document 1) to each participant, and in addition, Observer Sheets (Document 3) to the observers

Allow individuals time to read the instructions. Do not enter into discussions of what can and cannot be done under the 'rules'; these must be interpreted by the teams.

Step 5: Ask implementers to go to the waiting room(s)

If you have two extra rooms at your disposal, you may wish to keep the two implementing teams separate, but the activity works just as well – better sometimes – if the two teams are in one waiting room. Ensure that there are paper, pencils, newspapers or magazines available (and if possible, access to tea and coffee making facilities with paper cups. This is not essential, but encourages implementers, too, to consider the task in hand).

Step 6: Instruct observers that they are free to circulate between rooms from now on

They can be reminded that they can communicate with each other, but not with the teams during the planning and reconstruction phases of the activity. As the next few minutes will be occupied with issuing materials to the planners, it may be useful for them to start by seeing how the implementers are settling in.

Step 7: Issue materials and set planners to work; note the time the exercise started

Remind the planning teams that by the end of the allotted time they will have to have precise instructions for the implementers, as they will not be allowed to participate, physically, in the reconstruction.

Step 8: Give a time check after 20 minutes

Suggest that, if they have not already done so, planners should begin to write up instructions for the implementing colleagues.

Step 9: After 30 minutes instruct planning teams to stop working and place their 'towers' out of sight

Allow an extra five minutes for this re-grouping and distribution of materials before starting the implementers on their task.

Step 10: Ensure that the main course room has two tables on which implementers can work; set out new sets of materials exactly similar to those used by the planners

Arrange the tables so that the whole team, planners, implementers and observer can be together for the reconstruction of their 'towers'.

Step 11: Instruct implementers to begin the task of reconstruction

Remind implementers that they have 15 minutes maximum to achieve the task set them. Every team member must keep to the rules as laid down in step 2 and on their briefing sheets.

Step 12: At the end of the allotted time, instruct implementers to stop work

Step 13: Measure the 'towers'; announce the winning team

Step 14: Process the activity beginning with participants' experience of the exercise itself

Explain and stress that the exercise may have been fun for some and annoying for others, but the main point of the activity was not the construction of the 'tower', or who 'won' – built the tallest structure – but in the processes involved in the planning and implementation of a task.

Questions you might use:

- *What system did you use to build your structures?*
- *What processes did you try and reject?*
- *How similar were the reconstructions to the originals?*
- *Did either team utilize other resources found in the course room or materials such as personal pens, combs, etc in the assembly of their 'tower'?*
- *Nowhere did it say in the 'rules' that the items issued were the only ones to be used, so if you didn't utilize other resources, why didn't you?*
- *Would it have helped if you had used creative thinking in this way, ie looking at the problem from a different perspective to the one presented?*
- *Can you see applications in the workplace for this first learning point?*

Step 15: Begin to draw out the main learning points of the activity

Questions you might use:

To the implementers:

- *How did you pass your time while you were waiting to be called?*
- *What were individuals' feelings during this time?*
- *How did the group react?*
- *How good were the instructions given to you by the planners?*
- *Throughout the activity, and also on your briefing sheets, teamwork has been stressed. Did you feel part of your team at all times during the exercise?*

- *If not, why not?*
- *Did you realize that the rules did not exclude you from being involved in the planning and design of the project?*

To observers:

- *What were your perceptions of the implementing groups during their waiting period?*
- *What evidence was there of excitement, frustration, boredom, opting-out and so on?*
- *Did you see the implementers and planners as separate work groups or as a cohesive team?*
- *Was any team member less involved than the others?*
- *What, if anything, was done by other team members to involve them in the project?*

To the planners:

- *At what point did your focus change from task-content to the process involved in instructing the implementers on your team?*
- *At what point, if at all, did you consider involving your implementers in the planning and design of the tower?*
- *If you did not consult them at all, or only in the latter stages of the planning time, why was this?*

To the implementers:

- *Had you discussed methods of constructing the tower while in the waiting room?*
- *How did you feel about having ideas, but not being consulted?*
- *Did anyone go to the planners with your ideas, or to see how they were progressing?*
- *If not, why not?*
- *If you did, what reception did you get?*
- *What were your feelings about having to follow the planners' instructions to the letter?*

To the planners:

- *Was it difficult giving instructions without being able to assist?*

To the observers;

- *Did the actual reconstruction cause any conflict?*
- *Who was committed to the task?*
- *Was anyone not involved?*

To the whole teams:

- *Do you consider that you worked as a cohesive team, or were you separate work groups?*
- *What would have been the advantages of involving the implementers from the outset?*

- *Have the observers any other observations regarding the commitment, motivation or lack of these things within the teams?*
- *What have you learnt from this activity?*
- *How will you apply the learning back in your place of work?*

Step 16: Issue and discuss Document 2

Hopefully, most of the points in Document 2 will have been discussed at Step 14. Point out any areas not already covered.

Invariably, this activity demonstrates a double standard operating under the heading 'teamwork'. Within 'the team' the planners usually gel and see individual and mutual benefit in sharing ideas, opinions and so on in an open way. Implementers often feel outsiders – not part of the main team – and usually continue to function as a work group at best (although dissatisfaction can often draw people together, but in a negative way). The lesson to managers and supervisors is to see the team in its widest context, involving, or at least informing, everyone at every stage. This will help generate maximum commitment and sustained motivation – especially important when introducing change of any kind.

Step 17: (Optional) Issues such as leadership, effective communication, motivation, conflict, creativity and so on implicit in the activity could also be discussed

All of these points will have been touched on if the suggested questions are followed. However, the main theme of the activity, as written, has been to show the benefits of planning and implementation working in parallel when introducing new concepts and managing change.

Step 18: Close the activity referring to the objectives

Towers of Strength – Document 1

Team brief

Your team has been divided into *planners* (thinkers), *implementers* (doers) and an *observer*. Your team objective is to design and build as tall a free-standing structure as possible, in competition with one other team.

Each team has two sets of materials; one set for planning and designing the prototype, the other for reconstruction of the prototype by the implementers. These materials are:

- 20 sheets of A4 paper (plus spare sheets with which planners can experiment)
- 8 paper cups
- 1 roll of Sellotape
- Pair of scissors
- Tape measure

Each team has an identical set of materials.

Planning time – 30 minutes to include design, trial constructions, and compilation of implementation instructions.

At the end of 30 minutes, prototype towers will be put out of sight. All participants will reassemble in the main course room and a new set of materials will be issued. Implementers will have 15 minutes to reconstruct their team's 'tower'.

At no time may the planners physically assist the implementers in reconstructing their team's design. Written or oral instructions only are permitted.

You are in competition with the other team. The exercise will be stopped at the end of the 15-minute reconstruction time. The team with the tallest construction (measured on a vertical plane) will be declared the winner.

The observer has her/his own brief and will circulate throughout the exercise. Observers must not communicate with their team-mates during the planning and implementation stages of the exercise, but will assist the trainer in offering feedback to the teams later in plenary session.

Towers of Strength - Document 2

Change - introducing any new concept

Good communication within work teams is a key to the effective management of change. The communication should begin with the discussion and setting of objectives. Even if it is not practical for every member of the team to be involved with this process, it is crucial that they be kept informed of progress and decisions – the whys and wherefores – if commitment and motivation are to remain high. Even if there is nothing concrete to report, being informed of *something* is better than a silence into which can be interpreted all sorts of misconceptions. Better perhaps to explain that there is a hold up in planning or the decision-making process because of certain difficulties, explaining what these are. In this way, everyone will feel involved at every stage; someone may even come up with an idea not before considered.

Once objectives are established, to maintain a sense of common purpose and ownership of the project, it is important that teams *really* perform as teams, not just as work groups.

Work groups exist when individuals are not sufficiently involved in objective setting and planning. They comprise of individuals who just happen to work together, often independently, and who are limited, often by 'the system', to applying their skills to tasks dictated by others.

Teams, on the other hand, are groups of individuals who achieve tasks through interdependence, and who recognize that tasks are accomplished more efficiently and effectively through open communication, a sharing of ideas, opinions – even disagreements, with mutual support and encouragement.

When implementing change, of whatever kind, effective teamwork is a prime factor to its success. Planning, designing and implementing are elements which, if considered in parallel, aid this process. If they are considered as separate entities, friction can occur, and friction, as any student of physics will know, slows down the process – can even scupper the enterprise altogether!

If planners of change continually consult and inform those who will be responsible for the implementation of that change throughout the process, they are likely to achieve early team commitment to the project, they may well gain the advantage of ideas from those not as close to the planning and design of the task, and they will sustain motivation as the project progresses, achieving high task results.

Towers of Strength - Document 3

Observer sheet

Please read carefully

You may speak with the other observer, but during the planning and implementation stages, you must not communicate with other members of your team. You certainly *must not* divulge the content of the following paragraphs to other members of your team.

The real object of the activity is not to see which team creates the tallest tower. Rather it is about the processes involved in achieving the task – how effectively each of the two groups work *as a team*, how much co-operation, consultation and communication exists between the planning and implementing branches of the team, and whether lack of involvement, if this exists, demotivates, lowers commitment to the common cause, even causes disharmony or conflict.

Note: Nowhere in the rules does it state that planners and implementers should not consult and work together in the planning and design of the structure. In fact, everywhere teamwork is emphasized.

Please observe both planners and implementers as they work, and record your observations. Look out for the following:

- How do the implementers occupy their waiting time?
- During the initial 30 minutes planning time, do the planners get bogged down in the task, or do they consider the needs of the implementers too?
- Are the implementers involved in any stage of the planning?
- What does the body language of the implementers tell you about their frame of mind during the planning stages?
- How involved is each member of the planning side?
- Who takes which role – leader, thinker, doer etc?
- Are there different levels of motivation between implementers and planners? At what stages? How can this be recognized?
- Is there any evidence of competition or conflict between members of the team?
- How does this level (if it exists) compare with levels of competition between teams?

Activity 33

Where do you stand?

Description

This is a very simple but very powerful activity of relevance to anyone responsible for managing the process of change who is going to have to contend with people's attitudes and prejudices. It doesn't suggest that there are easy solutions – there aren't – but it *does* make people more aware of the strong resistance, or fierce driving force, which can spring from people's feelings (as opposed to rational thoughts). People need to be alert to the polarization which can occur within a group faced with a controversial topic.

The activity should be used with people who are already comfortable with each other – well into a two- or three-day course, or who belong to an existing team – and it can draw people closer together. It tends to work best with single-gender groups and this point is picked up in the processing notes which follow.

The activity, although simple, must be used with care and the rules observed scrupulously.

Objectives

By the end of this activity participants will:
- have expressed and considered a personal view on a controversial topic and have helped others to do the same
- be aware of the strength of feeling which has to be dealt with in tackling people's attitudes and prejudices towards controversial topics
- be alert to the polarization of views which can result from group reaction to personal attitudes and prejudices.

Participants

Number: Between 10 and 20
Type: Managers who are involved in managing organizational change

Time

1 hour 15 minutes

Resources

- Set of pre-prepared topic cards (see trainer's notes)
- Piece of string long enough to stretch across 30ft
- Sufficient room for a 30ft long space to be marked out and for people to observe in a semi-circle without crowding

Method

Step 1: Introduce the activity

The activity actually works best with single-gender groups – all male or all female. If you have a large group (say up to 20) it might be worth dividing up into two groups of around 10 each if the gender balance is roughly equal. A trainer would be required with each group. A minimum of 10 people are required for the activity to work properly. However, the activity will work perfectly well with mixed groups, which tends to be the work norm, although the outcomes may be different.

The activity is best not introduced at length; simply state that you are going to run an activity which will look at people's attitudes and how they can impact on group thinking. You should seriously consider gaining group commitment to a contract of confidentiality, and it should be mandatory if you are dealing with a group of people working for the same organization.

Step 2: Ask the group to stand in a semi-circle while you stretch out the string in a taut line; weight down each end and place the 'Unacceptable' card at one end and the 'Acceptable' card at the other, both face up so that the words are showing clearly; mark a rough centre point with a marker pen or some such item

Step 3: Explain the rules to the group

The rules are:

1 *The string represents a continuum of acceptability between the two extremes indicated. So, the position of the card at one extreme showing 'Acceptable' means 100 per cent acceptable and the position of the card at the other extreme showing 'Unacceptable' means 100 per cent unacceptable. All other positions on the line represent degrees of acceptability.*

2 *The first person in the group will draw a topic card, unseen, from the pile. She or he will show it to the group and then decide where to place it face up along the line marked by the string, according to how acceptable or not they feel the topic to be to them. For example, a participant may draw the topic card marked 'Euthanasia' which they would then place according to whether or not they find the concept of euthanasia acceptable or unacceptable together with an indication (by the exact position on the line) of how acceptable/unacceptable the concept is.*

3   *The person will then stand by their card and, for two minutes, will take questions from the group as to why they feel that way. The questions must be* clarifying *questions only. They must under no circumstances be challenging or hostile, whatever people may personally feel. State that you, as trainer, will rigorously reinforce this particular rule. (You can explain that their chance to change a card's position will come later!). Each person has the absolute right to refuse to answer a particular question if they so choose.*

4   *After two minutes the person will return to the group, leaving their card where it is.*

5   *The next person will repeat these stages until the whole group has had its turn. No card may be obscured by another and no placed card may be moved.*

Step 4: **Run the first part of the activity according to the rules outlined in step 3**

Be on your guard to rule out anything approaching aggressive or hostile questions. People must feel *reasonably safe in declaring their views at this point. (This is why single-gender groups often work particularly well since perceptions and levels of unspoken understanding are often similar.)*

Enforce the 2 minute timing but do not insist it runs to two minutes if things dry up before then. Ask questions yourself if you feel you genuinely need to know something or if you feel you need to set a tone.

Questions you might use:

- *Why do you feel that?*
- *Did you ever feel differently?*
- *What changed your view?*
- *Are there any circumstances where you might place the card differently?*

Questions which may be valid but which may which may not be answered:

- *Do you have personal experience?*
- *Do you know someone who is involved in. . .?*

At the end of this step you should have a set of topic cards placed along the line. It is unusual for there to be any serious degree of polarization (towards either end) at this point.

Step 5: **Explain the next step**

Each person now has a second go. The stages are:

1   *The first person selects a topic card from those already placed. It must not be their own original card and it must be one whose current placing she or he disagrees with. She or he picks it up and then places it according to their own view of its acceptability or otherwise.*

2   *She or he stands by the new position and takes two minutes of clarifying questions. The same rules apply as at step 4.*

3 *She or he returns to the group and the next person takes their turn in the same way until the whole group has had its turn. Any card* except their own *may be moved and it is not uncommon for a particularly controversial card to be moved several times during this phase of the activity.*

Step 6: Run the second part of the activity according to the rules shown in step 5
Remain alert for the same issues as in step 4, and be especially watchful of the person whose card has just been moved!

By the end of this stage it is normal to find a strong degree of polarization, with cards positioned at the extreme ends and very few, if any, in the middle.

Step 7: Process the activity
Allow up to 30 minutes. Allow the group to sit down and draw out comments and reactions.

Questions you might use:

- *How did people feel about that activity?*
- *Did people feel threatened? Why? Or why not?*
- *How difficult was it for questioners to avoid getting worked up or emotional?*
- *What happens when people do get worked up or emotional when discussing attitudes or prejudices?*
- *If it happened, why did the polarization occur?*
- *What have people learnt about handling people's prejudices and attitudes?*
- *What have people learnt about the influence of a group on discussions about prejudices and attitudes?*
- *Change is often controversial; what are the implications for managers who have to implement change and win support for it of handling attitudes and prejudices? Thus, for example, it is important to be aware of the impact of 'group think' on the extent to which attitudes may become more extreme/polarized. It is also important for managers not to underestimate the strength of feeling generated by controversial issues and these feelings are best brought out in an atmosphere of understanding and genuine questioning as opposed to thinly veiled hostility, put-downs and so on. These are just three examples of the kind of learning points which this activity may generate and the group will identify some of their own.*

Step 8: Close the activity by referring briefly to the objectives

Trainer's notes

You will need to prepare topic cards before this activity. A4 paper with the topic in marker pen is best.

In addition to the topics themselves you will need two cards marked 'Acceptable' and 'Unacceptable'.

ACCEPTABLE   UNACCEPTABLE

You can, of course, design your own topic cards. It would be possible to use controversial, in-company topics, but personally we would probably never take that risk! Internal politics and relationships could be wrecked for ever, so we suggest you avoid that particular minefield unless you feel very strongly that the activity could be used or modified so that it is a catalyst for revealing blockages to change. But do handle it with extreme care as this is adding risk to an already risky activity.

What follows is a list of 10 topics which we have used to good effect. You can use these or add/substitute some of your own. The list is provided mainly by way of providing a flavour for the kind of topic you should be aiming to use.

- Fox hunting
- Homosexuality
- Soft Drugs
- Smoking in public places
- Private health care
- Euthanasia
- Abortion
- Genetic engineering
- Medical experiments on live animals
- Factory Farming

Activity 34

Why me?

Description

An activity which should be run early in a course concerned with managing change. By using scenarios as a starting point it explores the reasons behind resistance to change.

Objectives

By the end of this activity participants will:

- have identified and discussed some of the reasons individuals fear change, are reluctant to embrace change or actively resist change
- have considered ways of introducing change to reduce the anxiety often associated with it
- be aware of the need to view change as a positive aspect of life rather than as an imposition to be resented or feared.

Participants

Number: Any
Type: Any

Time

120–150 minutes

Resources

- Space to work in small syndicate groups
- One copy of Document 1 for each participant
- Sheets of A4 paper
- Pens/pencils (at least one per syndicate group)
- Flipchart stand, paper and marker pens
- Means of duplicating participants' work (optional)

It is suggested that rather than issuing pre-printed handouts, participants' own work be written/typed up and duplicated for distribution later in the course. See step 8.

Method

Step 1: Explain the purpose of the activity

Most people, if asked, would say that quite often change is for the better – it's progress – it's essential to surviving and thriving. It is equally true that all of us can accept the concept of change in the abstract, or if it's happening to someone else, but when faced with the prospect of change ourselves it's a different story. We hear cries of 'What's wrong with the way we're doing it now?' or 'But we've always done it this way' or 'Why upset the status quo?' or 'Why me?'

Coping with change is a fact of everyday life. Whether we like it or not, daily we are getting older; our bodies and minds are adapting naturally to this, without too much strain for most of us. The seasons will change from spring through to winter and there is nothing we can do about it. Interest and bank rates change; market values alter; shop prices fluctuate. We may not like the results of this sometimes, but it affects everyone and we adapt accordingly, again, for most of us, without too much stress. If change is from personal choice; a new hairstyle, or a change of location – a holiday for example – we not only cope, but usually enjoy the change.

However, if change is announced *or* imposed *on us, invariably we feel threatened, unsure of ourselves, alarmed, angry, and so on and our first reaction is to dig in our heels and try to maintain the status quo no matter what.*

Why is this? Why do people initially resist change, sometimes quite forcibly? There are several very human and understandable reasons for this phenomenon. These will be looked at in a non-threatening way, by using scenarios, the subjects of which everyone will recognize, as starting points for discussion.

Step 2: Explain procedure and timings

Participants will each be given a copy of Document 1 which carries six scenarios. They will work in small syndicate groups of three or four, discussing the scenarios and preparing from them a list of reasons why people resist change. One person from each syndicate group should therefore be nominated as 'scribe'.

Obviously, not all reasons for resistance will be covered, but studying the scenarios will give a starting point for more general discussion of the issues involved. Hopefully, other ideas and reasons for resistance will flow from this. Syndicate groups will have between 45 minutes and 1 hour to discuss the scenarios. A time check will be given at 45 minutes when more time can be negotiated as necessary.

The syndicate groups will then re-convene for a plenary session to share their views and to form a combined list of reasons why people resist change. As a group participants can also consider ways of introducing change so that it is less threatening for those who will be affected by it.

Handled wisely, change can be accepted as a challenge and a motivating force.

Step 3: Issue copies of Document 1; split group into syndicate groups of three or four
Issue also sheets of A4 paper and a pencil or pen to each syndicate group. Only one list need be made which should be the combined work of each member of the syndicate group.

Step 4: Start the exercise
Give a time check after 45 minutes, re-negotiating deadlines with syndicate groups if more time is required.

Step 5: When syndicate groups have finished discussing the scenarios, or when the allocated time is up, end the exercise. Re-convene participants as a large group for a plenary discussion.

Step 6: From the work done in syndicate groups, draw up a combined list of reasons people might resist change
Head a flipchart sheet 'Why People Resist Change'. Ask each syndicate group in turn to call out one reason identified. Write up reasons on flipchart. Continue to circulate round syndicate groups, asking for causes of resistance identified until all syndicate groups' lists have been exhausted.

Step 7: Lead a plenary discussion on the issues revealed by the exercise; ask syndicate groups if they wish to add other reasons why people might resist change, not covered by the scenarios, but revealed by the syndicate group discussions
Go through each scenario one by one. (See trainer's notes on p. 227 for guidance if required). Ask syndicate groups what assumptions they made, on what these assumptions were based, what issues arise from situations similar to the one quoted, and so on. Discuss what measures could be taken by the instigator of change, in each instance, to make the proposed change more acceptable, the transition easier and so on.

Step 8: (If appropriate) explain that the flipcharted lists will be duplicated as handouts to be issued later in the course
Any training which looks at the concept of change invites individuals to look to their own perceptions and receptivity and asks for a flexibility of attitude. Participants are far more likely to act on their own findings. To this end it is valuable for handouts not to be pre-printed 'words of wisdom', compiled by person or persons unknown at some earlier date. Participants are more likely to respond positively to guidelines for which they have shared ownership, and to which they can relate directly having been through the process of devising them.

Step 9: Close the activity, referring back to the objectives

By understanding resistance to change for what it is – a natural human reaction experienced by us all – and by recognizing the very real reasons why people may be wary, fearful or even obstructive,

(a) *we won't be surprised when even our most positive proposals meet (to us unwarranted) opposition*

(b) *we will be empathetic to those who are going to be affected by change, recognizing their needs and fears*

(c) *we will be able to pre-empt a lot of the arguments against changes we need to instigate*

(d) *we will be better equipped to introduce change in a manner which will be acceptable*

(e) *we will be more able to cope with change within our own lives, seeing it as a positive force, and a challenge rather than as a threat.*

Trainer's notes

The following is intended as a guide for leading group discussion. These are *suggestions, not definitive answers* to the scenarios set. Many other issues will no doubt be raised by your group.

1   Jo Francis
What are the possible reasons why Geoff 'hit the roof'?

- care of children
- loss of status as sole bread-winner
- fear of wife's possible success
- she may not be as available to play hostess etc
- he may have to spend more time sharing domestic responsibilities
- threat to stability as he's known it
- may go against peer group norms (other senior managers' wives don't go out to work)
- historical factors (his mother may not have worked, at least while bringing up a family).

Lack of information/consultation/discussion are all reasons why people resist change. An explanation of why it is important for Jo to get a job may help the situation. Put in this context, her desire to apply for a job could be received more favourably. Eg 'The boys are both in full-time education now [stating indisputable fact] I need something to stimulate my mind [expressing own needs in unequivocal terms]. When the boys are old enough, I'd like to resume my career [stating long term plans] but for now I'm going to look for part-time work – to get myself back into the world of employment, set myself a challenge [stating intention]. I thought I'd apply for a job in a school or educational establishment where the hours would match the boys' and I'd have the same school holidays [showing she's thought it through. She's also preempted any criticism of neglecting the children's interests]. I'll be home in plenty of time to help you with your work as usual – I might even be able to offer a bit more stimulating conversation at dinner with a new interest! [humour, plus showing Geoff that his interests won't be affected]. I know we don't actually *need* the extra cash, but it will come in handy for holidays; maybe we could save and go skiing this winter [showing him the benefits].

2 John
Why might John resist going on the course?

- fear of the unknown
- fear of failure
- fear of looking stupid
- been 'out' of studying for some time; could be worried about essays, exams etc.
- practical rather than academic – feels he won't be able to cope with study
- fear of losing face
- meeting others in same profession, but more up-to-date, could be a threat to his core-skills and competence, therefore self-esteem.

It may have been a more appropriate approach if the Principal had (a) thought through John's likely response, ie rather than delight him it might fill him with fear and self-doubts; (b) obtained as much information as possible about the course and methods of assessment to give John to read prior to a discussion on his attendance; (c) discussed the possibility of his attendance rather than presenting John with a fait accompli. In this way John could, if he desired, have expressed his doubts and talked through the options with the Principal.

3 Anne
What could be the *real* reason for Anne's refusal to go on the training course?

- fear of being 'found out' (she's muddled through until now, but is possibly aware of her shortcomings. This is possibly why she is defensive of her work, and getting increasingly bad-tempered)
- threat to her power base (if she goes her deputy will take over and might do the work better)
- poor working relationships (indicated by high staff turnover)
- reluctance to let go (doesn't delegate; is possessive about the work)
- low trust organizational climate (Smith Jr is checking her work – she takes her subordinates' work home)
- plus many of the fears listed above under *John*.

This is poor management practice on behalf of the directors. They can't really expect an external training course to solve their problems – or Anne's. She is likely to be a resentful, uncooperative student, determined from the outset that 'They won't be able to teach me anything!' She could return to the office with an even bigger chip on her shoulder.

This has to be handled by discussion in-house. Anne needs to be convinced that the directors care for her well-being; that they recognize her loyalty and long service, and that they are constantly looking for ways to improve working conditions, working systems and so on – as indeed she should as office manager. By convincing her that training would help both her and the company she is more likely to accept the opportunity to 'further her career'. Open communication should be encouraged (for the reasons listed under *John*.)

4 Petra

Why do you think Petra received a negative response from her staff?

- historical factors (they are used to Frank Hughes' methods, systems, and their own areas of responsibility as they see them)
- threat to their own preferred areas of work
- fear of the unknown
- reluctance to experiment with new ideas
- change for the sake of change (why rock the boat?).

Any 'new broom' that tries to 'sweep clean' in such a sudden and abrupt way, however enthusiastically, is going to meet resistance. Far better to go gently, bringing your team along with you in generating ideas, creating new systems and so on. A better approach would be for Petra to bring her team together for a democratic discussion of the issues involved, reaching, if possible, group decisions on the way forward. Of course, ultimately it is up to Petra to decide how her section is to be run, but by explaining the whys and wherefores, collecting all the facts from her staff, consulting them individually and as a group, at all times communicating decisions, Petra is more likely to create a productive cohesive and supportive team.

5 William Barton

William has had change forced upon him. What are his main areas of difficulty?

- coming to terms with redundancy
- deciding what both he and his wife really want from life from now on
- his wife – a problem in itself as she seems far more status conscious than he. She also has a new role (brought about by necessity? How resentful is she?)
- whether selling caravans is a viable proposition for a future career
- perceived drop in standard of living
- 'you can't teach an old dog new tricks'

If William is going to pursue his idea of a partnership in the caravan business, what areas of resistance to change will he have to confront, both in himself and with his wife?

- fear of the unknown
- threat to status
- threat to social standing
- fear of failure
- further possible loss of capital/earning potential.

William and Kate have got a lot of talking to do! They *must* establish what their own needs are in this situation. It would seem that William has already decided, in his heart, that he does not want another senior management post similar to the ones held recently. In that frame of mind, he is hardly likely to succeed in landing one anyway! He seems to care less for social standing than his wife – this needs thrashing out between them. It is only by expressing his needs truthfully and honestly that he and Kate can begin to adapt to the changes, make the best of, and eventually benefit from them.

6 Jason White
What assumptions has Jason made about the situation?

- that his career is more important than Veronica's
- that a wife automatically moves to fit in with husband's career
- that he can make major decisions without consulting her
- that the situation may prove a lever to change her decision about having children.

What other reasons might Veronica have for resisting the change?

- lack of consultation
- lack of information
- personal loss of status
- personal loss of earning power
- possible enforced 'redundancy'.

One should not introduce this sort of major upheaval as a fait accompli. Matters such as these should be researched and thoroughly discussed before any decision is reached, and of course, should be acceptable to all parties. This will involve negotiation and compromise, and may, in fact, result in change for the other party. In this case, for instance, it may be more appropriate for Jason to find another position – easier in central London – than for Veronica to seek a post in Wales comparable with the specialist tax adviser post she now holds.

Why me? - Document 1

Using the following scenarios as the basis for discussion, chat over each situation in your group, compiling a list of the reasons why the individuals might resist change. From discussing the issues involved, begin to think about how change could be introduced and implemented to minimize resistance and maximize co-operation.

Scenario 1: Jo Francis has been married for 10 years to Geoff who is production manager for a large industrial company. He is very successful – the youngest person to attain his position in the history of the company. His work frequently takes him abroad, or to meetings in other parts of the UK, meaning overnight stops. Several times a year, Geoff and Jo entertain his business associates. Geoff is well liked and successful socially as well as in the business world. He has made many useful contacts through membership of his golf club – a game which he enjoys playing in his leisure time. Jo has kept in touch, by letter, with some of her friends from university days, but her main friends now are the wives of Geoff's colleagues who she meets at dinner parties and company functions, and the mothers of other small boys who she knows from collecting her two sons, aged 8 and 6, from school.

Jo has decided that she wants to resume her career, or at least to get a job which will get her re-acclimatised to the world of work. She is surprised and dismayed when Geoff 'hits the roof' when she suggests applying for a job.

Scenario 2: John has been a specialist photographer for over twenty years, most of which time has been spent at the same place of work, a college of higher education, where his work has been admired and appreciated. Despite financial cutbacks, meaning that he has had to make do with the same photographic equipment for years, John has maintained very high standards both for himself and for the students he teaches. He has great technical expertise, so has been able to repair and maintain the department's photographic equipment. He also has an imaginative, inventive mind so that what has been lacking in up-to-the-minute equipment has been made up for by his ability to show students how to make do and adapt.

One morning, John is called to the Principal's office. He is told that, because of his standing within the college, it has been decided that he is the best candidate to attend a course of specialist training in photomicrography in order that this can be included in the college syllabus the following year. The course, lasting three months, is partly on a day-release basis, with two residential sessions. It is a certificated course, qualifications being attained by a combination of continuous assessment, course work, and a final examination. Provided John attains the qualification, ('and of course, you will!', says the Principal) he will be eligible for an upgrading when he begins teaching photomicrography at the start of the next academic year. John is dismayed at the prospect.

Scenario 3: Anne has worked at Smith, Smith & Weston for 28 years. She has, in fact, been there longer than any other member of staff (including the second Smith). She has worked her way up from junior clerk to office manager, a post she has held for the last four years. She is personally responsible for finance, and is accounting officer for the company. She is in charge of eight staff, two accounts clerks, three administrative officers, one of whom (a graduate management trainee) is her deputy, two clerical officers and one receptionist/word processor operator. ('And to think that when I started, there was only me and Janet plus the two bosses, Mr Smith the elder and Mr Weston').

Smith, Smith & Weston had been growing steadily, with healthy profits. Over the last five years however, things have begun to slide. The atmosphere in the office has been dreadful at times, and staff turnover has increased dramatically. Anne has invested in her own electronic typewriter and has been taking more and more work home just to get it done ('Well you can't trust youngsters of today with important tasks like drafting reports can you? I tell them that their work just isn't up to Mr Smith's standards – Mr Smith senior that is'). On a personal level, Anne is getting increasingly bad-tempered, 'having to do the work of half of the office as well as my own'.

Mr Smith junior has had occasion to check and double check financial statements recently. He knows that Anne is largely self-taught but can't understand either her methods or why she has reached such daft conclusions sometimes. He is also concerned about staff turnover. He has suggested to the other directors that Anne be given some external training. Anne is appalled when she learns she is to attend an 'Introduction to Management' course ('to include things like *Interpersonal Skills* and *Teambuilding*. Never heard such nonsense, sending me on a training course when I've been doing the job for umpteen years. And them with a cashflow problem too! I shall refuse to go')

Scenario 4: Petra has just been promoted. She has 'inherited' what is known to be a difficult section from Frank Hughes who took early retirement. Among her staff are two women who have been in the section for several years and who have chosen the tasks they like to do, two more junior staff, who have tended to be given the jobs that are either repetitive and boring, or those which no one else wants, a workaholic who keeps the section together and could run it single handed if there were sufficient hours in the day, plus two willing and able staff, at present understretched and therefore a bit apathetic and slip-shod.

At first Petra, although aware of the problems, could see no way of changing a situation which had gone on for years. 'Frank should have dealt with it' she told her husband. 'It's not my fault if things have been left to deteriorate like this'. However, two weeks after her promotion, Petra was sent on a training course. The trainer pointed out to her that she could not, in all fairness to her staff and the organization, make lame excuses for not making sweeping changes to improve things. She learnt about concepts such as job design and redesign, the process or outcome of grouping together work tasks to form individual jobs. She learnt about motivating staff through job extension, giving each person greater job satisfaction through job enlargement, where additional tasks are given to provide more variety. She learnt about job enrichment, where subordinates are given greater scope in deciding how tasks should be performed. She learnt about job rotation, where employees rotate around all the jobs in the section, so that everyone understands all the work and processes, and has a regular share of each, variety giving extra job satisfaction. Also, everyone has a chance to do the interesting as well as the boring jobs.

Fired with enthusiasm, Petra returns to her section, and calls a meeting to explain that she requires everyone to list all their tasks as a first step to re-allocating the section's workload to facilitate a fairer and more appropriate distribution of tasks. She is dismayed at the negative response she gets from her staff.

Scenario 5:   William Barton has had it easy for most of his 53 years. Born into a well-to-do family, he went to public school, but decided to skip university or military service and go straight into industry. He immediately secured a middle management position, and soon reached directorial level. For the last four years he had been Managing Director of a leading manufacturing company.

William owns a large house in the country, and belongs to many prestigious clubs – local and national. He is married to Kate, who enjoys the entertaining which such membership brings. She taught Geography before their marriage. Since that time she has been 'lucky not to have had to work', as she tells her acquaintances.

That was all until the fateful day six months ago when William was made redundant. Profits had fallen; the shareholders were unhappy, and answers had to be produced. According to William, the solution to such situations often means a shake-up of top management. 'They needed scapegoats; heads had to roll' he said. 'The heads in question happened to be mine and the Marketing Director's'.

William has applied for many positions at a similar level since his redundancy, although secretly he is relieved to be 'out of that particular rat race'. Although his redundancy payment was generous, his position has meant retrenchment. Kate applied for, and obtained a teaching position at a private school, 15 miles away. Because she found the travelling tiring, she has taken a flat in town which she stays at during the week (and recently, weekends when there has been a concert or function in town she wanted to attend).

Recently, William has had the chance to buy into a partnership with a drinking friend he met at his local pub. The business, about which William knows nothing, is selling caravans and mobile homes. The idea of being his own boss has always appealed to him, although in this case it would mean being boss and secretary, salesman, book-keeper – 'head cook and bottle washer'! It would also mean a fall in living standards, at least initially until he got on his feet – even possibly the sale of his house ('we don't really need a six-bedroomed house now that the children have left') to buy something smaller in order to raise the capital to set up the business.

William is surprised that Kate is less than enthusiastic about the venture, and continues to badger him about 'finding a suitable position' in industry.

Scenario 6: Jason White is a finance officer who works for one of Britain's leading cosmetic houses, at present based in central London. Although he is not a high flier, he has done well in the company, considering he had no formal qualifications and has worked his way up from clerical assistant when he left school, to his present position. At 31 he is now in line for promotion. He hopes to be appointed deputy head of finance when that position becomes vacant later in the year.

Jason is married to Veronica. They met when she was a student and went out together for two years before they decided to share a flat, mainly so that Veronica could give up her part time job and concentrate on her studies for her final year at University. 'I'll pay the bills now – you can keep me later' joked Jason. Veronica did well, and is now a tax adviser for a multinational company. Although she is not 'keeping' Jason, her salary is treble his; they have a comfortable life style.

They now have a problem. Jason's company is closing its London offices and moving its factory to Darlington, and its offices to Wales. Everyone's job is secure, and generous relocation allowances will be paid. After the initial shock of being told, Jason agreed to the move, and soon saw the bright side of the venture. 'We'll be able to afford a larger house with some land, away from London's pollution – might even start a family, although I know Veronica's never been keen on having children – she's lived for her work' thought Jason as he travelled home that evening. He stopped at the off licence to buy a bottle of champagne to toast their new life.

Jason had Veronica's favourite meal prepared, and the champagne on ice by the time she arrived home. 'I've got great news - we're moving to Wales!' was his greeting as she came in, weary after a hectic day. 'We're *what*?' The expression on her face was not what he had expected, but said it all!

Activity 35

X, Y or Z?

Description

Based on a self-report questionnaire this activity is designed to help identify present individual managerial styles and compare them with alternative methods perhaps more appropriate to managing organizational change.

Objectives

By the end of this activity participants will:

- have assessed 75 statements against their present approach to management
- have identified their present preferred managerial style
- have considered, in small group discussion, the reasons for using their present managerial style, and the pros and cons of alternative approaches
- be aware of some behavioural scientists' theories regarding management style, and of some current trends influenced by Japanese methods of working.

Participants

Number: Any
Type: Junior-middle managers, and supervisors

Time

120–180 minutes

Resources

- Space for participants to work alone, in small groups, and for plenary discussion
- Table/desk top or clipboard on which participants can rest questionnaire

- Pen/pencil for each participant
- One copy of Document 1 for each participant
- One copy of Document 2 for each participant
- One copy of Document 3 for each participant
- One copy of Document 4 for each participant

Method

Step 1: Introduce the activity

This activity is designed to help managers and supervisors recognize their present management style and to see the reasons for it. It may well suggest alternative approaches which could help improve staff relationships and motivation, productivity, quality of goods or services offered and so on, and also encourage positive change – gradual continuous improvement; setting and achieving higher standards.

Step 2: Tutor input; a brief outline of factors which influence managerial style. A suggested format follows.

There are many factors that influence managerial style. The first, and most basic, concerns individual conditioning. From infancy we have all developed beliefs, biases, prejudices, feelings of confidence, or inferiority; self-worth or poor self-esteem, and so on. This is bound to influence our managerial style. Some individuals will have or adopt a dictatorial style; others will need to be liked at all costs, and will be in danger of being considered 'a soft touch'; others will adopt a firm but fair approach. These are the clear cut approaches; there are countless variations on each theme.

Another factor which influences our managerial style is our own experience of being a subordinate. Some, who have been given a hard time by a particular boss think 'When my turn comes, I'll have the chance to make others squirm as I have!' Others will learn by the mistakes they have witnessed, and vow to be a better boss to their staff when their opportunity comes along. Again, there are countless gradations in between. Most of us can think of a boss we've liked working for, or admired, or respected. We also know of bosses who have been poor managers of human resources. Hopefully we have learnt positively from these experiences; but all have contributed to our present management style.

Our own self perception – whether we like ourselves, are secretly comparing ourselves (favourably or unfavourably) with other managers, whether we are generally placid or stressed, and how this affects our relationship with others – these things all have relevance to our management style.

Other elements which affect our approach to management obviously connect to our view of the organization we work for and where we fit into the structure. Ask yourself questions such as 'Am I fully committed to the aims and objectives of my company?' 'Does the company, and my position *within it, meet my personal needs and wants?' 'Are my opinions and those of my team, asked for, considered and valued?'*

The point of this analysis is to begin to recognize that your present management style has been influenced by many factors. It may have been thrust upon you by circumstance – the ethos of the organization for which you work, for example – or you may find yourself acting a part which is really alien to your nature (or even, better judgement).

The following exercises are designed to help individuals recognize their present management style, to identify the alternatives available, and to begin assessing the possibility of change, if this is relevant or appropriate for individuals at this time.

Step 3: Explain procedures and timings of the first exercise, and issue the questionnaire, Document 1

Participants will now complete a self-report questionnaire. There are a lot of questions – 75 in all – so it is best not to dwell for too long on any one question. A gut reaction is what's called for.

There are two columns to choose from. Participants should put a tick in the column which most closely represents their feelings on the issue in question.

Stress that the questionnaire, the results, and the outcome of the following discussions, have to be based on trends rather than absolutes. The activity is designed to give an indication only of management styles and practices.

Participants will have 15 – 20 minutes to complete the questionnaire.

Step 4: After 15 minutes, re-negotiate times if necessary; when participants have completed their self-report questionnaires, issue Document 2, the Score Sheet

Participants should allocate marks, following the guide on Document 2. Allow 15 minutes for marking the questionnaires and reading the assessment of scores.

Step 5: Issue and discuss Document 3

Explain that this handout gives a brief, explanation of the three management styles: McGregor's Theory X and Theory Y, and Japanese management practice, called in this activity, Theory Z.

You could either leave participants to read through Document 3, and then open it up for discussion, or go through it systematically with them, asking for observations as you go.

Step 6: Issue Document 4, 'Evaluating your Scores'

Review results, asking individuals for their reactions.

Step 7: Instruct participants to look at the questionnaire again, and to identify any statement or response which demonstrates an attitude which they would like to change in their management style, given appropriate support back at their place of work

Participants should circle the number of the statement which identifies an area of their working practices they would seek to change. Another five minutes should be allowed for this.

Step 8: Divide group into syndicate groups of three or four

Use any arbitrary method to choose groupings.

Step 9: Instruct syndicate groups to look at the circled statements of each person and discuss why individuals are unhappy with that aspect of their work, and what processes need to be undertaken in order to change their management style back at the workplace

The timing of this part of the activity depends on the number of statements circled by individuals, and will vary from group to group. A minimum of 30 minutes is suggested, however. Where groups have identified few aspects they would wish to change, discussion should centre around the pros and cons of the different management styles identified as Theory X, Theory Y and Theory Z.

Step 10: After the agreed time for completion of Step 7, ask participants to re-group for a general plenary discussion of the activity

Ask if any individual would like to share observations from syndicate group discussions.

Look at the benefits and disadvantages of Theory X, Theory Y and Japanisation as management styles.

Lead a discussion on why some people felt that their management style was appropriate for their work situation; why some would find it difficult, although desirable, to modify their management style; why some recognize a need to adapt their approach to management. Use the group as a source of support and advice to individuals who would like to introduce a change of approach on return to the workplace.

Step 11: Close the activity, referring to the objectives

X, Y or Z? - Document 1

Questionnaire

Please respond to all the following statements as honestly as you can. In most cases you would not be able to respond with absolutes to any issue, so the alternatives are phrased *mostly agree* or *mostly disagree*. There will be a chance later to discuss and qualify your choices. Don't spend too long on any one statement – your initial reaction is what is called for here.

Note: it is impossible to answer *mostly agree* to all questions (or *mostly disagree*) because some statements are diametrically opposed to others.

There are 75 statements in all. You have 15–20 minutes to tick the answers which most closely represent your opinions.

	Mostly Agree	Mostly Disagree
1 Job specifications providing precise responsibilities of each job, restrict rather than expand what people do		
2 Generally speaking, employees expend as little physical and mental effort as possible at work; they just do enough to get by		
3 Most employees will exercise self-direction and self-control if committed to the objectives of the organization		
4 The ultimate need in business today is not so much efficiency, but effectiveness		
5 Most subordinates prefer to be given clear, precise directions with little scope for initiative or creativity		
6 Motivation is enhanced if rewards reflect achievements		
7 People should be treated as members of an organization, not as employees		
8 The average employee values security above all else		
9 If I'm away from the workplace, my subordinates continue to function as if I was there		

	Mostly Agree	Mostly Disagree
10 Shared opinions and values in the workforce is more important than detailed procedures and controls to guide operations		
11 Most subordinates are happy just ticking along; they avoid responsibility where possible		
12 Given appropriate conditions, individuals not only accept, but seek responsibility		
13 Managers should listen to the opinions of all their staff – executive, administrative and operative. Some of the best ideas come from 'the shop floor'		
14 Both processes and people need close managerial control		
15 Individual goals should be integrated with those of the organization		
16 Retired staff should still be considered part of the organization, and kept informed of its plans and progress		
17 'Write it, don't say it' should be the preferred operating style. It is more efficient and saves time		
18 Management is more about training and coaching than controlling and directing		
19 It is more important to have generalists than specialists in key managerial positions		
20 It is management's responsibility to control the actions of staff, modifying their behaviour to fit the needs of the organization		
21 It is important for an employee to see a job through to completion if one is to expect commitment to the task		
22 It is sound management practice to		

	Mostly Agree	Mostly Disagree
consult everyone involved with the implementation of a project, and get their agreement on a chosen course of action, before attempting to put it into practice		
23 Management means getting things done through other people		
24 Job enlargement, where an employee is given a greater range of tasks of approximately the same level of difficulty and responsibility, results in higher motivation		
25 Open plan offices, where the supervisor or manager is available to subordinates at all times, aids staff effectiveness and productivity		
26 Most employees want to work as little as possible for the greatest financial reward		
27 I think it best for my staff to resolve their own work problems where possible, either alone or by consulting the team, without my intervention		
28 If subordinates have total responsibility for their area of work, quality improves and motivation and commitment increase		
29 Most employees are basically indifferent to organizational needs		
30 Subordinates should be given scope to use initiative, even if this means learning by their mistakes. Human error can be accepted so long as it is within reasonable bounds.		
31 The physical environment plays an important role in motivation and job satisfaction		
32 Every position in the organization should have a tightly worded job		

		Mostly Agree	Mostly Disagree
	specification; the holder should keep to the duties and responsibilities as laid down		
33	My staff are self motivated and need little supervision		
34	It is important for work teams to meet frequently and regularly with their supervisor or manager to discuss problems and exchange ideas		
35	The 'carrot and stick' approach to management is an effective and productive motivator		
36	While managers should control the process, staff need freedom to use their initiative in the planning and implementation of tasks.		
37	Terms and conditions of work should be common to all employees – blue- and white-collar workers; junior to senior management		
38	A fair day's work for a fair day's pay is all most employees want		
39	My staff see me more as an adviser than a boss		
40	There should be a company-wide approach to quality improvement		
41	Because ultimately I 'carry the can', I expect my staff to follow my directions and accept my decisions		
42	My staff know what's expected of them, and get on with their work with little need of supervision from me		
43	Management should enable all employees to participate in the preparation, implementation and evaluation of its activities		

	Mostly Agree	Mostly Disagree
44 I exercise close supervision to ensure staff are keeping on target and working to specified directions		
45 It is important to learn about subordinates – a bit about their out-of work activities, home life, what makes them 'tick'		
46 People are the most important part of an organization; its most appreciable asset		
47 My subordinates work best when their work is planned for them, and assigned to them		
48 Most people would go to work even if they didn't need the money		
49 Promotion should be linked to seniority		
50 If I don't monitor work closely, output suffers		
51 Most employees would welcome the opportunity to have more control over their work		
52 Organizations should concentrate more on customers and users, both outside and inside the company		
53 Managers need to keep a distance between themselves and their staff. This is essential to maintain discipline, quality of work, and the respect of subordinates		
54 Part of my function as a manager of staff is to train them for promotion		
55 When individual contributions are encouraged and recognized, it follows that employees become more committed to, and co-operative with, organizational objectives		
56 If I consider it necessary (to meet a		

	Mostly Agree	Mostly Disagree

59 deadline for example) I recall work, re-assign it, or do it myself

57 If employees are encouraged to exercise responsibility for their own work, superior organizational performance can result

58 Regular in-house training and education is necessary to ensure improvement both of quality and of productivity

59 Most employees 'work to live' rather than 'live to work'; work is simply a means to achieve material ends

60 There should be mutual trust and respect between manager and subordinate

61 Organizations should be seen as collections of people rather than mechanisms for quick profit

62 Efficiency, improved output, profitability and so on must take priority over subordinates' needs

63 It is part of my function to draw out ideas and contributions from my team

64 Consensus agreement should be reached before change is implemented. If people agree to a proposal, they are more likely to be committed to its implementation and success

65 Provided their job is relatively secure, employees are not interested in organizational objectives, long-term plans and goals

66 Subordinates should be encouraged to set their own objectives and targets in line with organizational goals

67 The prospect of life-time employment with one organization increases commitment to the success of the company

	Mostly Agree	**Mostly Disagree**
68 My job as manager means getting the job done, by whatever means I think appropriate		
69 Subordinates' views should be considered in the decision-making process		
70 Managers should become less progress chasers, more leaders (and members) of work teams		
71 Staff meal breaks, and time away from the desk/bench need to be tightly controlled or there is loss of productivity		
72 Managers should encourage subordinates, giving them confidence that they can do a good job		
73 Recognition of effort is as important as recognition of results		
74 It is important to have tight control and disciplinary procedures so that all employees know what can happen if they don't measure up to the job.		
75 Staff turnover and grievances are greatest where managers are task oriented, and closely control the work of their staff		

X, Y or Z? - Document 2

Score Sheet
Allow yourself one point for every time you ticked the *mostly agree*
box against the following numbers:

1 _____	2 _____	3 _____
4 _____	5 _____	6 _____
7 _____	8 _____	9 _____
10 _____	11 _____	12 _____
13 _____	14 _____	15 _____
16 _____	17 _____	18 _____
19 _____	20 _____	21 _____
22 _____	23 _____	24 _____
25 _____	26 _____	27 _____
28 _____	29 _____	30 _____
31 _____	32 _____	33 _____
34 _____	35 _____	36 _____
37 _____	38 _____	39 _____
40 _____	41 _____	42 _____
43 _____	44 _____	45 _____
46 _____	47 _____	48 _____
49 _____	50 _____	51 _____
52 _____	53 _____	54 _____
55 _____	56 _____	57 _____
58 _____	59 _____	60 _____
61 _____	62 _____	63 _____
64 _____	65 _____	66 _____
67 _____	68 _____	69 _____
70 _____	71 _____	72 _____
73 _____	74 _____	75 _____
TOTAL _____	TOTAL _____	TOTAL _____

X, Y or Z? - Document 3

Theory X, Theory Y, and Theory Z - Japanization
Douglas M McGregor was an American psychologist and Professor of Industrial Management. In 1960 he published *The Human Side of Enterprise* which discusses two sharply divergent concepts of management. The conventional (at that time) approach to management he called Theory X, based, he says, on traditional assumptions about human behaviour, ie that human beings are essentially lazy and will avoid work if they can; that they will shun responsibility, are unambitious, prefer to be directed and controlled, and value job security above all else. In a nutshell, Theory X managers work on the assumption that employees function best when told *what* to do, *how* to do it, and then suitably rewarded financially *when* they do it.

McGregor questioned this and proposed a new theory of management which he called Theory Y, based 'on more adequate assumptions about human nature and human motivation', ie that work is a natural and welcome activity which, if the employee is adequately motivated, need not be closely supervised and controlled. He further surmised that, given the right conditions, subordinates not only accept, but seek responsibility to give them more job satisfaction, and that they can give valuable help in ensuring the team and the organization run efficiently and effectively. Managers who practise Theory Y style management believe that an organization functions best when it allows employees to develop through full participation. People before products and profits could be their motto, because if people are happy at work and presented with adequate challenges, improved productivity and profits should automatically follow.

Theory Z is a name given to the application of a Japanese style of management to western organizations. There is no single formula for Japan's economic success; no two companies operate identically, but there are underlying principles based on the management style of large, private-sector companies.

In society in general, and in the workplace, harmony is a key word in Japan. They foster a unified sense of purpose and a dedication to company policies and philosophy. Life-time security of employment is still a reality in Japan. Individuals are unlikely to change organizations; in fact a potential second employer may doubt an applicant's loyalty if she or he has resigned from one organization to seek an alternative post. The benefit of staying with one company, however, is the loyalty this produces when one's future prosperity depends on the success of your employing organization. The benefit to employees is that the company will stand by them in the event of personal crisis. Employees are considered valued

members of the organization; human relationships are of utmost importance; individuals' views are valued; there is consultation at every stage of
decision making processes involving everyone likely to be affected by the
decision.

Pay and promotion systems are based on seniority. This may seem unfair
by western standards, but at least no one has to worry about the new
'bright spark' being promoted over one's head; everyone knows where they
are likely to be in the hierarchical structure 5 or 10 years hence.

Western companies have rarely adopted the above policies in full, but
some have adapted them with great success. Other aspects of Japanization more easily transferred to western company culture are concepts such
as consensus seeking in decision making. Theory Z emphazises quality
control which is directly linked to worker involvement. Top managers
formulate strategic projects, but don't finalize plans until lower managers
refine and revise them as they think necessary. This is done by ensuring
that everyone affected is consulted. In this way potential problems are
identified and ironed out of the system before implementation. If considerable modification is required, those affected will be consulted again before
change is made, and so on until everyone is in agreement. Each person
then fixes his or her seal to the proposal (the *ringi* system) and is then
committed to its implementation and success.

Other aspects of work organization adopted now by many western
companies, are Quality Circles, Quality Assurance, Total Quality Control,
Total Customer Service, Just-in-time (Kanban) production. These are all
designed to improve quality, worker involvement, customer care, and the
ability to adapt quickly and appropriately to changing customer and
market requirements.

Some of the keys to Japanese economic effectiveness lie in its flexibility,
quality consciousness, and teamworking, with care both for the consumer
and the workforce. Harmony, and unity over individuality are vitally
important themes, a further example of which is single status, or common
terms and conditions for all staff. This eliminates the 'them and us'
situation often found in western companies, where white collar workers
receive different holiday or sickness conditions from blue collar workers,
for example. Japanese organizations are seen to value all their workforce
equally.

★　　★　　★

A further examination of the statements contained in the questionnaire
will give you a better understanding of the three Theories, X, Y and Z. It
will help you to identify the issues related to the three different management styles represented by these statements, if you now put the appropri-

ate letter in the left hand margin against the relevant statements

- Z against questions 1, 4, 7, and so on
- X against questions 2, 5, 8, and so on
- Y against questions 3, 6, 9, and so on.

For more information on Theory X, Theory Y or Theory Z the following reading is suggested: Douglas M McGregor's *The Human Side of Enterprise* (1960), *Dealing with the Japanese* by Mark A Zimmerman (1988), and *Theory Z* by William Ouchi (1993) (see Bibliography details).

X, Y or Z? – Document 4

Evaluating your scores

The statements relating to column 1 were compiled from studies of Japanese management styles, Theory Z; those from columns 2 and 3 respectively, from Douglas M McGregor's Theory X and Theory Y – two opposing views of management and organization.

Most people will have points in every column. If you have more points in column 1 (the Z statements), your approach to management favours the Japanese approach, adopted by many western companies today. As Japan is a leading manufacturing nation and economic power, with high financial growth, high productivity, low staff turnover, and an excellent record of producing low-cost, top-quality goods and services, it is hardly surprising that more and more organizations are trying to match its success by emulating its management style.

If you had more points in the second column, you probably feel that employees need to be tightly managed, needing close supervision and control. Managers who adopt this style may feel that because they are in a position of authority, therefore power, subordinates are, by definition, dependent and need have little say in the way the section is run, in setting its objectives, in problem solving or decision making. These are tasks for management. You probably favour task-centred management rather than people-centred management.

There are many reasons why the Theory X approach to management is still to be found today. It should be recognized that there are some jobs which are so closely defined, limited in their application, or integral to a complex series of functions, that this approach is essential. This may be how it is with your section. However, it has been shown that more of a teamwork approach, as favoured by the other two management styles described here, has benefits, certainly in terms of staff turnover, commitment and morale in the workplace. If you have a high score in this column, it may benefit you to look to a more people-centred management style in the future.

If you had more points in the third column, you favour the Theory Y style of management. You have a positive view of human nature, believing that individuals, given encouragement, support and respect can be self motivating, will enjoy and be able to set their own objectives and targets, and will actively respond to responsibility and to a teamwork approach to problem solving and decision making. Given the opportunity, your subordinates can become committed to organizational goals.

If you had a fairly balanced number of points, ie no high scoring column or one with just a few points, you probably have a well-balanced approach to management. Different situations need different approaches and styles. If, however, you scored highly in the centre column, your Theory X approach to management could produce difficulties for you when managing change unless a directive, authoritative style is adopted. A 'them and us' situation is likely to result, however. A high score in the first column, Z, combined with an above average score in the Theory Y column indicates that you are happiest operating in a flexible, changing environment as leader of a mutually supportive team, and active member of the larger team – the organization.

Note: These analyses should be used as indicators only. The statements reflect trends, not absolutes.

SECTION 4

HELPING ONESELF TO MANAGE CHANGE

Activity 36

Camouflage

Description

A short, 'fun' activity which is useful as a vehicle for beginning some work on change.

Objectives

By the end of this activity participants will:

- have identified three positive and three negative reactions to change
- have identified the key concept of transferability of skills as critical to an individual's handling of change.

Participants

Number: Any
Type: Any

Time

1 hour

Resources

- One copy of Documents 1 and 2 for each participant
- One pen/pencil for each participant
- Flipchart stand, paper and marker pens
- Optional: small token prize, eg chocolate bar

Method

Step 1: Introduce the activity
Refer to the objectives but do stress that the exercise itself is not a profound one!

Step 2: Issue Document 1 to each participant; use a flipchart

and examples to explain the idea of a wordsquare – refer to the solution in Document 2 if you're unsure yourself!
Words in a wordsquare can appear in any direction: across, down, diagonally, forwards and backwards.

Step 3: Divide the participants into syndicate groups of between two and six people; draw attention to the explanation on Document 1
As this is more of a game than a serious activity you may like to offer a small token by way of a prize to the winning team.

Step 4: Start the exercise
Stop the exercise after 10 minutes or after any team declares it has found all 10 items.

Step 5: Establish which team has found the highest number of words or phrases to do with change, check for accuracy and award any prize

Step 6: Issue Document 2: the solution
Allow each group a few moments to check their own answers and to find the ones they missed.

Step 7: Reassemble the group in plenary session; lead a discussion
Allow 20 minutes.

Questions you might use:

- *Do the words 'transition' and 'new direction' suggest different ways of looking at change? For example, transition could imply a gradual moving from one situation to another, possibly over a long time, while new direction might suggest leaving the old behind and moving quickly into something quite new. How might people be influenced in their attitude to change by the words used to describe it?*
- *What examples can people give, from their own experience, of 'stress', 'fear of the unknown' and 'inadequacy'? Why were these feelings experienced? Did they prove groundless in the end?*
- *What examples can people give, from their own experience, of 'coping', 'adapting' and 'learning'? Were those experiences painful? Exciting? Challenging? Which? Why?*
- *Why might 'transferable skills' be important in confronting change? Can people give examples of situations where they have made use of skills in a new situation which were acquired in other, quite different situations (eg interpersonal skills, time-management skills and so on)?*

Step 8: Summarize the discussion and ask for contributions to

the following two questions, which it would be helpful to write up on a flipchart

- *How can organizations help reduce fears about change?*
- *How can individuals reduce their own fears about change?*

Allow 10 minutes. The first of these may produce ideas such as:

- *consultation*
- *keeping people informed about plans*
- *training people in new skills.*
- *training people to brush up on old skills*

The second may produce ideas such as:

- *reflect on the extent of change in one's life so far and how it has been coped with*
- *admit and discuss anxieties with others who will be supportive*
- *identify skills which will be useful in a new situation*
- *identify shortfalls in skills or knowledge and take action to remedy them.*

Step 9: Close the activity by referring to the objectives

Camouflage - Document 1

The square below contains 10 camouflaged examples of words or phrases that have to do with change. There are:

- three words or phrases for change (including the word 'change' itself)
- three words or phrases that describe possible positive reactions to change
- three words or phrases that describe possible negative reactions to change
- one word or phrase that describes an important idea connected with change.

The first team to find all 10, or the greatest number after 10 minutes, will be declared the winner. Beware: there are several red herrings in the puzzle - words or phrases that have nothing to do with change!

```
I  C  G  E  I  L  C  H  A  C  D  E  L  D  F  A  T  Z  Q  L
N  H  A  G  N  O  L  A  U  D  A  C  I  O  U  S  O  S  U  K
A  A  D  N  E  O  O  N  D  U  N  O  I  T  I  S  N  A  R  T
D  N  A  I  P  N  S  G  I  N  S  P  O  R  T  I  N  G  S  N
E  G  P  C  T  E  E  G  O  D  C  I  N  A  M  I  N  D  O  W
Q  D  P  T  I  W  T  L  S  O  O  N  O  N  C  E  I  N  T  O
U  E  O  P  A  D  A  P  T  I  N  G  O  S  P  O  R  T  I  N
A  L  C  L  N  I  L  I  N  G  E  R  T  F  R  A  I  T  A  K
C  F  G  E  T  R  I  D  E  F  E  R  D  E  N  I  G  R  O  N
Y  C  L  A  L  E  E  E  R  I  E  S  T  R  E  E  T  S  B  U
E  L  E  S  C  C  T  R  E  S  T  O  R  A  B  I  N  G  E  E
C  C  E  T  O  T  O  S  S  O  P  H  O  B  T  R  E  E  S  H
S  H  C  A  Y  I  O  C  R  A  J  O  N  L  C  I  E  N  C  T
T  A  T  L  R  O  T  H  O  R  S  E  S  E  I  T  T  L  X  F
A  N  G  L  O  N  I  O  O  E  E  S  O  S  N  S  E  C  T  O
G  D  L  E  A  Z  I  O  F  A  C  E  S  K  O  O  S  E  E  R
E  L  A  A  M  T  N  N  E  S  T  C  P  I  I  C  H  E  N  A
R  T  N  C  H  E  G  E  G  A  O  R  Y  L  S  R  O  T  D  E
Y  Z  C  T  M  A  U  E  G  N  A  H  C  L  E  O  R  O  E  F
E  E  F  F  N  M  M  S  L  O  E  T  O  S  S  P  E  A  R  O
```

Camouflage - Document 2

Solution

```
I C G E I L C H A C D E L D F A T Z Q L
N H A G N O L A U D A C I O U S O S U K
A A D N E O O N D U N O I T I S N A R T
D N A I P N S G I N S P O R T I N G S N
E G P C T E E G O D C I N A M I N D O W
Q D P T I W T L S O O N O N C E I N T O
U E O P A D A P T I N G O S P O R T I N
A L C L N I L I N G E R T F R A I T A K
C F G E T R I D E F E R D E N I G R O N
Y C L A L E E R I E S T R E E T S B U
E L E S C C T R E S T O R A B I N G E E
C C E T O T O S S O P H O B T R E E S H
S H C A Y I O C R A J O N L C I E N C T
T A T L R O T H O R S E S E I T T L X F
A N G L O N I O O E E S O S N S E C T O
G D L E A Z I O F A C E S K O O S E E R
E L A A M T N N E S T C P I I C H E N A
R T N C H E G E A O R Y L S R O T D E
Y Z C T M A U E G N A H C L E O R O E F
E E F F N M M S L O E T O S S P E A R O
```

Activity 37

Career move (1)

Description

This is in some ways similar in concept to Activity 40 'I am, therefore I can', but the processing is different, rather more analytical in nature and it leads to a more detailed outcome. You may like to read both before determining which to use with your particular group. This is one of two (potentially) linked activities. Its aim is to assist participants to plan for their next career move. It can be used with two main groups of people:

1 those who are confronting change at work, whether it be a new job or new responsibilities
2 those who have been, or are about to be, made redundant, perhaps with between one week's and three months' notice.

To contend with either of these situations people need the confidence and high self-esteem that results from knowing, and being able to articulate, their skills, strengths and achievements. Add to this the concept of transferability of skills and the result is a feeling of empowerment to handle major change.

The activity is therefore targeted at managers who are managing some process of change.

Note: There is an optional element to this activity (Step 22) which would normally be used only for managers in the second situation described above. This activity, and its linked Activity 38, 'Career move (2)' should not be used with managers who are to be made redundant *and for whom outplacement is to be offered*, since the approach may conflict with that of the outplacement company, who will cover similar ground but in a different way.

Objectives

By the end of this activity participants will:

- know what transferable skills they possess and be able to describe them succinctly
- be able to list their achievements (work and non-work)

- (optionally) be able to construct an effective CV.

Participants

Number: Maximum of 8
Type: Any managers who either (a) need to assess their skills and achievements to date in order to know clearly what weapons they can call on to confront organizational or career change or (b) are to be made redundant and who are not to be offered outplacement

Time

2 hours 30 minutes

Resources

- Flipchart stand, paper and marker pens
- Pens and at least one A4 sheet of paper for each participant
- Ready-prepared flipchart paper as specified in Step 19
- One copy of Document 1 for each participant if using the optional Step 22

Method

Step 1: Introduce the activity
Spend only a moment or two on this, relating the activity to the appropriate situation as outlined above.

Step 2: Brainstorm responses to the question 'What does a job mean to you?' and flipchart them
Allow five minutes. Write up the responses as they come from the group. Usually you will elicit responses such as. . .

'Security
'Job Satisfaction
'Money
'Social Contact

and so on.

Step 3: Brainstorm responses to the question 'What does a job mean to you as a manager?' and flipchart them
Allow five minutes. Explain that you are now seeking a different perspective to that employed in step 2. You are asking participants to consider why a job exists. Ask them to think about jobs under their own control – why do they exist? This is a rather more demanding step but, with a little prodding if necessary, you can usually elicit 'Task', 'Objective', 'Profitability'. In other words, a job exists because there is a task to be done or

an objective to be met. Linked to this is the need for enhanced profitability. Jobs do not normally exist unless there is a clear task or objective, effective discharge of which will result in increased profits, even after salary deduction.

Step 4: Compare the two lists

Simply make the point that the two perspectives contain very little common material. If you are working with redundant managers it is worth stressing the point that candidates who market themselves with the step 3 perspective in mind rather than step 2 are likely to secure more interviews.

Step 5: Ask the group to identify what companies are paying for (in salaries and wages) in order to fulfil the perspective of step 3; flipchart the replies

Allow five minutes. You should identify at least the following:

- *Experience*
- *Knowledge*
- *Skills*

and that it is these items that people draw on when confronting and handling change.

Step 6: Explain that participants are going to take stock of their own experience, knowledge and skills so that they can be aware of what they can draw on and, if appropriate, what they should be marketing to their next potential employer

It is not unusual for able and experienced managers to deny that they have any skills at all! The results of this exercise often surprise such people. For all participants the exercise normally raises self-esteem and confidence, simply through the process of identifying and listing what they have to offer.

Step 7: Ask each participant to work on their own for a few moments and to list all the activities which they get involved in outside work. Ask people to list at least five

Allow two minutes. You will often need to 'unblock' people here. Give examples and encourage people to list even the most commonplace. Examples are: shopping, cooking, housework, reading, working with children, playing football, sailing, theatre, socializing, member of Parent Teacher Association, local politics. . . the list is endless.

Step 8: Now ask each participant to underline the activity they derive most enjoyment from. Go around the group and ask each participant which activity they underlined and list it on a flipchart

This will only take a few moments. It is useful to divide each flipchart page into four roughly equal squares and place an activity in each square, thus:

Sailing	Reading
Theatre	Dancing

Step 9: Agree a definition of 'Skill' with the group
Allow two minutes. Usually 'Something I do well', or a close variant, emerges and will suffice.

Step 10: Now add to the flipchart, under each activity in turn, the skills required to do the activity effectively; use the whole group to brainstorm
Allow two minutes per participant. Don't allow the one person who has offered the activity to be the only one to brainstorm. Part of the value of this exercise lies in the perspectives of others, especially in dealing with those of the 'haven't got any skills' variety. An example:

Sailing. . .

Skills: *Navigation, technical knowledge, physical strength, teamwork, forward planning/anticipation, flexibility, crisis handling, etc.*

Step 11: Now move on to the world of work; go through steps 7, 8 and 10 again, but this time taking a work activity or task identified from a list and teasing out the skills on a flipchart

Allow 15 minutes. Step 10 is designed to orientate participants' thinking into what skills are and what sorts of words are commonly used to describe them. Step 11 builds on this process. It is suggested that you pair participants (ideally those who do not know each other) to work together in identifying the skills required for the identified task and that you then flipchart the results. Allow 10 minutes for paired discussions (five minutes each way) and then five minutes to flipchart.

Step 12: Get reactions to the results of the exercise
Allow five minutes.

Questions you might use:

- *Do you think it was easier having a dialogue about this rather than trying to do it on your own?*
- *How often did common terms such as 'forward planning', 'communication skills', 'time management' occur – probably in most people's lists? What is the value of this if everybody comes out looking much the same? Step 13 will address precisely this issue.*

Step 13: The most difficult part of this activity; get people back in their pairs and take one skill that appears on most people's lists, eg 'communication skills'; tell participants you want this skill put in context for each person on whose list this appears; any participants who do not have the skill on their list should take another generic term and use it similarly.

Allow 15 minutes. Participants can use any method they like (analysis, brainstorming and so on) but examples like those below may help. Essentially you are looking for movement from something bland and generic like 'communication skills' to something specific and in context and appropriate only to the person who is laying claim to it. Thus, for a personnel officer, 'the ability to listen effectively, through open and probing questioning techniques together with observation of body language' would be a much more informative statement to a selector than 'communication skills'. Alternatively, a sales representative might use 'the ability to understand the needs of others and to be persuasive in suggesting how those needs can be met' as opposed to 'communication skills'. Another example, for a merchandise manager in retailing, would be 'motivating and managing a task-orientated team in a demanding profit environment'. Compare this with 'staff management skills'.

This is not an easy exercise, and pairs may require guidance from the trainer.

Step 14: Flipchart the results for each participant. Make such observations as seem necessary
Allow 10 minutes. It's important participants can compare their own material with others'.

Step 15: Ask participants to identify at least four (and preferably more) skills in context. They should work individually, drawing from their work-task lists, for about 20 minutes and should then work in pairs for another 20 minutes to refine the process. Allow participants to take at least a working tea or coffee break during this step.
Allow a minimum of 40 minutes. The intensiveness of Step 13 means that a tea or coffee break will be much needed by this stage. If it coincides with lunch, you could extend the lunch break by 30 minutes and ask them to work on their lists over lunch.

Step 16: If you haven't yet had some sort of break, you must do so now, or you will be asking too much of your participants

Step 17: Go swiftly round the group and ask for one example of a skill in context from each participant; get others' reactions and give your own and then move on
Allow 10 minutes. It's worth stressing that these are first drafts *and that, in practice, people often need to go through two or three cycles of refinement before they feel happy with their lists. This will have to be done after the activity is over, however.*

Step 18: Ask participants how they react to interview questions like 'What are you most proud of?'
Allow only a few moments for this. It's a favourite with potential bosses and personnel officers and most people are thrown by it. Another way of putting it is to ask 'What do you feel you have achieved in your current post?'. Many people panic when faced by such questions. Step 19 pursues this further.

Step 19: Display a prepared flipchart showing the following two statements:
  - **Responsible for filing system**
  - **Raised user confidence in filing system through a review of its operation and making user-driven changes**

Get people's reactions to the two statements
Allow five minutes. Of course, not everyone who is in charge of a filing system can necessarily lay claim to the second description, but pose the questions 'Which is the more interesting to read?' and 'Which would prompt you to want to find out more?' The answer is, usually, the second. Both statements apply to the same person but one is achievement-orientated *while the other is not. Too often we describe our careers in 'job description' terms that are boring to read and which simply describe what*

we were required to do. They do not do us justice. It's perfectly possible – and highly desirable if we are trying to persuade ourselves and others of our ability to handle change – that we describe what we did in proactive terms which say something about how we contributed to the company's performance and profitability. Remember the different perspectives from steps 2 and 3?

Step 20: In pairs (preferably different ones from those set up earlier) ask participants to role-play the question 'What are you most proud of in your present job?'

Allow only five minutes. Ask people how easy it was to find answers. Often, it is not easy and you can suggest that the time to reflect on such issues is now before the interview or the impending change and not once into it. Knowing the answers to this, or similar, questions serves to raise our confidence in how we have handled change in the past (provided the answers are honest, of course!) and in assessing our capacity to cope with change in the future. It will also help others to assess this as well.

Step 21: You can now draw the activity to a close OR you can go on to Step 22 which is optional and for use mainly with participants who need to produce a good CV

Allow five minutes. Although your participants have put their skills in context, ask to what extent they are transferable to other situations. How well have people adapted to change in the past through drawing on their skills and experience elsewhere? Suggest that people now have the ability, on their own or with others, to work out full skill lists and achievements which they can articulate clearly and confidently and possession of which will stand them in good stead in confronting change.

Step 22 (Optional): Issue Document 1; discuss it as a possible vehicle for using the skills analysis and career achievements already undertaken as a basis for constructing a short CV which concentrates on the potential employer's perspective rather than the applicant's

Allow 10 minutes, running through each section of the example CV in turn, checking on:

- *Are the skills clear and in context?*
- *Is the career history a catalogue of tasks or something rather more interesting?*
- *What do the sections on education/training and personal information convey?*

There is usually agreement over this. Sometimes people resist the idea of a one-page CV but most employers and agencies welcome them provided they pack useful information on experience, knowledge and skills into the space available and they thus address the company's perspective rather than the applicant's.

Step 23: Close the activity by referring briefly to the objectives

Career move (1) - Document 1

KIM SMITH

42, Adams Road,
East Finchley,
LONDON N99 2GG

Telephone: 081 123 2345

Date of Birth: 1 April 1958

Skills offered

- Strong analytical approach plus attention to detail for effective problem-solving.
- Ability to manage an annual multi-million pound budget to maximize profit and to meet stringent financial targets.
- Motivating and managing a task-orientated team in a demanding profit environment.
- Negotiating effectively between parties of different considerations to ensure a workable and profitable conclusion.
- Ability to work under pressure to meet deadlines whilst maintaining a calm and balanced overview.

Career history

Merchandise Manager: Vendors group plc 1986–date

- Managed a team initiating the introduction and development of major new retailing concept.
- Planned and organized a new reporting structure for analyzing overseas group performance.
- Promoted effective liaison with computer programming team to develop an integrated system which satisfied requirements of all users.
- Successfully managed team to achieve bonus targets for stock control.

Buyer A N Other Vendors Ltd 1980–1986

- Planned and controlled introduction of a new product range.
- Trained and developed several cohorts of new trainees, launching them into successful careers within the group.
- Developed sophisticated sales analysis system resulting in significantly enhanced feedback to all levels of management.

Education

MA (Hons): Social Sciences – Lincaster Polytechnic 1976–1980

Several in-company training programmes on specific skills and product knowledge

Interests

Archery, computing, pub quizzes.   Married with one son aged 2.

Activity 38

Career move (2)

Description

This activity is about the job market and looks at how to manage the practical process of getting the next job offer.

It is linked to Activity 37, 'Career move (1)'. It would normally be appropriate for use only with managers who are to be made redundant. It follows on naturally from 'Career move (1)' and would be most useful where step 22 of that activity has been carried out, since participants would then have a useful document (a succinct CV) with which to launch themselves on the job market.

As with 'Career move (1)' this activity should *not* be used with any manager who is to benefit from outplacement, since its approach may conflict with the approach of the outplacement company. Please read the introduction to 'Career move (1)' before attempting to use 'Career move (2)'.

Objectives

By the end of this activity participants will:

- understand the nature of the job market
- possess a strategy for dealing with each facet of the job market.

Participants

Number: Maximum of 8
Type: Managers who are to be made redundant and who are not to be offered outplacement

Time

1 hour 30 minutes

Resources

- Flipchart stand, paper and marker pens

- One copy of Document 1 for each participant
- One copy of Document 2 for each participant

Method

Step 1: Introduce the activity

Before tackling the job market it's important that people understand its nature and operation. By and large it is not a system worthy of the title 'system'. 'Market' gives a rather better flavour – of a noisy set of apparently related activities but frequently with many different and conflicting messages that many people find hard to understand or interpret. The passage through the job market for many people is an unhappy and disillusioning experience. But by analysing its nature and looking at some of the 'rules of the game' it can be turned to advantage.

Step 2: Get the group to brainstorm opportunity sources (or 'leads' which may result in job offers ultimately)

Allow two minutes. You will normally end up with the following 4 basic routes into the Job Market, and it is suggested that you group them on your flipchart as people call them out.

Adverts	*Agencies*
Contacts	*Direct Approach*

So, for example, 'Newspapers' would go under 'Adverts'. 'Job Centre' or 'Headhunter' would go under 'Agencies'. 'Contacting companies direct' would go under 'Direct Approach' and 'Friends' or 'Colleagues' would go under 'Contacts'.

Step 3: Canvass the group's views on the following:

1 *What percentage of jobs are filled through the two routes above the line?*
2 *What percentage of routes are filled through the two routes below the line?*

3   *Are there any other key differences between the above the-line and the below-the-line routes?*

Allow up to 10 minutes on this as there are some key concepts, and possibly some surprises, here. The widely accepted answers to the above questions are:

1   *Something like 30 per cent of managerial posts in the UK*
2   *Something like 70 per cent of managerial posts in the UK*
3   *The above-the-line routes are* competitive, reactive *and require a* less-skilled *approach.*

By contrast, the below-the-line routes involve less competition – *maybe even none –* are proactive *and require a* skilled *approach.*

Questions you might use:

- *Which routes are the most satisfying and why?*
- *Should the above-the-line routes be ignored, or are they useful? How? (See next step.)*

Step 4: Divide the participants into two groups; ask one group to take Advertised Posts and Direct Approach and the other to take Agencies and Contacts; brief each group to discuss and list the 'pros and cons' of using each route and to flipchart their results

Allow 15 minutes. Check understanding of the terms. Definitions used by the authors of this activity are:

Advertised posts: *Any vacancy advertised in the media by an employer or by an agency*
Agencies: *Any agency, government or private, in the business of placing people in work through identifying suitable candidates to fill vacancies notified by employers*
Direct Approach: *Identifying and approaching a company which it is considered may be interested in employing the person using the approach. Not linked directly to an advertised vacancy*
Contacts: *Making a wide range of contacts, mainly in person, with people who may be useful in providing intelligence, advice, further contacts and conceivably job leads. Starting with a small number of people the development of a network of contacts can grow exponentially provided each contact leads to more contacts.*

Step 5: Bring the participants back together and process the flipcharted results

Allow 20 minutes. Get each group to outline its findings in turn. Refer to Document 1 as a checklist and pose appropriate questions if you identify missing elements.

Step 6: Re-form the two small groups and brief them to

**discuss and formulate a short set of 'Good Practice Rules'
which they would recommend to job hunters using each route;
ask for at least three on each; they should be flipcharted**
Allow 20 minutes. See Document 2 for examples if necessary.

Step 7: Bring the participants back together and process the flip-charted results
*Allow 20 minutes. Get each group to outline its findings in turn. Refer to
Document 2 as a checklist and pose appropriate questions if you identify
missing elements.*

Step 8: Issue Documents 1 and 2

Step 9: Close the activity by referring briefly to the objectives

Career move (2) - Document 1

Four routes through the job market: the pros and cons

Advertised posts

Pros
- Source of real vacancies
- Source of intelligence about salary levels – or 'what you are worth' on the job market – can help with salary negotiation
- Means of identifying employers who are currently recruiting even if not at your level (for Direct Approach)
- Means of finding out about career opportunities in unfamiliar sectors
- Means of identifying named contacts in companies (for Direct Approach)
- Means of identifying agencies/consultancies active in the industry or at your level
- Often very explicit about what they want in terms of skills and experience

Cons

- Competitive
- Reactive
- The 'ideal candidate' specified may not exist but you may be put off applying because you feel you are not 'up to scratch'
- Job may not exist – it may have been invented by an agency in order to boost its bank of CVs
- Only a minority of managerial level jobs are advertised

Agencies

Pros

- They will use their own network of contacts to promote you
- Can reduce to some extent workload on you
- Valuable source of intelligence about your sector of the job market

Cons

- Competitive
- Reactive
- The marketing of the product – you – is in someone else's hands
- Your CV may be hacked around and put in a standard format
- You may be put forward for unsuitable vacancies
- You may not be put forward at all
- Only a minority of managerial jobs are notified to agencies

Contacts

Pros

- Proactive
- Raises your profile
- Can result in leads to be followed up as a Direct Approach
- Chance to acquire and develop substantial intelligence base on job market
- Keeps self-esteem high
- Meet some really nice people!

Cons

- Time consuming
- May be expensive in terms of travel

Direct approach

Pros

- Proactive
- Minimal competition
- Company may not realize they have the vacancy yet – until you come along. . .
- Raises your profile

Cons

- Hard work for minimal return
- Easy to get disillusioned
- Expensive (postage and stationery)

Career move (2) – Document 2

Good practice in tackling the job market

Advertised posts

- Read widely; don't just look for vacancies that suit you
- Analyse adverts that *do* interest you carefully
- Look for 'key words' in the advertisement that suggest the skills, knowledge and experience they are looking for
- Don't be put off by the 'ideal candidate' syndrome. Probably nobody exists who will meet all their selection criteria
- Follow the instructions carefully – method of application, closing date and so on
- Deal with a named person if you can – try and find out who the anonymous 'general manager' or whatever is
- Beware of seductive 'informal chats' on the phone – they may be used to screen you out. If you *have* to do them, be prepared mentally
- If you have to fill in an application form make sure it is error-free and completed in full. It's no use sending it back blank with a copy of your CV stapled on the front. Keep a copy
- Be business-like in your correspondence
- Telephone to check that your application has been received safely
- Research and prepare thoroughly before attending any interview
- Ask for feedback if you get an interview but are unsuccessful. Use the information to improve your campaign and/or interview technique

Agencies

- Select a small number (two or three) with care. Shop around, talk to other people, use directories in public libraries
- Be clear what it is you want from your agencies
- Be realistic about your salary needs and expectations and discuss them with the agency
- Check to see if they are going to use your original CV or a processed copy. If the latter, get a copy of it
- Follow up with each agency regularly – call them once a week to make sure they know you are still in the market
- Once registered with a good agency use them to develop your job market intelligence
- Ask for feedback if you get referred and are unsuccessful at interview. Use the information to improve your campaign and/or interview technique

Contacts

- A useful 'agenda' for dealing with contact meetings is:

- I want *intelligence* about a market sector or company
- I want *advice* about how I might proceed, or how suited I may be, or how good my CV is, or. . . the list is endless
- I want some *suggestions as to more contacts* I can follow up with. Try to get at least three from each interview
- Contact meetings should not be about 'Have you got a job for me?' – the answer is probably 'No' and posing the question will embarrass. Be clear about the agenda outlined above
- Start with people you know well. You can use:
  - Business contacts (colleagues, suppliers etc)
  - Relatives and friends
  - Contacts through clubs, societies, associations
  - Local business community
- If you get a good lead – someone who may have a job – treat as a Direct Approach and use the rules for that
- *Always* write and thank people for their time afterwards
- Try to retain the initiative about contacting others suggested, or the lead may dry up, however well-intentioned the other person may be
- Enjoy the process! It's an established, recognized way of operating and most people are entirely comfortable with it

Direct approach

- Research target lists using business directories, local library, contacts, advertisements, etc
- Identify named personnel within a target organization, even if it means research
- Always make the first contact in writing, enclosing a brief CV
- Stress what you have to offer (Knowledge, Skills, Experience) *and* show how these could benefit the company. Most people fail to do this second part
- *Never* use 'The Personnel Department' for this approach
- Recognize it's a high-volume, low-return route; send out plenty of business-like letters, ten per week at least.
- If you get called in for interview remember they may not have an identified vacancy. They will want you to take the initiative in the interview.

Activity 39

How will I cope?

Description

The focus of this activity is the individual change manager. A manager has a range of techniques available to her or him; many of the activities in this volume concentrate on how the manager can handle the process: managing the environment, the organization, processes, others. But what about the individual manager's ability to cope? The 'macho' model of management prevalent in western culture allows little time to show, let alone admit, any doubts about one's own ability to cope. This activity will allow this process to happen. It needs to be done in a supportive atmosphere and it will only achieve its objectives if you have created such an atmosphere. Otherwise people will not be honest in answering the questions which lie at the heart of the activity.

The activity will not work *unless* each participant has some kind of identifiable change ahead of them.

Objectives

By the end of this activity participants will:

- have considered their own personal reactions to change
- be able to develop a strategy for coping with change at a personal level, through recognizing what stage they are at and what stages are likely to follow.

Participants

Number: Maximum of 10
Type: Anyone who has to cope with change. The activity is not restricted to those who have to manage change but it can be usefully done by anyone who is facing or undergoing some kind of transition, whether in their personal or in their organizational lives. It is, however, important that your participants are of a sufficient ability that they can discuss and understand some relatively abstract concepts.

Time

2 hours

Resources

- One copy each of Documents 1, 2, 3, 4, 5, 6 and 7 for each participant
- Paper and pens for people to make notes if they wish

Method

Step 1: Introduce the activity

Cover the material outlined in the Introduction and Objectives for this activity. You might like to add that the questionnaire which you are going to use is based on the work of Hopson, Scally and Stafford (1988), authoritative English writers on transition and managing personal change.

Step 2: Form the group into pairs (or pairs and one triad if you have an odd number); arrange the seating so that pairs can talk without being disturbed by others

You can either allow self-selection or you can set up the pairings yourself. What you should be aiming for is pairings of people who will feel comfortable with each other and who will be mutually supportive. A trap to avoid here is pairing men and women because you feel women may be particularly supportive. Remember the women will have needs just as much, and it can often work especially well if you pair off men with men and women with women for this activity.

Step 3: Explain that the activity is split into seven short sessions of 10 minutes. Each pair will be asked to have a dialogue based on a number of questions that you, as trainer, will pose

Stress that, although you will ask for general feedback afterwards, no pairing will be asked to divulge anything confidential. It's often a good idea to have a coffee or tea break in the middle of this, often intensive, activity. (The best place for this is suggested in the processing notes below.)

Step 4: Negotiate a contract of confidentiality

This is essential if the activity is to work. Participants need to be sure that they can be open with their partners without fear of the discussion going any further. It may be worth flipcharting some conditions that all are willing to be bound by. For example: The trainer will not report back to management views expressed by participants and/or Participants will not discuss individually expressed opinions outside the course room and so on.

Step 5: Issue Document 1 to each person

Explain that each pair now has 10 minutes to use the questions raised in the document to focus their thinking and discussion on the change that each of them confronts. Say that you will not impose a structure on the discussions apart from operating the 10-minute rule. What each pair should aim to do is to cover the 'agenda' set by the document and for both parties to explore, through dialogue, the issues raised.

Step 6: Take any questions
You may find people anxious about approaching this activity, and this sometimes reveals itself in terms of excessive questioning about the process, which can be a form of avoidance! There may come a point when you have to say 'Suck it and see'. Rest assured that, in most cases, this activity leads to some powerful learning, an increase in self-confidence and a breaking down of destructive stereotypical thinking about managers and how they 'must' cope.

Step 7: Start the activity
Allow 10 minutes. Check that each pairing is happy during this time, but do not listen in on conversations. Try to avoid being drawn into answering questions on the issues raised in the documents: one aim of the activity is to encourage the idea of sharing coping strategies with peers, and you will not necessarily be around to help that process in the 'real world'.

Step 8: Issue Document 2
Allow another 10 minutes.

Step 9: Issue Document 3
Allow another 10 minutes.

Step 10: Undertake a brief review of the activity so far
Allow 5 minutes. Explain that the issues raised so far have been about taking a 'snapshot' of the situation as it appears to be. The remaining steps are about how to develop a strategy for coping with the situation. Take questions and reactions so far by all means, but we suggest you don't actually encourage in-depth processing at this stage.

Steps 11 – 14: Issue Documents 4–7 in order and allow the usual 10 minutes of discussion on each
You may like to take a refreshment break – perhaps with people taking their drinks back into the pairings and continuing so that the momentum is not lost – after step 13. You may need to adjust the time if people are discussing well – particularly when focusing on the issues in Document 5 which is a long one and which raises quite intense issues.

Step 15: Re-form the main group; get reactions to the activity; avoid concentrating on outcomes (strategies and so on) and ask people what sorts of issues emerged earlier on, but

without demanding specific examples

Allow 30 minutes. You may like to re-cap on the structure you have taken the group through:

- *Knowing about the change or transition that lies ahead*
- *Knowing your attitude to the change or transition ahead*
- *Identifying who else can help*
- *What can we learn from the past?*
- *How good are we at looking after ourselves?*
- *Can we let go of the past?*
- *Setting goals and targets.*

If you have set up a supportive atmosphere people will be forthcoming on the sorts of issues they discussed without prompting from you, maybe even giving specific examples.

Questions you might use:

- *How useful was the seven-stage approach as a way of structuring thinking about coping with change?*
- *Which were the most useful sections? Why?*
- *Which were the least useful? Why?*
- *How unfamiliar/uncomfortable were people with the idea of sharing their vulnerabilities and uncertainties with others? Why?*
- *Can people see advantages in discussing coping strategies with others in future? What advantages?*

Step 16: Explain that the model explored in this activity can be helpful in getting people to identify what stage they are at in a transition and being able to see what may lie ahead; this in itself can assist the process of planning for the next phase (or phases beyond the next one) and possibly discerning practical steps which might promote that forward process

Step 17: Close the activity by referring briefly to the objectives

How will I cope? - Document 1

Coping with change and transition

Ask yourself, and discuss with your partner, the following questions about the forthcoming change or transition. Ensure you allow your partner to explore their ideas, views and feelings too.

Adopt the same approach throughout the series of agendas (seven altogether).

Agenda 1: Knowing about the change or transition ahead

- Can I describe the change or transition clearly?
- Are the boundaries clear or blurred?
- Who else is involved?
- Do I know how I'm expected to behave?
- Is there any way I can try out facets of the new situation in advance?
- Can I find at least one thing which is positive about the situation?

How will I cope? - Document 2 & 3

Agenda 2: Knowing your attitude to the change or transition ahead

- Would you have chosen for this change or transition to happen if it had been up to you?
- How do I tend to react to new situations? Do I grab things by the scruff of the neck and get on with it or am I more cautious - reactive, even - to see how things will turn out?
- Am I clear on what I'd like to see from the new situation?
- Am I clear on what I *don't* want from the new situation?
- If I experience stress do I know how I can help myself handle it?
- Do I allow my feelings to influence my thinking on where I am at as I go through the transition?

Agenda 3: Who else can help

- Is there anyone I can depend on in a crisis?
- Is there anyone at work I can discuss my concerns and anxieties with? Regularly, or just in a crisis?
- Is there anyone I can feel close to - not necessarily a work colleague - and whose opinions and support I can value and respect? A friend, in fact.
- Is there anyone who tends to make me feel competent, valued and generally good about myself? Apart from me, that is?
- Who can supply me with the information I need?
- Who will force me to take a long, hard look at myself and what I'm doing? In a constructive way?
- Who can I celebrate my successes with?

How will I cope? - Document 4 & 5

Agenda 4: Learning from the past

- Have I ever been through anything remotely like this before?
- What are the similarities with the present situation?
- What are the differences?
- What helped me get through the previous situation?
- What would I have done differently and why?

Agenda 5: Looking after myself

- Do I talk to myself supportively, or do I tend to keep putting myself down, doubting my every action?
- Do I exercise regularly or have some sort of programme for keeping fit?
- How important do I think it is to keep fit at times like this?
- What's my diet like? Should I modify it? Is now the right time to put myself on a serious diet? How will it affect my performance if I do?
- Do I know how to relax? Do I do it?
- Do I have a regular schedule of some sort that gives me some kind of stable structure?
- Do I have stability zones in my life – things that I know are not currently changing and will always be there as I face this transition?
- Do I treat myself occasionally when under stress? How?
- Do I have other people around me who will worry about me and be concerned for my welfare?
- Do I know how to let off steam – particularly anger – but keeping my self-esteem intact?
- Do I *honestly* think I will pull through this OK?

How will I cope? - Document 6 & 7

Agenda 6: Unhooking from the past

- How easily do I let go of old situations?
- Do I still feel bitter about unpleasant things that have happened to me before?
- Do I commonly feel that 'these things shouldn't happen to me'?
- Do I learn from my mistakes, or do I tend to feel it is usually someone else's fault?

Agenda 7: Setting goals and targets

- Do I know what goals and targets are?
- What's my experience of setting goals and targets?
- What are my goals for this transition or change?
- Do I have any life goals that will influence, or may be influenced by, the process and outcome of this transition?
- Do I know how to make and carry out action plans?
- Do I know how to set priorities and to adjust them if necessary?
- Am I an effective decision-maker?
- Can I generate alternatives? Develop contingency plans?
- What opportunities will exist after this change that don't exist now?
- What do I think I will learn from the experience that lies ahead?

Activity 40

I am, therefore I can

Description

A broad-based, morale boosting activity, to instil confidence, help recognize self-worth and generate motivation in participants who may be faced with career change, or different job direction. It could usefully be run early in a course concerned with re-training, job search or interview technique.

Objectives

By the end of this activity participants will:

- have identified at least five things they are good at, five achievements, and long-term ambitions
- have shared details of their accomplishments with at least one other person
- have analysed achievements in terms of skills used
- have begun the process of seeing how utilization of key skills fits in with short-term plans and long-term ambitions.

Participants

Number: 8–12
Type: Any

Time

3–4 hours

Resources

- Sufficient space, seating and table space (or clip-boards) for participants to work individually, and in pairs/small groups for discussion
- Flipchart paper and marker for each participant
- Pen/pencil and A4 paper for each participant
- One copy of Document 1 for each participant

Method

Step 1: Introduce the activity, explaining the procedures and timings

This is a broad-based activity which introduces processes (which could usefully be followed up by more detailed exercises) necessary to understanding where individuals are now, what are their strengths, and marketable skills. It also allows individuals to begin to look objectively at future goals and ambitions.

This exercise is in three parts. Each participant will be given a sheet of flipchart paper and marker and asked, in the first instance, to work individually, recording five things she or he is good at, then five achievements. This will take about 15 minutes. The second part of the activity is again performed individually, enlarging on the information recorded on the flipchart sheet, but participants will then be asked to share their thoughts with a partner or within a small group, and to work together. This part of the exercise is likely to take the longest, an hour or more. Finally, participants will be able to identify their major skills, strengths and attributes using a pre-printed grid/profile.

Throughout, there will be opportunities to share thoughts with the whole group, and the activity will conclude with the plenary session.

Step 2: Divide group into pairs, triads or fours

Use your knowledge of the activity and of the group you are working with to decide whether pairs or small groups would work best. Use any arbitrary method to choose groupings, or if the participants are known to you, choose supportive partners for those less obviously secure. It is important that individuals' feelings of self-worth are enhanced by the exercises.

Step 3: Once participants are sitting with their partner/in groups, issue each with a sheet of flipchart paper and a marker

Although participants will be working individually during this first part of the exercise, it may be useful to share ideas with at least one other person, hence the security of being with a partner/group from the outset.

Step 4: Instruct participants in what they have to do, remind them of how long they've got to do it, and set them to work

Working individually, participants should write their names on the top of the flipchart sheet, then

(a) write I AM: listing five things (not necessarily work orientated) which they are good at, or five positive attributes, eg I AM good at gardening, or I AM loyal.

(b) write I AM PROUD OF: then list five achievements (gained at any

time, in or out of work). Just a phrase will do at this stage, eg I AM PROUD OF being picked for the school athletics team.

Explain that if they want to bounce ideas off someone in their group, that's fine (the exercise should be as non-threatening as possible).

They have 15 minutes to complete this first part of the exercise. Do not give time checks as this could cause stress in what should be an unpressured exercise. Do circulate amongst groups, giving encouragement and assistance if necessary.

Step 5: **When all participants are ready, ask them to pin their flipchart sheets to the wall**
Ensure that everyone has had time to list all five I AM statements attributes and, at least three achievements.

Step 6: **Ask each participant in turn to choose just one of the things she or he is good at, or a positive attribute which is listed on their sheet, and to state it aloud to the group.**
It may sound like a simple thing to ask participants to do, but for many whose self-esteem is low, or whose confidence has been shaken, to assert publicly a personal positive quality is often very difficult. It is a necessary first step, however, in selling oneself – to a new boss, or at interview for example.

Step 7: **(If appropriate) acknowledge the difficulty some may have had, but stress the importance of positive self-image**
This part of the activity can be used alone, as it stands, as an icebreaker, an introduction to assertion, of where groups are particularly vulnerable and need to be eased gently into positive self-awareness.

Step 8: **Issue A4 paper, pens/pencils as necessary; explain the second part of the exercise**
Working individually, participants will now put 'meat on the bones' of their achievements, explaining the whys and wherefores. Eg. I AM PROUD OF being chosen for the school athletics team because:

> *Apart from proving to myself that I really was good at sport, it was the first time that people other than my parents had recognized an achievement. I was pleased for my parents too, as they were really proud and there to cheer me on. I felt that I could compete as an equal, and even win!*

Participants will have 20 minutes, initially, to complete this (further time may need to be negotiated).

Step 9: **Give a time check at 20 minutes, re-negotiate times if necessary**
Inevitably participants will work at different speeds. Ensure that this part of the activity is concluded within 30 minutes however.

Step 10: When everyone has written a few sentences qualifying their achievement statements, direct them to work together, in pairs or small groups, to ascertain what each achievement 'says' about that person; stress that first impressions are often very telling, so there is no need for a knowledge of psychology to undertake this task!

Up to one hour should be allowed for this part of the activity. Encourage discussion of the listed achievements within the partnerships/small groups. To continue with the athletics team example, given above, it would seem that that person needs recognition; possibly lacked confidence in her/his own abilities at that stage in her/his life, and needed reassurance; is nevertheless competitive, and successful in that field; was good at individual achievement (with the exception of relays, athletics tends to concentrate on individual achievement rather than team effort). Does this individual, therefore, function better alone or as part of a team? Is there a preference for individuality or teamwork? Does 'winning' matter to this person?

These are the sorts of issues which can be discussed within the partnerships/small groups. Initially, participants may need guidance from the trainer, who should circulate among groups for the duration of this part of the activity, ensuring that group members' perceptions of another's achievement are tested against that individual's own self-perceptions, and are of a positive and constructive nature.

Step 11: Close this part of the activity after one hour
Be sensitive to the requirements of the group, and flexible regarding timings. Some participants will relish this sort of discussion; others will need more guidance/less time. Most groups, however, will need about an hour in order to give adequate attention to each person's work.

Step 12: Ask the group if anyone would like to share anything they have gained from the above process
Individuals should not be pressured into talking about their analyses, but it is necessary to hold a discussion with the whole group in order that individuals can begin to translate their self-perceptions and those of others into a recognition of their positive qualities, needs, skills and attributes which should, if possible, be pursued in their working lives.

Questions you might use:

- *Did anyone learn anything about themselves, from this exercise, of which they were previously unaware?*
- *Do you see a pattern in your behaviour/needs/drives?*
- *What do these patterns tell you about the sort of career or lifestyle you should/would prefer to follow?*
- *Are your needs/skills met, or used effectively in your present line of work?*

- *If not, which needs/skills are not being met or used?*
- *(If this is the case) is your immediate superior aware of these untapped resources? Would it be useful to talk this through with her/him or with the personnel section of your organization?*
- *If you are in the process of changing jobs, how can this information help you – how can you utilize your skills, qualities and attributes in furthering your career?*

Step 13: Explain the next part of the activity and its timings

In order to get a more complete picture of the skills and attributes each participant possesses, individuals will now be asked to think about their achievements and assess what skills were used and attributes needed in order to 'be chosen for the athletics team' or 'design and construct our own conservatory' or 'be the youngest manager ever to sit on the board of directors' or whatever else participants may have identified as achievements.

Participants will be given a pre-printed profile (Document 1) with skills and attributes listed. They will have 30 minutes to look at each achievement and put a tick against the skills and attributes used in order to accomplish that achievement.

Step 14: Issue and explain Document 1

Although this should be completed individually, again, it may be useful for participants to bounce ideas off their group colleagues, especially as by now they will have discussed the achievement and what was involved. For example, the person who, in the above example, built a conservatory may not tick 'communication' as a skill which was used. A colleague may be able to point out that in order to gain planning permission for the building, a good deal of communication must have been successfully undertaken.

Participants should consider all aspects of their achievements, and put a tick in the appropriate box for every time that skill was used. For example, if effective communication was necessary to gain planning permission (see above example), and in settling a dispute between a neighbour and delivery man who accidentally dumped two tons of sand on her drive instead of yours, put two ticks against 'communication'.

Again it may be necessary and beneficial to individuals if the trainer circulates, giving this kind of guidance.

Step 15: After 20 minutes give a time check, re-negotiating if necessary

As previously stated different individuals and groups will require different amounts of time to complete exercises such as these. If necessary, the profiles can be completed at a later date by participants for their own information. Provided enough time is allowed for two or three achievements to be analysed in this way, sufficient patterns should have emerged for individuals to see where their strengths and weaknesses lie.

Step 16: Discuss the implications of the completed profiles

Even after analysing just two or three achievements, patterns will start to emerge. Some skills and attributes will feature in each achievement; others will not figure at all.

Generally, people enjoy doing what they are good at. They are most effective when bringing into play aspects of their personality with which they are comfortable and confident. Once completed, the profile should give a clear indication of skills which, by definition, individuals are competent/good at, are confident about and from which they derive pleasure. These skills should obviously be utilized to the full, and form a solid basis for job progression or job search. Similarly, attributes should not be ignored, and emotional and intellectual needs are an important part of job satisfaction, and thus effectiveness. Skills and attributes which received no ticks on the profile don't necessarily indicate that an individual doesn't possess such a skill; it is just unlikely to be a strength compared with others.

Step 17: Lead a short discussion on the value of building on strengths, and of recognizing areas where skills are not so strong or where personal needs are at odds with present work or goals

The group can be reminded that they should now have a much clearer picture of the direction they should be taking in order to satisfy their own needs and aspirations. Also, of what they have to offer their present or future employer in terms of skills, and have examples at their fingertips of how these skills have been demonstrated in the past (very useful for interviews, whether in-house, or for a new position). They should be aware of skills and expertise which is being under-utilized at present but would be of benefit to an employer – a good selling point, this!

If participants are in the situation where a change of job is a possibility, this analysis of skills and needs may well reveal that 'more of the same' is not what they want from their working life. It is the first step necessary in deciding new directions.

Most importantly, participants will leave the activity with a clearer idea of what they are good at and enjoy doing, and with an enhanced concept of self-worth.

Step 18: Close the activity

I am, therefore I can - Document 1

Go through each of your achievements, giving thought to the process
involved at each stage, and enter a tick in the appropriate box for each
time that the skill was used. In the same way, put ticks in the boxes
against attributes. The skills and attributes listed are extensive, but not
exclusive, so please add any other skill or attribute you have used in the
spaces provided at the end of the lists.

SKILLS		*ATTRIBUTES*	
Communication	☐	Hard working	☐
Interpersonal	☐	Work well under pressure	☐
Analytical	☐	Common sense	☐
Problem solving	☐	Determination	☐
Negotiating	☐	Foresight	☐
Creative	☐	Personality	☐
Innovative	☐	Gregarious	☐
Time management	☐	Firm, but fair	☐
Planning	☐	Courage	☐
Organizing	☐	Loyal	☐
Objective setting	☐	Honest	☐
Financial	☐	Perceptive	☐
Leadership	☐	Flexible	☐
Team building	☐	Versatile	☐
Motivational	☐	Approachable	☐
Human resource management	☐	Assertive	☐
Numeracy	☐	Supportive	☐
Business acumen	☐	Persevering	☐
Manual dexterity	☐	Patient	☐
Costing	☐	Enquiring mind	☐
Prioritizing	☐	Empathetic	☐
Counselling	☐	Dependable	☐
Decision making	☐	Caring	☐
Technical expertise	☐	Resilient	☐
Coordinating	☐	Sense of humour	☐
Directing	☐	Can laugh at myself	☐
Other. . .	☐	Other. . .	☐

Activity 41

Jeopardy

Description

A competitive activity, involving two teams, based on the TV quiz programme of that name. Because the trainer gives a statement encapsulating an *answer* to which the participants have to supply the *question*, it does not require in-depth knowledge of the subjects in order to run the activity. A handout with additional information to issue to all participants at the end of the activity also eliminates the need for the trainer to get involved in discussions of the topics tested.

The subjects in question are all concerned with change and the way forward in the world of management. Statements are from the *Penguin Business Dictionary**, *Collins Dictionary of Business***, and BSI Quality Assurance – BS5750 – documents.

Objectives

By the end of this activity, participants will:

* have experienced a challenging game in competition with a group of their peers
* have reinforced knowledge of, or learnt facts about, five different topics relevant to progress and change.

Participants

Number: 6–12
Type: Junior/middle managers

Time

30–60 minutes

* *The Penguin Business Dictionary*, Penguin, 1985.
** Collins Dictionary of Business, HarperCollins, 1991.

Resources

- Seating for two groups of up to six people
- Flipchart stand, paper and marker pens
- Copy of questions and answers, as contained in the trainer's notes (p. 294)
- One copy of Document 1 for each participant

Before the session it will be necessary to draw the subject grid as shown in the trainer's notes on a flipchart sheet, leaving enough room to write in the accumulating scores of each team

Method

Step 1: Explain the activity

This is a competitive quiz run on lines similar to the game-show Jeopardy *as seen on TV. Participants are divided into two teams who will take it in turns to answer questions chosen from the grid, points scored as per category chosen, eg if a team asks for Japan 15, and answers the question correctly, 15 points will be awarded to them. If that team fails to answer, or gets it wrong, the opposing team have the chance to gain 15 bonus points if they answer correctly. The second team then has its own turn in choosing and answering.*

The categories and questions all have connections with progress and change in the context of management. Japanese management style is being adopted increasingly by western organizations, for example, and an awareness of what this involves is useful for all managers.

The questions are graded in difficulty, 5 being the easiest; 25 the most difficult, although, of course, any question is easy if you know the answer, and considered difficult if you don't!

The twist is that the trainer will give the answer *and it is the task of the teams to supply the correct* question *in order to gain the points. For example, if there were a category on 'Motivation' the trainer might say: 'A manager giving a subordinate responsibility with authority for a task or project'. The team would need to respond with the appropriate question – 'What is delegation?'*

Teams can confer before answering. The spokesperson must prefix her/his response with the words 'What is. . .' or 'Where is. . .' as appropriate. Failure to do so results in 10 additional points being offered to the other team.

Step 2: Divide group into two teams

Counting round the group, all 1s being in group A and all 2s forming group B might be a fair way of choosing teams.

Step 3: Arrange seating so that teams can confer without

being heard by the opposition
Teams must, of course, also be in sight of the flipchart!

Step 4: Flip a coin to decide which team is to choose and answer first

Step 5: Ask team to confer, and choose a subject and point category
As each team chooses, cross off that subject and category from the grid.

Step 6: Give the statement relating to the chosen subject and category
If the team can give the correct question applicable to the 'answer' given by the trainer, mark the flipchart sheet with the appropriate number of points, remembering to award 10 points to the opposing team if the question isn't prefixed by 'What is. . .' etc.

If the team whose turn it is fail to respond with the right 'question' or do not know the answer, offer the statement to the opposing team. Award the points to them if they respond correctly; if they do not, supply the answer. Explain that both question and answer, plus additional information if relevant, will be issued, as a handout, at the end of the activity.

The trainer should alternate between teams to give each group an equal chance of choosing and responding, picking up bonus points if appropriate.

Step 7: When all categories from each subject have been attempted, add up the total scores of the two teams and declare the winners

Step 8: Issue Document 1
Explain that this gives a little more background information to the questions and answers set.

Step 9: Close the activity referring to the objectives
Remind participants that though not necessarily essential to their present roles, it is advisable to keep informed about changes in management styles, in aspects of management which could give competitors an edge, of advances in technology and so on. The purpose of this activity is not so much to instruct in the subjects covered, as this can only be very superficial, but to raise awareness of the need to keep abreast of changes in these, and other areas of management.

Trainer's notes

Reproduce this grid on a sheet of flipchart paper, leaving enough room at either side, or at the bottom of the sheet, to note the scores of both teams.

EUROPE	QUALITY	TECHNOLOGY	JAPAN	BUSINESS
5	5	5	5	5
10	10	10	10	10
15	15	15	15	15
20	20	20	20	20
25	25	25	25	25

Scores: **Team A**   **Team B**

The Statements (correct responses are shown in italics below)

Europe

5 A regional bloc, established by the Treaty of Rome in 1958, with the general objective of integrating the economies of member countries.

What is the EC (Formerly EEC)?

10 The unit of account used to value the exchange rate of member countries.

What is an ECU?

15 The free trade in goods and services through the removal of tariffs, quotas and so on, and the free movement of labour and capital across national boundaries.

What is the Common Market?

20 The subsidization and protection of the farming sector by operating a price support system.

What is CAP (Common Agricultural Policy)?

25 Bonds that were introduced because of the need of American industry to raise money in Europe for investment there.

What are Eurobonds?

Quality

5 A statistical method of ensuring that each product or service is consistent with specified criteria.

What is Quality Control?

10 An organizational commitment to the detection and prevention of quality problems in order to maintain specified levels of quality.

What is Quality Assurance?

15 Small groups of supervisors and employees who meet periodically to discuss ways in which quality can be improved.

What are Quality Circles?

20 An entire business philosophy which seeks to instil in every employee, individual and collective responsibility for high standards in product, service and customer care.

What is TQM (Total Quality Management)?

25 An American term now internationally used to describe the aim to produce perfect goods and services.

What is zero-defect production?

Technology

5 Has largely replaced the typewriter in offices of today.

What is a word processor?

10 The generic term for programs or instructions that make a computer system perform particular tasks.

What is software?

15 Capable of transmitting an exact copy of a document via a telephone link.

What is a FAX or facsimile machine?

20 The 'brain' of a computer which stores, processes and manipulates data.

What is a CPU (Central Processing Unit)?

25 Encodes and decodes the signals one computer sends to another via the telecommunications system.

What is a modem?

Japan

5 When addressing a Japanese businessman, the correct title is not 'Mr' as in western society, but his surname followed by this word.

What is – San (eg not Mr Sanshi, but Sanshi – san)?

10 The theory regarding the application of the Japanese approach to management by western organizations.

What is Theory Z?

15 The term used for the principle whereby several Japanese companies target a particular foreign product, and concentrate their efforts on capturing that market in order to dominate that sector.

What is the 'laser beam effect'?

20 In this system, the quantity of stocks is kept to the minimum level necessary for immediate production.

What is Just-In-Time (or Kanban) production?

25 Meaning literally 'improvement' this word is used in Japanese management circles to describe the umbrella concept covering most of the uniquely Japanese management practices, such as Total Quality Control, Total Customer Service, Just-In-Time production, Zero-Defect production, and so on.

What is Kaizen?

Business

5 The movement towards relocation of managerial authority to a lower level in the organization.

What is decentralisation?

10 A form of external growth involving organizations expanding in a horizontal, vertical or conglomerate direction.

What is a merger?

15 The collection and processing of information, from within an organization, and from the firm's environment, using computers, communication devices and so on.

What is IT (Information Technology)?

20 An organizational sub-unit of a firm, given responsibility for minimizing costs and maximizing revenue within its limited sphere of operations.

What is a Profit Centre?

25 The firm or company which has the biggest share of the available market for a specified product or service.

What is a Market Leader?

Jeopardy - Document 1

Jeopardy - Answers, questions and explanations

Europe

5   A regional bloc, established by the Treaty of Rome in 1958, with the general objective of integrating the economies of member countries.

What is the EC? (formerly the EEC)

The EC is the leading economic grouping in world economy. Policies are formulated by member countries' governments by the Council of Ministers (one appointed member per country) and the democratically elected European Parliament. The main developments to date include the Common Market, the free trade philosophy, the Common Agricultural Policy, a regional policy to achieve a more even spread of prosperity within and among member countries, the establishment of the European Monetary System and the creation of the ECU. Issues such as the replacement of individual national currencies with the ECU, and the formation of a federal Europe, are still under debate at the time of writing.

10   The unit of account used to value the exchange rate of member countries.

What is an ECU?

The creation of a special monetary unit, the European Currency Unit (ECU) was to provide a common basis for inter-country settlements under the CAP and the EMS.

15   The free trade in goods and services through the removal of tariffs, quotas and so on, and the free movement of labour and capital across national boundaries.

What is the Common Market?

In 1957, six countries put their name to the Treaty of Rome to form an economic community which became active from January 1958. This community was collectively called the Common Market. The present 12 member-country Common Market has a population which exceeds that of the combined former Soviet republics and that of the USA. The Common Market is one of three types of free trade blocs and is a customs union which also provides for the free movement of labour and capital across national boundaries.

20   The subsidization and protection of the farming sector by operating a price support system.

What is CAP (Common Agricultural Policy)?

One of the conditions of membership of the Common Market was acceptance of this policy which was written into the agreement in order to protect the European farming industry. The EC fixes minimum prices for various farm products through the European Commission, and imposes tariffs on imported goods. There has been much criticism of CAP, and at the time of writing, reform of the policy is under discussion by member countries.

25 Bonds that were introduced because of the need of American industry to raise money in Europe for investment there.

What are Eurobonds?

The main instrument used in the Eurocurrency Market to finance long-term investment is the Eurobond, a form of fixed-interest security. They are issued and subscribed for on the international market, and are often used by companies wishing to raise money abroad.

Quality

5   A statistical method of ensuring that each product or service is consistent with specified criteria.

What is Quality Control?

Quality control involves a number of activities, in particular the interpretation of product specifications, the inspection of products at each stage of production, co-operation with design, marketing, production and R&D over improvements, and undertaking audits to check the efficiency of quality control procedures.

10 An organizational commitment to the detection and prevention of quality problems in order to maintain specified levels of quality.

What is Quality Assurance?

Quality assurance involves managers, supervisors and employees from all functional areas in collaborating to design and produce more reliable goods and services.

15 Small groups of supervisors and employees who meet periodically to discuss ways in which quality can be improved.

What are Quality Circles?

These consist of individuals from a particular functional area, who meet formally at regular intervals to assess the effectiveness and efficiency of its part of the production or service process, and to discuss and suggest possible improvements. For quality circles to work, it is essential that there is organizational commitment to them, including commitment of top management.

20 An entire business philosophy which seeks to instil in every employee, individual and collective responsibility for high standards in product,

service and customer care.

What is TQM (Total Quality Management)?

The success or failure of an organization relies on its ability to satisfy customers. Quality of product, service and customer care are deciding factors. TQM seeks to establish a unity of interests and commitment to the maintenance of the highest possible quality standards, throughout every section and department, in order to generate and sustain competitive advantage. TQM attempts to minimize the amount of time and money spent on quality control by the prevention of problems arising in the first place.

25 An American term, now internationally used to describe the aim to produce perfect goods and services.

What is 'zero-defect' production?

Everyone in the organization is expected to aim for 'right first time' work, with no scrap or corrective operations. Zero-defect production assists the attainment of minimal overall costs of products and services. 'Zero-defect' is an Americanism for a Japanese management concept.

Technology

5 Has largely replaced the typewriter in offices of today.

What is a word processor?

A word processor is basically a computer with software designed for the manipulation and printing of text.

10 The generic term for programs or instructions that make a computer system perform particular tasks.

What is software?

Hardware in very basic terms, is the components of the machine itself – the electrical circuits, and electromechanical devices that make up a computer system and includes the disk drives, the keyboard and the VDU (visual display unit). Software is what makes the computer system operate; specialist software packages allow the computer to perform various functions, eg word processing, spreadsheets, databases and so on.

15 Capable of transmitting an exact copy of a document via a telephone link

What is a FAX or facsimile machine?

Two FAX machines can be connected to one another over the telephone network thus enabling the instant transmission of documents from one location to another.

20 The 'brain' of a computer which stores, processes and manipulates data.

What is a CPU (Central Processing Unit)?

Together with the monitor, keyboard and printer, the CPU is an integral part of computer hardware.

25 Encodes and decodes the signals one computer sends to another via the telecommunications system

What is a modem?

A modem is a device used to connect a computer to the public telephone network, to enable that computer to receive and transmit information from other computers similarly connected but sited some distance away.

Japan

5 When addressing a Japanese businessman, the correct title is not 'Mr' as in western society, but his surname followed by this word.

What is – San?

Thus, if your name is Jones, you may well be referred to as Jones-san, rather than Mr Jones. A Japanese with the name Sashki should be addresses as Sashki-san, not Mr Sashki. Similarly, the correct form of greeting is a slight bow from the hips, or lowering of the head, not a handshake which many Japanese businessmen still find offensive.

10 The theory regarding the application of the Japanese approach to management by western organizations.

What is Theory Z?

Change and constant improvement are ways of life for Japanese managers. Japan is so successful economically, Japanese manufacturers being market leaders now in so many areas, that some western organizations are seeking to emulate their success. Theory Z type companies adopt elements of work organization and employment practices usually found in large Japanese companies, such as TQM, zero-defect production, quality circles, total customer service, just-in-time production and so on. They generate and sustain commitment in their staff by employee participation, and consultation. They invest heavily in employee care, and training.

15 The term used for the principle whereby several Japanese companies target a particular foreign product, and concentrate their efforts on capturing that market in order to dominate that sector.

What is the 'laser beam effect'?

This has been used to great effect in areas such as watch making, where Switzerland once had a large percentage of the market. With the introduction of digital and now computerized watches, Japan has a virtual monopoly; other countries largely rely on sales of very high quality timepieces now. By a similar 'laser beam' approach, Japan has an almost total monopoly on production and sales of video recorders in the west.

20 In this system, the quantity of stocks is kept to the minimum level necessary for immediate production.

What is Just-In-Time (or Kanban) production?

This is a production management system in which materials, components and products are produced for, or delivered to, the next stage of production at the exact time they are needed. It requires a highly systematic approach to organizing production, but reduces stock-holding costs and storage space requirements. Another advantage is faster manufacturing rates.

25 Meaning literally 'improvement' this word is used in Japanese management circles to describe the umbrella concept covering most of the uniquely Japanese management practices, such as Total Quality Control, Total Customer Service, Just-In-Time production, Zero-Defect production, and so on.

What is Kaizen?

Kaizen means gradual, unending improvement; doing little things better; setting and achieving even higher standards. It has been claimed that *Kaizen* is the answer to Japan's success in being able to adapt swiftly to changing customer and market requirements.

Business

5 The movement towards relocation of managerial authority to a lower level in the organization.

What is decentralization?

There has been an increase in decentralisation during the past decade, the rationale being that it would increase the motivation of lower-level managers, and enable the organization to respond faster to market developments.

10 A form of external growth involving organizations expanding in a horizontal, vertical or conglomerate direction.

What is a merger?

A merger is an amalgamation of two or more firms into a single business on a basis that is mutually agreed by the firms' managements, with a view to increasing overall efficiency. In this way it is different from a takeover bid where one company buys up another, often against the wishes of the latter's directors or shareholders.

15 The collection and processing of information, from within an orga-

nization, and from the firm's environment, using computers, communication devices and so on.

What is IT (or Information Technology)?

Improving information technology has enabled firms to collect more data than previously could have been handled, and to analyse it quickly and accurately. Various IT methods have allowed firms to gain competitive advantage over less-advanced companies, by responding more rapidly to changing customer requirements.

20 An organizational sub-unit of a firm, given responsibility for minimizing costs and maximizing revenue within its limited sphere of operations.

What is a Profit Centre?

Profit centres are independent business units, controlled by a local manager, but financed by the parent company. They differ from other organizational sub-units brought about by decentralization, such as cost centres, where costs are ascertained and used for purposes of cost control, and investment centres which are profit centres with the additional responsibility for raising capital and for long-term investments.

25 The firm or company which has the biggest share of the available market for a specified product or service.

What is a Market Leader?

The term is usually used in the context of sales in one country, eg the market leader for video recorders in the UK is Japan.

Activity 42

Lifeline

Description

This activity is best used early on in a course where change is a major dimension. It is not suitable as an ice-breaker but it could perhaps follow such an activity.

Objectives

By the end of the activity participants will:

- have spent some time reflecting on their life to date
- have identified significant life events
- have ascribed to those events degrees of significance
- have acknowledged the extent to which change has been a factor in their lives
- have begun to consider the extent to which they have managed – or not – major change
- be aware of the relative stress levels attaching to significant life events.

Participants

Number: Maximum of 12
Type: Any

Time

45 minutes (6 participants) to 75 minutes (12 participants)

Resources

- One piece of flipchart paper for each participant
- At least enough marker pens to allow each participant to use two colours on their own chart
- Flipchart stand
- One copy of Document 1 for each participant

Method

Step 1: Introduce the activity

Explain that each participant is to be asked to complete, on their own, a flipchart which will show, in graphic form, a representation of their lives to date.

You need to explain that each person will be asked to share the results with the rest of the group. This means that, although you want to encourage people to include significant events, it is not mandatory to do so. For example, if a participant would prefer not to include an event that is traumatic to discuss, or would simply prefer not to declare, then that is fine.

Step 2: Give an example on the flipchart of what you want; you can use the first three or four events from the example on p. 307 if you wish but it is not advisable to issue the example contained in the example as this may condition participants' thinking and approach

The example of a completed 'Lifeline' chart on p. 307 is simply intended to give you guidance on the format required. In your own example on the flipchart draw attention to the Time Axis (across the page – where the axes cross is the origin, in this case representing birth and the right-hand end is the present time) and the Significance Axis (down the page). Participants should always return to the central axis after each event since this will assist in highlighting changes, even if a return to complete equilibrium after major change is probably not a fair representation of reality!

This graphical approach enables people to plot events according to three criteria:

- *when the event happened relative to birth and the present time*
- *how significant it was (ie how far above or below the time axis: the greater the distance the greater the significance. In the example the redundancy was seen as more significant than the accident)*
- *whether it was a negative experience (below the line) or a positive one (above the line).*

Participants may use dotted lines to show changed perspectives, ie how it felt at the time compared with hindsight. The examples shown would be explained as follows:

- *The* first job *seemed great at the time, but it was actually three years of wasted time when I could have been doing something much better*
- Redundancy *seemed terrible at the time but it actually turned out to be an opportunity to do something I'd never otherwise have had the courage to do, ie set up in business on my own.*

Step 3: Ask participants to work on their own and to produce their own Lifelines

Allow between 5 and 10 minutes, but extend the time to 20 minutes if people are investing considerable thought and reflection in the activity. Don't allow this step to exceed 20 minutes, however. Optionally, you can also join in this exercise and produce your own Lifeline.

Step 4: Stop the individual activity; ask for a volunteer to display their Lifeline and get them to give a short explanation of their material; clarify and question and then move on to the next person until all participants have had a turn; produce your own chart last if you have done one – after all, the participants are more important than you are!

Allow each person three or four minutes 'air time' then move on to the next. With a group of 12 this will take about 45 minutes; any longer will become tedious and repetitive.

You and the group can interrupt to explain or clarify. You might want to use questions such as:

- *Why was that event more/less significant than another?*
- *Why has the perspective changed with hindsight?*
- *Are you surprised by the amount of change so far in your life?*

But impose an important rule on your own and the group's questioning: it must be clarifying and not judging. So questions like 'Why on earth did you go along with that?' or 'What a terrible thing to do!' – however tempting – must be curbed, or people will not be forthcoming and the exercise will lose its power.

Step 5: Process the whole activity briefly

The processing should not be too formal or academic. It is possible to draw up a list of learning points on a flipchart if you want to but our experience is that an informal discussion and an acknowledgement of the following points is all that is needed. There will – if the activity has been run sensitively – have been a high degree of self-exposure and risk-taking and a very analytical conclusion tends to be anti-climactic.

Allow no more than 10 minutes for this final stage. Use the following checklist of questions – many points will emerge naturally as people reflect on what they have seen, but you can also introduce the ideas if they do not occur naturally:

Questions you might use:

- *Have people been surprised by the amount of change in their lives so far?*
- *What determines whether or not change is perceived or experienced as positive or negative?*
- *Does self-imposed change tend to be seen positively?*
- *Is change imposed by circumstances or events outside one's own control experienced as mainly negative?*

- *How important is a sense of having control as a determinant of whether or not change is perceived as positive or negative?*
- *Why does our perspective sometimes change with hindsight?*
- *What support, professional or otherwise, have people used to help them manage change or its effects? Are sources of potential support clear?*
- *What have people learnt from major changes or significant events in their lives?*

Step 6: Issue one copy of Document 1 to each participant

Allow about five minutes and see if you can relate the information in this document to the significance levels ascribed to such events by participants in their Lifelines. Events like these are recognized sources of stress and that it is not abnormal or weak to feel stressed by significant life changes. Acknowledging this can help people to cope.

Step 7: (Optional and recommended only where the group is small, maximum of 6)

Ask each participant to identify one positive point emerging from the discussion which would help them cope with the next significant event in their lives. If the group is larger than 6 this will take too long relative to the length of the activity so far.

Step 8: Close the activity by referring briefly to the objectives

Trainer's notes

Example of a completed Lifeline

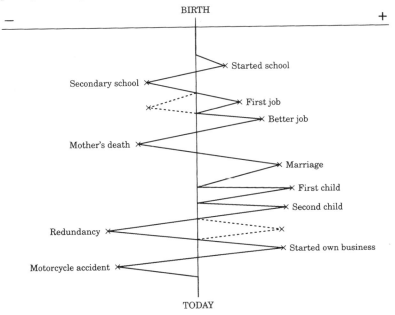

Lifeline - Document 1

Stress scores for adults for significant events

Research suggests that the following stress scores can be ascribed to the events shown:

Event	Stress Score (out of 100)
Death of spouse	100
Divorce	73
Separation	65
Death of a close family member	63
Imprisonment	63
Personal injury or illness	53
Marriage	50
Losing a job	47
Reconciliation after separation	45
Retirement	45
Family member becoming ill	44
Pregnancy	40

Activity 43

Relax

Description

Change always involves additional pressure – not in itself a bad thing, but pressure can lead to stress, which *can* be detrimental to effectiveness and health. Relaxation is one method of dealing with stress. This activity offers four relaxation exercises (especially suited to *individual* use – some *group* relaxation exercises are included in Section 1 of this volume) and which can be used as part of a training course on stress management or managing change. Trainers can choose one or more, appropriate to their group and the nature of the course.

Objectives

By the end of this activity participants will be aware of, and/or have practised, at least one relaxation technique.

Participants

Number: Any
Type: Any

Time

Variable

Resources

- Comfortable chair with space to stretch and relax
- (For Exercise 2) floor space to extend arms without touching neighbour
- (For Exercise 4) pillows, cushions, clean socks made into 'balls': see trainer's notes

Method

Step 1: Explain the purpose of the exercise(s)

One of the ways to combat stress is to learn to relax. Techniques are not difficult to learn, and can be carried out quite easily several times a day, or when the need arises. Most relaxation techniques do need practice, however – and patience. Too often managers say 'I haven't time to just sit and relax!' It is often these same managers whose bodies eventually say 'enough is enough' and force them to relax – often in a hospital bed!

Step 2: Choose an exercise, and run it as directed by the instructions (see Documents 1–4)

These sheets are in a form which could be reproduced as handouts. Four exercises are included to suit every group from the most sombre to the extrovert.

The exercises can be run first thing on day one to relax course members, after lunch, in the session always difficult to fill (although relaxation may put participants to sleep altogether!) at the end of the day to send course members home relaxed, or, indeed, any time during the course if the trainer feels it appropriate.

Trainer's notes

To make a 'ball' from an old (clean!) sock take, for preference, a long, woollen sock. Simply push the toe into the open top and keep feeding it in until you have a 'ball'.

Relax - Document 1

Exercise 1: The Breath

When people are under stress, they tend to breathe more shallowly and rapidly than at other times. If gripped with panic – when the computer goes down, and there is just one day to an important deadline, for example – this shallow breathing can become serious hyper-ventilation and cause real distress and illness. Breath control is a way of overcoming feelings of panic, and helps ease other symptoms caused by the feeling of events getting on top of you. Breath control can be practised any time, anywhere.

Just taking in great lungfuls of air in strained gasps can do more harm than good, however – it can leave you feeling faint and dizzy – so practise this simple method of controlled breathing.

1　Choose a relaxing posture that can be maintained with maximum comfort and minimum strain.
2　Close the eyes, and concentrate on regular breathing, from below the belt-line, not just from the upper chest. Do this for about a minute.
3　Now control this breathing, taking in air, holding the breath, and breathing out to the ratio 1:4:2. So, begin by breathing in for the count of 2, holding breath to the count of 8, and expelling air to the count of 4. As your breathing gets easier, and your chest feels less tight, increase the count to 3:12:6, remembering to fill up with air from the stomach, not just the chest.

This is a variation on a Pranayama Yoga theme. The primary source of Prana (life-force) is air, and the exercises practised include breathing, and abdominal muscle control which combined help eliminate tension, stress, and all forms of panic. The following are just the initial steps to give you an idea of what is involved.

1　Sit with a straight back, arms in a relaxed position at your sides.
2　Pull the tummy in as far as possible, then flick it out again to the relaxed position. Do this several times while maintaining normal, regular breathing.
3　Now begin to develop a rhythm while maintaining normal breathing patterns – IN, 2,3,4; OUT, 2,3,4 – building up to the count of 6. Do this gradually, perfecting the rhythms before each increase.
4　Combine breathing with stomach control. Hold tummy in for the count of 1, breath in and out deeply through the nose, let tummy out for count of 1. When this is perfected, begin to increase the stomach control times – tummy in for count of 2, breath in and out deeply through nose, tummy out for the count of 2, and so on.

Relax - Document 2

Exercise 2: The Shake

1   Find standing place with enough room to swing your arms without touching anyone or anything.
2   With your hands straight down at your sides, shake your right fingers and hand, from the wrist. Continue to do this for a minute.
3   Now shake your lower right arm, from the elbow down, for another minute.
4   Shake your whole right arm, from the shoulder down, for a further minute.
5   Now throw your arm away from you, out to the side, with as much vigour as you can manage.
6   Lower your arm; feel the tension draining from it.
7   Let both arms hang limply by your sides. There should be a marked difference in length between the arm freed of tension, and your left arm which is yet to have 'the treatment'.
8   Repeat the above steps with the left arm. The exercise can be continued if desired, shaking out legs, kicking from the knee at step 5, and omitting step 7.

Relax - Document 3

Exercise 3: The Clench

For this exercise, sit comfortably with hands at sides. You will be required alternately to clench parts of your body, in sequence, and then relax that part, letting the tension flow out.

A word about the word 'relax' - relaxing is passive; you should not use *actively* any muscle to relax. In other words, don't *try* to relax; just let it happen.

1 Clench your fists so tightly that the knuckles show white. Hold this for a count of 5, then let your hands go limp. Uncurl your fingers gradually, feel the hands relax.
2 Bend your arms and clench your biceps as tightly as possible. Hold for a count of 5, then release the tension and let your arms relax.
3 Tense the muscles of your feet. If your shoes allow it, curl up your toes. Hold for a count of 5, maintaining the pressure, then release the tension and let your feet go limp.
4 Clench the muscles in your legs, firstly the calf muscles by pulling the foot up at the ankle to the count of 5, then the thigh by straightening the leg and pushing your foot away from you, again for the count of 5. Consciously allow the feet and legs to go limp. Relax.
5 Squeeze the buttocks tightly together for the count of 5. Relax.
6 Pull in the tummy as far as you can. Make your waist as small as possible. Now push the tummy out, making yourself as large as you can in the abdominal area. Relax your tummy muscles.
7 Clench your chest muscles by inhaling deeply, then holding your breath to the count of 5. Exhale slowly, consciously relaxing these muscles as you do so.
8 Push your shoulders back as far as they will go for the count of 5; then push them forwards for 5; then pull them up to your ears, again for a count of 5. Relax the shoulders. (If the exercise is working, your shoulders should settle lower than when you started.)
9 Sit as tall as you can, stretching the spine, for a count of 5. Relax.
10 Now concentrate on your head and neck. Gently move the head from side to side, backwards and forwards, to stretch the neck muscles. Screw your eyes up tight, and hold this for 5 seconds. Frown for a count of five, then raise the eyebrows as high as possible. Wiggle your nose, waggle your jaw, smile broadly until your grin almost hurts! Relax.

You should now feel less tense, and refreshed - ready to face the rest of the day with renewed vigour.

Variations

This exercise can be condensed and used at any time when you feel the need to release tension. Just stretch, clenching every muscle you can, simultaneously, and hold for three to five seconds. Quickly release the pressure – let go, and relax.

A similar method of releasing tension can even be used, without detection, during a meeting, or while dealing with a stressful telephone call. In the former case, grip the sides of your chair and exert as much sustained pressure as you can for a few seconds, then release as before. If you are holding a telephone receiver, squeeze it as tightly as possible for a few seconds, then quickly release the pressure and relax your hand and arm. You can feel the tension draining away, and provided you don't drop the receiver, the person at the other end of the line will never know!

Relax - Document 4

Exercise 4: Gunnysacking

This exercise has its origins in handling-conflict training, Assertiveness training, and in various therapies for the release of tension. It requires a brave trainer, and an extrovert set of participants!

In these days of rapid growth and change, managers hardly have time to recover from one crisis before the next is upon them. This constant pressure can lead to stress. When under stress, our brains alert our bodies that our hormone levels need to be appropriate to 'fight or flight' action. More adrenalin and other chemical substances are released, by the endocrine system, into our bloodstream, resulting in a number of physical symptoms.

Thus stress and tension build up, sometimes without our recognizing these symptoms. We also feel taut and fraught, often irritable and snappy, but try to keep these feelings and emotions hidden. Our bodies have needs; these repressed feelings need an outlet. If not released, the outlet often takes the form of illness, or an increase in smoking, drinking, etc.

Most people undergoing change will feel concerned, or threatened, or resentful, or otherwise stressed, but will feel unable or unwilling to let out these feelings in an obvious or physical way – yet you *should* feel able to allow yourself some uninhibited release-time. Gunnysacking is a way of letting off steam, without hurting self or others, and feeling much better for this release of tension.

Take pillows, cushions or 'balls' made from clean socks and vent your aggression, anger, frustrations on them. If the trainer, or someone else, is willing, let them be the offending person (eg the boss who imposed those new rules that are making your life hell) or situation (eg the impending redundancies) and hurl socks at them until you feel better. Or if you prefer to punch, bite, kick, or jump on a pillow, or 'strangle' a towel, feel free! Let the emotions flow! You'll feel a lot better for it!

Variations

Other methods of Gunnysacking are to express your feelings verbally and forcefully, either, again, to a willing substitute, or in a sound-proof, closed room, perhaps to a wall or chair. Some prefer to scream and yell; best to do this in your own home, or in a moving car with the windows wound up!

The important thing is to give yourself permission to feel angry, resentful or threatened, and not to feel guilty about releasing the tensions in a physical, non-threatening way. One word of warning though. If you are already up-tight, competitive sport, like squash, may seem a good idea as a releaser of tension, but could send your blood pressure up that extra notch. Far safer to Gunnysack with an old sock!

Activity 44

Retirement (1)

Description

Few people plan for retirement sufficiently far ahead. The first part of this activity will suggest why this is often the case. The second part of the activity looks at the pros and cons of retirement so that people may approach it, and plan for it, in a balanced and rational way.

Retirement is a major life event, potentially a major cause of stress, and planning for it is the stuff of endless books and courses; the aim of this activity is modest – it is merely to get people unblocked in their thinking about it so that they can go on to plan for it properly by using other resources that are readily available either through their own company's training schemes or by reading the plethora of available literature. The activity links well with Activity 45, 'Retirement (2)'.

Objectives

By the end of this activity participants will be able to think about retirement in a balanced and rational way so that they can begin to develop plans for it.

Participants

Number: Any
Type: Anyone who is within 10 years of normal retirement or anyone who is thinking of early retirement as a response to organizational change

Time

45 minutes

Resources

Flipchart stand, paper and marker pens

Method

Step 1: Introduce the activity

Cover the points made in the introduction to the activity. In the UK the average life expectancy for a man is around 79 and for a woman around 82, so retirement, even at the normal statutory ages, can mean that many people still have a quarter of their lives ahead of them. Yet few plan for this final life phase in any positive way. Why?

Questions you might use:

● *How far ahead of retirement ought we to plan for it? (Financially, no time is too early. In other senses - what to do with it - planning ought to start ideally from about 10 years before the anticipated event.)*
● *Do we shy away from thinking about retirement? Why?*

Step 2: This part of the activity will help people focus on why thinking about retirement is often shunned: divide a flipchart into two and head it up as shown below; ask people to call out the kinds of phrases that we use to refer to retirement or to retired people; get agreement with each one as to which is positive and which is negative

Allow 10 minutes.

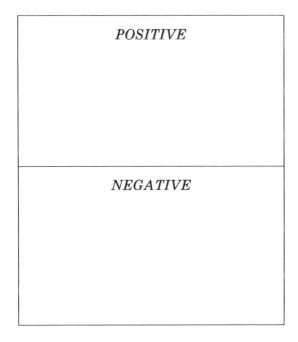

Step 3: Draw out the inevitable moral from a chart like that shown below - which is a common result of this first part of the activity; the fact is, we have, use and constantly reinforce, a multitude of negative images about retirement and about

retired people

A chart such as this will inevitably emerge:

POSITIVE
Third age
Golden age

NEGATIVE
Hang up your boots
Out to grass
Past it
Over the hill
One foot in the grave
Pensioners
Twirlies
Darby and Joans
Waiting for God
Oldies
Twilight of one's life
Evening years
My race is run
Wrinklies
On the scrapheap
. . . .
. . . .
. . . .
. . . .
. . . .

Step 4: Tell the group that you want to look more closely at why retirement has such a negative image; what exactly might the cons of a poor quality retirement be exactly? Get the group to think of them and call them out

Allow 10 minutes. Flipchart the results. The sorts of issues which will emerge are:

- *Less money to spend*
- *Boredom*
- *Isolation*
- *Intrusion into partner's domestic 'space'*
- *Lack of purpose*
- *Lack of structure/discipline which work provides*
- *Fear of the unknown*
- *Lack of clear goals*
- *Loss of self-worth*

- *Regret about things now not achievable*
- *Loss of status*
- *Loss of identity*

This is not a complete list but it gives some idea of what to expect. The last two often don't emerge at all, and it may be useful to get people to focus on, and not to underestimate the power of, these two items.

It is absolutely vital that you process the cons first and then move on to the pros, otherwise you end up reinforcing the negative view of retirement.

Step 5: Do a similar exercise, this time on the 'pros' of a good quality retirement

Allow 10 minutes. The sorts of issues which should emerge are:
- *Freedom of choice*
- *Chance to travel*
- *Living in and for the moment 'What is this world if, full of care, we have no time to stand and stare?'*
- *Hopefully reduced financial burden – children off hands, mortgage paid off and so on*
- *Chance to acquire new skills*
- *Ability to set own goals*
- *Chance to pursue old, or take up new, interests*
- *Further education*
- *Ability to respond quickly to opportunities (ie not having to take work priorities into account)*
- *Chance to try new experiences*
- *Another 'project' to manage*
- *Reduction in negative stress*
- *Able to take life at own pace*
- *Follow a healthier lifestyle*
- *Able to set, and change, own priorities*
- *Continued personal development*
- *Chance to grow closer to family and friends*
- *Freedom to do nothing if you want to.*

Step 6: Close the activity with a brief re-cap of the main points raised

Allow 5 minutes. Retirement should be planned for, despite its negative image. It only has this image because too many people fail at it precisely because they don't plan for it, and therefore don't have the necessary resources to see it through successfully. You might like to ask how people can plan to reduce the impact of important concepts like loss of status and identity.

Activity 45

Retirement (2)

Description

This activity complements Activity 44, 'Retirement (1)' although it stands alone perfectly well. It provides a structure for assessing the financial impact of retirement on the day-to-day resources of a family unit. It is not intended as a substitute for good investment planning and advice which should be carried out by a qualified person. Rather, the activity seeks to impart a sense of self-confidence that results from knowing that nothing major has been overlooked.

It is an activity that should *not* be carried out during a course but should rather be given to participants to work on privately, at home. The rationale for this is given in the processing notes below.

Objectives

By the end of this activity participants will:

- have conducted a financial analysis of the impact of retirement on the day-to-day resources of a family unit
- be confident that they have identified any major areas of concern.

Participants

Number: Any
Type: Anyone who is thinking of retirement in the near or immediate future; the activity is perhaps especially relevant and helpful for staff who may be considering early retirement as a response to unexpected redundancy

Time

Minimal during the course; up to 2 hours privately

Resources

One copy of Document 1 for each participant

Method

Step 1: Introduce the activity

Financial planning for retirement should take three forms:

1 *Long-term planning such as savings, life policies, personal pension plans and so on*
2 *Advice on how to invest lump sums*
3 *An assessment of the impact of retirement on income and outgoings.*

This activity covers the third area.

Step 2: Explain why the activity is to be carried out privately by participants, at home

There are two reasons for this:

1 *If a family unit is involved then it seems important to involve all the members in the analysis of the impact of retirement on the unit's day-to-day financial resources. The activity should therefore be carried out as a joint project.*
2 *The information generated by the activity is private and cannot possibly be generalized for group consumption. Nevertheless, in planning for retirement most people worry about how it will affect their day-to-day living and this activity is designed with this in mind.*

Step 3: Issue Document 1; ask participants to make use of it with whoever is appropriate to involve in it. Stress that – if participants are returning for a continuation of the course – they will not be asked to divulge their findings

Explain the structure and the basics of completing the form. These are covered in the document, but in our experience it helps to indicate the scale and nature of what is being asked for, by way of reassurance, otherwise participants may be intimidated by it, not carry out the activity, and thus not benefit from it.

Step 4: (Optional) Outline provisions of the State Pension Scheme

These are included in Leaflets FB 2 'Which Benefit?' and FB 6 'Retiring?', both issued by the Department of Social Security. Both are widely available at all main Post Offices. If you do decide to explain these provisions to your group try to be sure you have a good grasp of them: they are quite complex! It is, in our experience, far better to outline the main benefits, to draw attention to possible reasons for not receiving full benefits (as explained in the leaflets) and then to suggest people raise individual queries which they may have with the Department of Social Security's excellent Helpline: 0800 666555. All calls to this number are free. At all costs don't *get involved in advising people on their likely entitlements unless you're a qualified expert!*

Step 5: Close the activity by referring briefly to the objectives

Retirement (2) - Document 1

Financial aspects of retirement
The activity which follows in these pages is designed for you to be able to consider the immediate financial impact of retirement on your family unit's income and expenditure pattern.

Part A suggests a framework for you to use which will result in your listing all the *expenditure* you currently have. *If you are thorough in completing it then you can rest assured that you will not have overlooked anything major.*

Part B poses some questions for you to answer on your income together with some other important questions which you really cannot afford to ignore or overlook.

You are strongly urged to complete this activity with members of your family unit. It seems probable that they will be affected – not just financially – by your retirement and they therefore have a role in planning for the consequences of it.

You will probably need at least two hours to carry out this activity. It will require research unless you are one of those rare people who have all the facts and figures about your year's finances at your fingertips. You might like to spread the activity over 2 or 3 sessions. Whatever suits you personally.

Instructions for completing the activity

1   The aim of Part A is to present you with a 'snapshot' of your family's total outgoings, regardless of who is actually responsible for paying a particular bill at the moment. If your company pays for some things (eg car) at present that you will in future have to pay for be sure to include those too.
2   In Part A only enter a figure in *one* of the four columns. The column headed **W** is for weekly expenditure, **M** is monthly, **Q** is quarterly and **A** is annual. Round all your figures up to the nearest pound.
3   Part B consists of some important questions relating to your income but it also raises some other vital matters which you should think very seriously about.

Part A: Outgoings
CATEGORY

	W	M	Q	A
Home				
Mortgage/rent				
Community charge				
Water/drainage				
Ground rent				
Service charges				
Property insurance				
Contents insurance				
Sub-totals	....	....	....	....
Household/food				
Basic food				
Drink				
Pets				
Eating out				
Service contracts				
Audio rental				
Gas				
Electric				
Other fuel				
Telephone				
Other appliances				
Sub-totals	....	....	....	....
Travel				
Public transport/taxis				
Car(s):				
Petrol				
Road Tax				
Insurance				
MOT				
Servicing				
AA/RAC				
Depreciation				
Sub-totals	....	....	....	....

CATEGORY	W	M	Q	A
Personal				
Occupational pension: payments in				
Personal pension: payments in				
Life policies				
Private health insurance				
Savings schemes				
Other insurance premium				
School fees				
Bank charges				
Credit card interest instalments				
Other debt repayment				
Sub-totals	....	....	....	....
Leisure/other				
Socialising				
Clothes				
Hair/cosmetic				
Dental				
Medical treatment (private)				
Holidays				
Subscriptions				
Papers & magazines				
Books/records/video				
Christmas/birthdays				
Cigarettes/alcohol				
Outings				
Hobbies				
Luxuries				
Sub-Totals	....	....	....	....

Now bring forward your sub-totals from the previous 5 sections into the grid below. Perform the calculations.

SUB-TOTALS	W	M	Q	A
Home Household/food Travel Personal Leisure/other TOTALS				
Multiply by	× 52	× 12	× 4	× 1
ANNUAL TOTALS	....	....	....	....

Now calculate the annual expenditure figure by adding up your totals:

Total W	£
Total M	£
Total Q	£
Total A	£
Grand Total	£

Part B: income

Some questions

- Do you have any dependent relatives? How long are they likely to be dependent on you?
- Are there any elderly relatives who may have to depend on you in the future?
- What are the death benefits attaching to your present occupational pension scheme?
- Is your National Insurance record such that you will qualify for the full state pension benefits?
- Are you satisfied that you know exactly what the benefits from your occupational or personal pension scheme will be? Now? In the future?
- List all your *present* income from all sources:

Salaries	£
Fees	£
Investments	£
DSS Benefits	£
Other	£
TOTAL	£

- List all your anticipated income once you are retired:

Occupational pension £
Personal pension   £
Salaries   £
Fees   £
Investment   £
DSS Benefits/Pension £
Other   £
TOTAL   £

- How could you supplement this income if necessary?
- What is the difference between the two income totals above? What are the implications for your annual expenditure pattern, identified in Part A?
- Will you receive a lump sum or redundancy payment (or both)? How will you invest it?
- When will you receive any benefits from life policies or other regular savings plans which may mature? How much will you get? Do you know what terminal bonuses there may be?
- Do you currently save regularly? Will you continue with this?
- Do you plan to move house when you retire? Will this affect your mortgage if you have one? How? Do you know the area you plan to move to? Can you make friends easily in new surroundings?
- Have you and your partner made wills? If not, do you *really* want to impose the awfulness of intestacy on your family?

And finally. . .

- *What do you have to do ensure that retirement is financially secure for you?*

Activity 46

Skill stories

Description

This activity is suited to courses where participants are undergoing change in the workplace and need to look at areas such as re-training, applying for positions in competition with others, selling their expertise and skills and so on. It could complement, or be run as an alternative to Activity 40, 'I am, therefore I can'. It requires a good deal of time and thought, and benefits from participants being able to consult and discuss with someone who knows them well. It lends itself, therefore, to pre-course work, or 'homework' to be completed in the evenings during a course.

Objectives

By the end of this activity participants will:

- have up to 50 examples of their own accomplishments
- have a raised awareness of their capabilities, and skill strengths
- be better equipped to cope with career change
- have practised relating skill stories as an interview technique
- have a more positive self-image.

Participants

Number: Any
Type: Any

Time

60–90 minutes plus home preparation time

Resources

- Space for group to work in pairs, and for whole group discussion
- One copy of Document 1 for each participant
- Pen/pencil for each participant
- Flipchart stand, paper and marker pens

Method

Step 1: Explain the activity

Participants will each receive a copy of Document 1 on which is printed 50 verbs, in the past tense.

Thinking back over their lives, their achievements and accomplishments, participants will write a phrase or sentence against each of the words listed, demonstrating what they have 'researched', or 'negotiated', or 'directed' and so on in their lives. These experiences need not be work orientated. Participants should aim to have examples for all 50 words, and may 'pass' on only five. For this reason, the exercise can take quite some time and benefits from participants being able to bounce ideas off peers, friends, partners or relations. (It is therefore suggested that the exercise be set as pre-course work or homework.)

Step 2: Discuss why this exercise is important

When faced with change and upheaval, after the initial shock, anger, resistance and so on, morale tends to plummet. This is a natural phenomenon and happens to virtually everyone when in this situation. The 'why me?' syndrome often sets in, followed by the 'I won't be able to compete', 'I haven't enough to offer' type of thoughts. This activity is a great morale booster, because after completing the exercise, most people will realize that they have many hidden skills and talents, skills which are transferable to present and to new work situations. Meetings and interviews can be approached with increased confidence and feelings of self-worth.

In terms of writing formal applications, reports, letters, CVs or resumés, participants will have key 'power' words at their fingertips – words which they will be able to use with confidence because they will have examples from their own experience to reinforce their usage.

These examples, or skill stories, are invaluable in an interview. Having completed the exercise, plus follow up on the course, participants will have the ammunition to answer questions with confidence. In a meeting, or at an interview where the element of competition is present, it is vital to be memorable. Using stories to spell out achievements and skills makes individuals far more memorable than just quoting facts and figures – 'You remember Mitchell. He was the guy who created brumbling' or 'Let's recall Ms Jacobs; she was the one who solved the cromble problem by setting up the CADRIN project'.

Step 3: If using this activity as homework, issue Document 1 at the end of the first day for course processing at a later stage on the course

Each participant should be given a copy of Document 1 and asked to complete it, preferably at home in consultation with someone who knows them well. (If this is not practical or possible, the work can be undertaken during the course – it will take up to an hour to complete. Some participants may find it more difficult than others to think positively about their achievements, and may need help from the trainer, at least in getting started on the exercise.)

Step 4: In plenary, begin to draw out skills from the stories presented

Ask if any individual would be prepared to share one of their skill stories, as listed on Document 1. Ask who-what-where-how-why type open questions to encourage the individual to explain the skill story more fully. It will quickly be obvious that within every story exist many transferable skills, all of which will be morale boosters and also marketable traits. Begin a flipchart list of these skills. (These will be different from 'power' words and are likely to include skills like counselling, communication, manual dexterity, prioritizing and so on, but will add to participants' arsenals of material to produce in meetings, at interview and so on.)

Repeat this process with one or two other members of the group, asking them to quote a different word from Document 1, giving their skill story example.

Step 5: Divide group into pairs (one triad if necessary)

Step 6: Explain the next phase of the activity

Having witnessed the above process led by the trainer, participants will now work in pairs for the next 30 minutes conducting a similar process, ie one partner quizzes the other about what was involved in a particular story, making notes of the skills involved.

Step 7: After 30 minutes, re-group participants; draw out the learning points of the activity

Ask for comments on the work just undertaken.

Questions you might use:

- *What skills emerged as a result of these analyzes? (Add to collective flipchart list if appropriate.)*
- *Was anyone surprised at the number of achievements and skills they can now demonstrate?*
- *How will you apply this new-found self awareness?*
- *What impact do you think the use of 'power' words has in (a) writing about yourself and your achievements, (b) speaking about yourself and your achievements?*
- *Why does it help to talk through skill stories as you have just done in the main group and with a colleague?*

Step 8: Close the activity referring to the objectives

Using power words in self-marketing is useful only if you can back up statements with fact. If these facts can be presented as skill stories, you will be far more memorable. Skill stories should still quantify and qualify wherever possible. This was why time was spent asking why-what-who-where-how questions to assertions made against the power words on the exercise document.

The exercise just undertaken can, and should, be revised and rehearsed until individuals feel confident that they really do possess many transferable skills, and that they can sell these skills with confidence, sure in the knowledge that they can back up every statement with a skill story.

Skill stories – Document 1

After each of the following words, write a phrase or sentence to demonstrate how you have done the thing described by the verb, eg against 'Led'
. . . a successful salesforce. . . 'Redesigned' . . . my mother's kitchen.

NEGOTIATED

DEMONSTRATED

SOLD

INVENTED

PROPOSED

COMPLETED

BUILT

STRUCTURED

WON

SUCCEEDED

DEVELOPED

ORGANIZED

DOUBLED

ACHIEVED

INSTALLED

MAINTAINED

PLANNED

CREATED

REVISED

TRAINED

GENERATED

SET-UP

ESTABLISHED

DEVISED

INCREASED

REDUCED

WROTE

ACCOMPLISHED

DESIGNED

INTRODUCED

PROVIDED

STREAMLINED

BARGAINED

SOLVED

PRODUCED

MOTIVATED

IMPLEMENTED

CO-ORDINATED

CONTROLLED

LED

REDESIGNED

SCHEDULED

SIMPLIFIED

OPERATED

RESEARCHED

HEADED

RECOMMENDED

PRODUCED

ELIMINATED

MEDIATED

Activity 47

That's the limit!

Description

Anyone who has to manage change will testify to the stress involved. Most people would argue that some form of pressure is necessary, but there needs to be a balance between pressure (as a motivator to do something) and negative stress – when pressure gets out of hand.

Activity 43 – 'Relax' – in this manual offers some relaxation techniques for coping with stress. 'That's the limit!',however, focuses on identifying some of the underlying causes of stress, knowing the symptoms and suggesting some ideas for dealing with it. Since it is designed to address stress, it is deliberately low-key in its approach; we do not want to make the topic of stress even more stressful!

Objectives

By the end of this activity participants will:

- be able to identify common sources of pressure and stress at work
- be able to identify common signs of stress at work, in themselves and in others
- be able to describe simple techniques for alleviating personal stress
- recognize the stress factors involved in managing change.

Participants

Up to 12 managers who are involved in managing change

Time

1 hour

Resources

Flipchart stand, paper and at least two marker pens

Method

Step 1: Introduce the activity
Refer to the introduction and objectives.

Step 2: Discuss the concepts of pressure and stress
Allow five minutes.

Questions you might use:

- *What is the difference between pressure and stress?*
- *Do people need stress?*
- *Are techniques for handling stress enough – or is there a role for management in identifying and addressing the causes of stress?*
- *Why may change be seen as stressful?*

Step 3: Form two groups of up to six participants; ask the first group to identify and flipchart (for later presentation) the sources of stress at work; ask the second group to identify the signs of stress they would watch for, in themselves or in others
Allow 15 minutes. The trainer's notes on p. 335 give some idea as to the sorts of issues which tend to emerge.

Step 4: Re-form the main group and ask each group in turn to present and briefly explain their flipchart
Allow 20 minutes.

Step 5: In the main group, brainstorm some techniques which people might use to alleviate or handle stress of the kind identified in Step 4
Allow 10 minutes. Flipchart the suggestions as they arise. Clarify as you go along. Again, the trainer's notes suggest some of the most commonly suggested ideas.

Step 6: Check back on the list of sources identified at Step 3; address any which have not been covered by suggestions at Step 5
Allow 5 minutes.

Questions you might use:

- *Why was this not covered?*
- *Is it too difficult or too problematic to tackle?*
- *How could it be tackled and by whom?*

Step 7: Arrange to have the flipcharts reproduced by way of a handout for this activity
We think handouts like this are very effective since they represent the group's own thinking and participants will be more likely to identify

*closely with them after the training event. In the area of stress manage-
ment this is perhaps an especially desirable goal.*

Step 8: *Close the activity by referring briefly to the objectives*

Trainer's notes

Some common sources of stress at work

- Pressure of work
- Inadequate direction/leadership
- Insensitivity of others
- Ill health
- Change seen as inappropriate
- Change seen as appropriate
- Uncertainty
- Shortage of staff
- Personal problems
- Poor or alienating physical working environment
- Stressful travel to work
- Lack of proper resources to do the job properly
- Personality clashes
- Strong feelings about colleagues
- Lack of career opportunities
- Fear of redundancy
- Lack of recognition
- Lack of sense of being valued
- 'Them and Us'
- Isolation from colleagues
- Harassment
- Oppression/discrimination
- Perceived lack of skills and abilities
- Inadequate or inappropriate training

Some common signs of stress at work

- Ill health
- Forgetfulness
- Lack of concentration
- Aggression
- Sense of proportion lost
- Indifference
- Demotivation
- Mental 'blocks'
- Obsessiveness
- Passivity
- Lethargy
- 'Emotional' outbursts
- Lack of energy/enthusiasm

- Lack of will to help and cooperate
- Tiredness
- Headaches/migraine
- Lack of resistance to illness
- Lack of sleep
- Smoking/drinking/eating to excess
- Changes in 'normal' behaviour
- Not eating enough
- Lack of personal care
- Digestive problems

Some suggested ways to alleviate personal stress

- Acknowledge that others experience stress too
- Talk about it – share the problem
- Manage your leisure activities so that there is a balance of the mental and the physical
- Use relaxation techniques
- Spend some money on treats!
- Be nice to yourself
- *Like* yourself
- Identify others who could help – could they handle the problem aspect of the job better than you or can they advise you?
- Meditate
- Train to acquire/improve skills required
- Undertake education in areas which interest you but which will provide an antidote to work problems
- Seek specific help from line manager
- Explore if there is any way of moving from a situation where events are controlling you to a situation where you are in control of events, eg better time management, true delegation and so on
- Take a holiday (but take care that this does not in itself become stressful!)
- Switch off occasionally – and don't feel guilty about it
- Try a totally new experience
- Ask yourself: are you able to admit weakness or uncertainty to yourself, let alone others?

Activity 48

Transferable skills

Description

To illustrate to participants, especially those lacking in confidence, that they have innumerable skills, some of which will be untapped within their present positions. This is an effective activity for those desiring, or having to face, a change of career direction, or facing selection interview within their own organization.

Objectives

By the end of this activity participants will:

- be more aware of inherent and acquired skills
- be able to analyze tasks in terms of skills required and attributes needed
- have a raised awareness of their own capabilities
- have the means to develop a more positive self-image.

Participants

Number: Up to 12
Type: From junior staff to middle management

Time

45–60 minutes

Resources

- Notepaper and pencil/pen for each participant
- Flipchart stand, paper and marker pens
- Copy of trainer's notes on p. 339 for reference

Method

Step 1: Begin the activity without, at this stage, referring to the objectives; issue notepaper and pen/pencil to each

***participant and brief the group on the first part of the
exercise***

*Participants will list at least five things which they do well or enjoy doing
outside working hours. Check after four or five minutes that everyone has
several outside work activities recorded.*

Step 2: Record on flipchart paper one activity from each participant's list

*Work around the group asking each individual to call out one activity from
her or his list. It should be something they feel they do well. Record this,
leaving sufficient space between each for annotation (see trainer's notes).
To avoid duplication, if someone in the group has already said 'gardening', for example, ask others whose first choice was the same subject to
choose another activity they do well to add to the general list.*

Step 3: When everyone has added one item to the list, discuss each activity in the context of the skills involved and the attributes required to achieve results

*Some examples are given in the trainer's notes. You may have to prompt
the group, initially, until they begin to see for themselves how to break
down an activity (or any task) into component parts, then analyse what is
required to achieve success within each part. For example, if 'gardening' is
the first hobby to be discussed, these are:*

Questions you might use:

- *How do you ascertain which plants will grow well in your garden?
  (Possible answers: ask at a garden centre, or read seed packets/books/
  magazines/catalogues; do a soil test to find out if ground is acid or
  alkaline)*
- *What skills are involved in these processes? (Possible answers: forward planning; technical knowledge; judgement; selective, analytical
  skills; application of learning; communication skills; etc.)*
- *Is creativity involved? (Possible response: yes, in landscaping; planning flower beds; choosing colour schemes; etc.)*
- *What attributes should a gardener have? (Possible answers: stamina;
  patience; adaptability; being philosophical about setbacks; etc.)*

*Usually, by the time the third or fourth activity is discussed, input will be
from the group; you will just need to record their findings on the flipchart.*

Step 4: When everyone's activity has been discussed and skills and attributes recorded, lead a discussion to tease out the learning points

*Sometimes it's good to have a confidence boost. Often, especially when we
are faced with a career move, or having to compete for our own jobs
because of retrenching and so on, it is easy to adopt a negative attitude. It
is a useful exercise to look closely at what we like doing (usually tasks
which are enjoyed are performed well) and analyze just how we do that*

task, in order to recognize transferable skills. If you can manage a home, for example, you can organize, budget, prioritize, etc, even if you think you have never used these skills in your daily work.

Questions you might use:

- *Were you surprised at just how many skills you have at your fingertips? Why?*
- *How many of the skills and attributes used during leisure hours are not used during the working day? Why is this?*
- *What are the benefits of assessing strengths in this way?*
- *Would it benefit others – colleagues or subordinates – back at the workplace to go through a similar exercise?*
- *What application might the exercise have in a work situation? Could it help with career planning, for example?*

Step 5: Close the activity referring to the objectives

Note: *If it can be arranged, a handout should be prepared of the material produced, and given to each participant. This can be simply a handwritten record. This gives both a sense of immediacy and of ownership to participants, as well as providing a reminder of the methods used to assess transferable skills.*

Trainer's notes

Some examples of activities listed with a breakdown of some of the skills and attributes needed.

Driving
Manual dexterity; map reading; patience; assertiveness; courage; spatial perception; coordination; mental alertness; quick reactions; concentration; decision making; knowledge of relevant legal framework; forward planning; mechanical knowledge; confidence; courage; anticipation; observation; self control.

Socialising
Interpersonal skills – listening, empathy etc; being articulate; being informed; tact; real interest in people; able to meet a challenge; objectivity; honesty; fairness; approachability; discretion; loyalty; counselling skills; budgeting; entertaining; confidentiality; sense of humour.

Looking after grandchild
Creativity; energy; stamina; imagination; organizational skills; culinary skills; adaptability; improvisation; timetabling; balancing roles.

Activity 49

Transitions

Description

Major change, by its nature, creates upheaval, and the individual experiencing the change is likely to undergo several mood swings and transitional reactions. This activity introduces a model of transition which proposes that there are a number of stages which people can experience. This is often helpful, both in terms of people recognizing that there *are* established 'landmarks' in most transitions and also in being able to plot exactly where they are in terms of a current transition.

The activity is most suited to managers currently confronting, or about to confront, a major change or transition in their working lives.

Objectives

By the end of this activity participants will:

- understand a model of transition
- be able to apply the model to their own situation
- be able to help others apply the model to their own situation.

Participants

Number: Maximum of 12
Type: Managers who are currently, or are about to be, involved in managing a major change or transition at work

Time

45 minutes

Resources

- Overhead projector (OHP) and screen
- Pre-prepared OHP transparency (see p. 344)
- One copy of the transparency details for each participant

Method

Step 1: Introduce the activity

Allow two minutes. The work involved in this activity is based on the writings of Barrie Hopson and Mike Scally, who have undertaken a good deal of research on change and transition. They identify two major forms of transition:

1 *Stages of personal development*
2 *Major life events, challenge and stress.*

This activity concentrates on the second.

Step 2: Divide the group into pairs (have one triad if there is an odd number); ask each pair to share briefly with each other some major change at work which they have been, or are currently, involved in

Allow five minutes. The change can be recent or remote in time. It can be change which people have initiated or which they have had imposed on them. People should describe:

- *who initiated the change and why*
- *the high and the low points*
- *what the outcome was.*

Step 3: Re-form the group; introduce the model of the seven stages of transition p. 344

Allow 10 minutes. Present your OHP transparency (see p. 344).

Notes on each stage follow, using the example of redundancy throughout to illustrate a transition. Draw particular attention to the fluctuations in self-esteem as represented by the vertical axis. Encourage questions as you go along, or invite them as you finish dealing with each stage.

1 Numbness: Being unable to think clearly. Maybe an inability to understand what lies ahead. In negative transitions, such as bereavement, an absence of feeling is common at this initial stage. In more positive events, such as marriage, the numbness stage will be shorter and less obvious. People who experience redundancy are often unable to think clearly for a day or so and what's said to them after the news has been broken is often almost completely unheard.
2 Minimization/denial: A sense of 'this is not as bad as I thought' – even if it is! People sometimes trivialize the event, or even deny it has happened at all. People who have been made redundant will often concentrate on the benefits – loss of uncongenial work, no more commuting to the office, no more carping bosses, no more pressure – while it is not unknown for people not to tell family and friends, even to the extent, in extreme cases, of people still pretending to go to work each day. Positive changes, such as promotion, will often result in denial of some of the downside such as apprehension about the new job, loss of familiar

colleagues and so on. Minimization and denial is a high-energy phase, often involving intense feelings of joy and pleasure.

3 Self doubt/depression: Coming down to earth with a bang; a cliché but an acknowledged phenomenon in human experience. As the realities of the change become clearer uncertainty creeps in. Self-doubt stems from powerlessness, from feelings that some aspect of our life is now out of control. Anger and frustration are common emotional safety valves at this stage. In redundancy cases this stage is reached as the realities sink in; the practicalities of getting another job, how to set about it, the financial worries, 'how long can we last?' Even positive events, like moving to a cherished new career, can involve doubts about ability to do the new job.

4 Accepting reality/letting go: A process of 'un-hooking' from the past. Those experiencing redundancy commonly have strong, negative and bitter views about their late employers, but there comes a stage when such feelings begin to pass as nothing is achieved by them. This means that Stage 4 of the transition has been reached. The future may be uncertain but the reality of the situation is beginning to be accepted and some kind of forward planning is possible.

5 Testing: A phase involving much more proactivity, of projecting into the new situation, of trying out new ideas, new ways of looking at things. Looking for patterns, trying out new ways of dealing with people and situations. Trying to make the unfamiliar more familiar. High levels of personal energy often lead to quick emotional outbursts, such as irritation or feelings of frustration when small things go wrong. For people facing redundancy this is the stage of tackling a possibly unfamiliar job market, of testing themselves out against new employers' needs, of researching possible new career directions.

6 Search for meaning: After a good deal of energy has been expended in the earlier stages, this stage is a quieter one of reflection. How and why are things different now? Do I really want this? It's also a period of increased understanding of what has happened and of an attempt to put the transition into some kind of framework against which we live out our lives. Someone who has experienced redundancy may well now see some of the benefits, not just on the emotional rebound this time, but in the sense of recognising that they do perhaps have some choices which can influence their lives in the future.

7 Internalisation: We adapt our lives and routines in accordance with the new situation. It starts to become the norm. The redundant employee either accepts a pattern of job search for a period, or gains new employment which will mean settling down into the new job, with the routines and disciplines that both those situations bring. In other words, the transition is past and we accept the changes it has brought.

Of course, it's not usually the case that everyone progresses from step to step in orderly fashion. But we can detect those who have got stuck – the redundant manager who finds she or he is quite unable to move from depression to acceptance of reality, and who therefore does not even try to put themselves on the job market in any effective sort of way. Scally and Hopson take the view that, for a transition to be effectively managed, all seven stages have to be worked through.

Step 4: Get reactions to the model
Allow 10 minutes.

Questions you might use:

- *Can people identify with the seven stages?*
- *Would anyone like to give an example, either from their own or somebody else's experience?*

Step 5: Re-form the pairs from step 2; ask each pair to review the transition or change they shared earlier in the light of the model
Allow 10 minutes.

Questions you might use:

- *Can people identify with the seven stages and in what way?*
- *Can people discern the self-esteem changes suggested by the model?*

Step 6: Re-form the main group; draw conclusions
Allow 10 minutes.

Questions you might use:

- *How useful is a model like this?*
- *Can people see the process of transition more clearly as a result of the model?*
- *Would it help people in future to confront change and transition?*
- *How might it help managers who have to help others cope with change and transition?*

Step 7: Issue one copy of the transparency details to each participant

Step 8: Close the activity by referring briefly to the objectives

Prepare an OHP transparency by copying the diagram below.

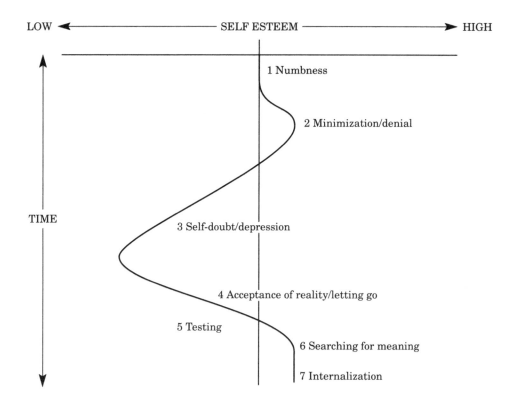

Activity 50

Work will be the death of me

Description

Most people have a regular pattern of work habits that is more, or less, healthy. Confronting change can upset or accentuate the regular pattern. This activity will help managers think about their normal work habits and consider how healthy (or otherwise) they may be. They will thus be better able to detect upsets – and remedy things – when change comes along.

Objectives

By the end of this activity participants will:

- be aware of their normal pattern of work habits
- be aware if change impacts on, or accentuates, the normal pattern of work habits
- be able to consider alternatives.

Participants

Number: Any
Type: Managers who may have to confront change

Time

30 minutes

Resources

- One copy of Document 1 for each participant
- One copy of Document 2 for each participant
- Flipchart stand, paper and marker pens
- Pre-prepared flipchart or overhead projector (OHP) transparency in accordance with the lists on pp. 348-9

- OHP if a transparency is to be used

Method

Step 1: Introduce the activity
Allow two or three minutes. Cover briefly the main points in the introduction and objectives.

Step 2: Issue Document 1 to each participant; ask them to complete it
This will only take two or three minutes.

Step 3: Give a short input based on your pre-prepared flipchart or OHP transparency
Allow five minutes. See lists on pp. 348–9. Make the point that these are extremes and no one is likely to be 100 per cent a Type 'A' manager or Type 'B' manager. However, it is worth recognizing that work tends to be structured towards requiring Type 'A' behaviour.

Questions you might use:

- *Is it true that work reinforces Type 'A' behaviours?*
- *What is the likely price that a high-scoring Type 'A' manager might have to pay if they carry on in this way? (Stress-related illness, ultimately ineffective work performance)*
- *How could an acceptable balance be achieved? (See step 5.)*

Step 4: Issue Document 2 and ask people to record their results
The document is self-explanatory and will only take few moments to complete.

Step 5: Suggest that people could now be alert to the impact of change on their normal work behaviour type, and to be especially aware of the tendency for work to require/push us towards the Type 'A' behaviour, especially if things are hotting up because change is in the air

Step 6: Brainstorm and flipchart ideas which people have and which may help move strong Type 'A' people towards a Type 'B' behaviour, and which could help get things more into balance; the list produced should be a good basis for a list of techniques to resist the push towards Type 'A' behaviour, or towards a more extreme form of it, the next time change comes along
Allow 10 minutes. Some ideas are listed here by way of starting the exercise off. But float these only if the ideas are not forthcoming. Ideas generated by the group are much more valuable.

- *Regular sleep habits*
- *Healthy exercise*
- *Good diet*
- *Sharing problems*
- *Treats*
- *Deliberately stepping out of the limelight for a day or so*

and so on.

Step 7: Close the activity by referring briefly to the objectives

Work will be the death of me - Document 1

Work habits questionnaire

Ring the number on each scale that describes your *normal* response at work. A score of 1 on the first entry would indicate that you feel that an uncompetitive, avoiding conflict behaviour pattern is very like you. A score of 2 would indicate this is perhaps sometimes how you behave.

Only use the middle score of 3 if you genuinely feel that is right; don't use it as a 'copout' score!

At work I...

am uncompetitive and avoid conflict.	1 2 3 4 5	*am highly competitive and thrive on battles.*
do things at an easy pace.	1 2 3 4 5	*do things at a fast pace, including walking, eating and driving.*
feel as though there is always plenty of time.	1 2 3 4 5	*feel there's never enough time.*
know I can go home to a wide range of hobbies and interests.	1 2 3 4 5	*am only interested in work. I think and talk a lot about my work when I'm away from it.*
always try and do one thing at a time.	1 2 3 4 5	*constantly have to juggle several balls at once.*
never hurry or rush.	1 2 3 4 5	*am always rushing about.*
use time off to relax and think things over in a reflective way.	1 2 3 4 5	*feel guilty about taking time off.*
am casual about time-keeping.	1 2 3 4 5	*am always in early, stay late.*

Work will be the death of me - Document 2

Work habits questionnaire - scoring

Simply add up the numbers you have circled. This is your total score.

Enter your score here:

Interpretation of scores

Definite Type 'B'	Score in range 8–15
Tendency to Type 'B'	Score in range 16–23
Well balanced	Score of 24 exactly
	(as long as you did not score 8×3!)
Tendency to Type 'A'	Score in range 25–32
Definite Type 'A'	Score in range 33–40

Type 'A' and Type 'B' Behaviour

The Type 'A' manager's most likely behaviours at work are:

- Highly competitive
- Always trying to achieve the best
- Always in a hurry
- Liable to flare up at the slightest provocation
- Tense
- Pressured
- Prone to stress-related illness
- Ultimately liable to burn-out and ineffective work performance

The Type 'B' manager's most likely behaviours at work are:

- Relaxed
- Able to stop without feeling guilty
- Recognizes value of non-work activity
- Unflappable
- Not easily roused to extreme emotions such as anger or frustration
- Has little need to display achievements in a high profile way
- Able to 'step up' the pace when required
- Capable of sustaining steadily effective performance

Bibliography

Helme, M (ed.) (1991) *Managing I/T for Competitive Advantage: Case Studies of Organizations in Japan, USA and Europe*, British Institute of Management.

Hopson, B., Scally, M. and Stafford, K. (1988) *Transitions: The Challenge of Change*, Lifeskills.

Lewin, K. (1951) *Field Theory in Social Science*, Harper.

McGregor, D.M. (1960) *The Human Side of Enterprise*, McGraw-Hill.

Ouchi, W. (1993) *Theory Z*, Avon Books.

Pedler, M., Burgoyne, J. and Boydell, T. (1986) *A Manager's Guide to Self-development* (second edn), McGraw-Hill.

Peters, T. (1989) *Thriving on Chaos*, Pan Books.

Peters, T. and Astin, N. (1986) *A Passion for Excellence*, Fontana.

Peters, T. and Waterman, R.H. (1988) *In Search of Excellence*, HarperCollins.

Rogers, C. (1951) *Client-centred Therapy*, Houghton-Mifflin.

Zimmerman, M.A. (1988) *Dealing with the Japanese*, Unwin Hyman.